WOMEN
ALL ON FIRE

The Women
of the
English Civil War

WOMEN
ALL ON FIRE

*The Women
of the
English Civil War*

Alison Plowden

SUTTON PUBLISHING

First published in 1998 by
Sutton Publishing Limited · Phoenix Mill
Thrupp · Stroud · Gloucestershire · GL5 2BU

British Library Cataloguing in Publication Data
A catalogue record for this book is available from the British Library

ISBN 0-7509-1221-9

ALAN SUTTON™ and SUTTON™ are the
trade marks of Sutton Publishing Limited

Typeset in 10/13 pt Baskerville.
Typesetting and origination by
Sutton Publishing Limited.
Printed in Great Britain
by MPG Books, Bodmin, Cornwall.

Contents

Note on Dates

There were two calendars in use during the seventeenth century. Continental Europe used the Gregorian or New Style system of dating, while England clung to the Julian or Old Style calendar and was thus ten days behind the rest of Europe. In this book I have used New Style for Continental events, Old Style for those in England and Scotland, indicating when the two overlap.

Chronology of Events

1640
3 November   Long Parliament meets

1641
22 March   Trial of the Earl of Strafford opens in Westminster Hall
2 May   Wedding of Princess Mary and Prince William of Orange
3 May   Parliamentary Committee set up to investigate so-called Army Plot
10 May   The king consents to Act of Attainder against Strafford
12 May   Execution of Strafford
10 August   The king goes to Scotland
23 October   Rebellion breaks out in Ireland
25 November   The king welcomed in the City on his return from Scotland

1642
4 January   Attempted arrest of the Five Members
10 January   The king and queen leave Whitehall for Hampton Court
23 February   The queen and Princess Mary sail for Holland
19 March   The king enters York
23 April   The king refused entry to Hull
August   John Hutchinson and others prevent the Sheriff and Lord Lieutenant from commandeering Nottingham's powder magazine
22 August   Royal Standard raised at Nottingham
                    War begins
23 October   Battle of Edgehill
13 November   Royal army retreats from Turnham Green
29 November   The king settles into winter quarters at Oxford

1643

22 February	The queen lands at Bridlington and is bombarded by the parliamentary ships
7 March	The queen arrives at York
18 March	The Earl of Derby storms Lancaster
30 April	Lord Derby defeated at Whalley
1 May	Unsuccessful attempt to surprise Corfe Castle
2–8 May	Siege of Wardour Castle
23 May	The Commons impeach the queen
4 June	The queen leaves York
18 June	Action at Chalgrove Field
23 June	Siege of Corfe Castle begins
30 June	The Earl of Newcastle defeats the Fairfaxes at Adwalton Moor
	Lady Fairfax is taken prisoner
5 July	Battle of Lansdown Hill
13 July	Battle of Roundway Down
	King and queen reunited near Oxford
26 July	Siege of Brampton Bryan begins
27 July	Bristol surrenders to Prince Rupert
4 August	Siege of Corfe Castle raised
7–9 August	Peace demonstrations in London
10 August	The king begins siege of Gloucester
8 September	Gloucester relieved by the Earl of Essex
9 September	Siege of Brampton Bryan raised
18 September	Royalist raid on Nottingham led by Sir Richard Byron
20 September	First battle of Newbury
	Lord Falkland and the Earl of Sunderland killed
11 October	Battle of Winceby
31 October	Brilliana Harley dies
6–13 November	William Waller assaults Basing House
30 November	Treaty signed in Edinburgh between parliament and the Estates of Scotland
8 December	John Pym dies

1644

16 January	Second Royalist raid on Nottingham led by Sir Charles Lucas
19 January	First Scots regiments cross the Tweed

26 January	Battle of Nantwich
27 February	Siege of Lathom House begins
17 March	Brampton Bryan Castle falls to the Royalists
21 March	Prince Rupert defeats Sir John Meldrum at Newark
29 March	Battle of Alresford (aka Cheriton)
17 April	The queen leaves Oxford
April–June	Lyme besieged by Prince Maurice
1 May	The queen reaches Exeter
18 May	Wedding of Ann Harrison and Richard Fanshawe
27 May	Siege of Lathom House is raised
28 May	Bolton sacked by Prince Rupert and the Earl of Derby
16 June	Birth of Princess Henrietta Anne
29 June	Battle of Cropredy Bridge
2 July	Battle of Marston Moor
10 July	The queen sails from Falmouth
11 July	Siege of Basing House begins
25 July	The king at Exeter
31 August	Battle of Lostwithiel (aka Castle Dore)
9–14 September	Relief expedition to Basing House
27 October	Second battle of Newbury
19 December	Self-Denying Ordinance passed by the House of Commons

1645

January	Abortive peace talks between the royalist and parliamentary Commissioners at Uxbridge
4 March	The Prince of Wales leaves Oxford for Bristol
February–July	Siege of Scarborough Castle
April	Formation of New Model Army
20 May	Ann Fanshawe joins her husband with the Prince of Wales at Bristol
14 June	Battle of Naseby
10 July	Battle of Langport
21 August	Basing House besieged by Colonel Dalbier
10 September	Prince Rupert surrenders Bristol
13 September	Montrose defeated at Philiphaugh
24 September	Battle of Rowton Heath
8 October	Cromwell arrives at Basing

14 October	Storm and destruction of Basing House
December	Lathom House surrenders

1646

3 February	Lord Byron surrenders Chester to Sir William Brereton
27 February	Corfe Castle surrenders
2 March	The Prince of Wales sails to the Scilly Isles
9 April	Sir John Berkeley surrenders Exeter
16 April	The Prince of Wales sails to Jersey
5 May	The king surrenders to the Scots at Newark End of First Civil War
25 June	The Prince of Wales goes to France
25 July	Lady Dalkeith escapes to France with Princess Henrietta Anne

1647

30 January	The Scots hand the king over to parliament
4 June	Cornet Joyce removes the king from Holdenby
11 November	The king escapes from Hampton Court and travels to the Isle of Wight
26 December	The king signs secret 'Engagement' with the Scots

1648

20 April	The Duke of York escapes to Holland from St James's with the help of Anne Murray
17–19 August	Cromwell defeats the Scots at Preston
30 November	The king taken into custody by the army and removed to Hurst Castle
6 December	Pride's Purge of the House of Commons
23 December	The king is taken to Windsor Castle

1649

20 January	The king's trial begins
27 January	The king is sentenced to death John Hutchinson is one of the signatories to the death warrant
30 January	The king is executed in Whitehall
5 February	The Prince of Wales is proclaimed Charles II by the Scots

7 February	The monarchy is abolished and replaced by a Council of State
10 July	Cromwell leaves for Ireland

1650

1 June	Cromwell returns from Ireland
23 June	Charles II arrives in Scotland
3 September	Cromwell defeats the Scots at Dunbar
8 September	Princess Elizabeth dies at Carisbrooke Castle

1651

1 January	Charles II is crowned King of Scotland at Scone
3 September	Battle of Worcester
15 October	Charles finally escapes to France after seven weeks on the run The earl of Derby is executed at Bolton

1658

3 September	Oliver Cromwell dies

1660

25 May	Restoration of Charles II
29 August	Act of Oblivion and Indemnity passed

1663

11 October	John Hutchinson arrested on suspicion of complicity in the Northern Plot

1664

11 September	John Hutchinson dies in Sandown Castle

Introduction

'Our women are all on fire, striving through a gallant emulation to outdoe our men and will make good our yielding walls or loose their lives.' So wrote an anonymous chronicler of the siege of Chester in October 1645, adding that 'our ladies likewise like so many exemplary goddesses create a matchlesse forwardness in ye meaner sort'. Certainly in the war between king and parliament which rent the fabric of English society in the middle years of the seventeenth century, the women of England played an enthusiastic part. A significant number of them indeed, exhibited a degree of courage (and belligerence) so far above their sex as seriously to surprise and disconcert their men.

Perhaps pride of place should be given to the queen. Henrietta Maria may have had many faults but pusillanimity was not one of them, and she flung herself unreservedly into the support of her husband's cause. Undeterred by threats of kidnap and impeachment, she braved storms at sea and enemy bombardment – the only Queen of England to have sheltered in a ditch while cannon balls whistled overhead and a man was killed not twenty paces away – and never gave up trying, never gave up hope.

Other prominent heroines include the formidable Countess of Derby, who held Lathom House for the king in an epic three months' siege; brave Blanche Arundell at Wardour Castle; Mary Bankes at Corfe, who, with her daughters and maids, heaved stones and hot embers over the battlements at the storming parties of Roundheads; the Puritan Brilliana Harley, left to guard Brampton Bryan against the royalists; and Mary Winter, who refused to surrender Lydney House to the parliamentarian Colonel Massey. Then there were the wives who shared the dangers and discomforts of a prolonged siege with their husbands – notably the Marchioness of Winchester at Basing House and Elizabeth Cholmley at Scarborough Castle, whose husband wrote admiringly of his dear wife's uncomplaining courage in much hardship and danger. Anne Fairfax, wife of the parliament's general, was actually present with him on the field of battle and was taken prisoner before his eyes by the Earl of

Newcastle's troops at Adwalton Moor; although his lordship, always the soul of courtesy, sent her back to her husband the next day in his own coach.

Women also acted as couriers in those intrigues which, as the Earl of Clarendon put it, 'could best be carried on by ladies'. At the time of the Waller plot to seize the City in the spring of 1643 Lady d'Aubigny, widow of the king's cousin killed at Edgehill, came to London ostensibly on family business but carrying on her person the Commission of Array, to be proclaimed as soon as the timing of a royalist advance on the capital was known. A daughter of the Earl of Leicester was able to obtain a pass to travel from London to Oxford, 'her sex being less open to suspicion'. But according to the Venetian ambassador, 'the officials who met her on the way, having carefully searched her, found a catalogue with the names of all His Majesty's partisans in London. She was able to escape arrest herself with the excuse that it was put in her baggage by her servants without her knowledge, but the king could not escape the mischief done.'

Some women have left their own record of their experiences. Lucy Hutchinson, wife of the parliamentarian Governor of Nottingham and who shared his Puritan zeal, wrote a classic account of the war as she saw it at his side. Committed though she was, Lucy tended the wounded royalist prisoners in Nottingham Castle, considering it her Christian duty; just as Elizabeth Cholmley nursed the sick during the siege of Scarborough. Ann Harrison, a refugee in royalist Oxford, who married the diplomat Richard Fanshawe in May 1644, also recorded her memories of wartime life. The Fanshawes waited on the king at Hampton Court in 1647 and Ann described her last sight of him there, when she could not refrain from weeping.

Ann Fanshawe had nothing to do with Charles's flight from Hampton Court, but Anne Murray, later Lady Halket, played a vital part in the escape of the young Duke of York from St James's Palace and Jane Whorwood tried hard but unsuccessfully to help the king break out of Carisbrooke Castle. Another young woman who famously risked her life in a royal escape was Mistress Jane Lane, riding pillion behind Charles II disguised as her servant William Jackson after the disaster at Worcester.

There were plenty of anonymous heroines, too. Women of all ranks turned out to help dig the fortifications around London in the autumn of 1642. The women of Gloucester and Hull drew much admiration for their work on the defences of their home towns, and the women of Lyme, besieged by Prince Maurice in 1644, became renowned for their courage – going into the thickest danger to take ammunition, provisions and encouragement to their men. As well as providing more traditional services – 'they had their whores with them' complained Bulstrode Whitelocke when a troop of royalist cavalry occupied his house at Henley – women carried messages and acted as look-outs, loaded muskets and sometimes fired them. A few adventurous spirits, the so-called She Souldiers, even dressed in men's clothes and fought alongside the men.

And, of course, there were the anonymous casualties: the maidservant killed by a stray bullet as she crossed St Margaret's churchyard on her way to fetch water during the peace demonstrations at Westminster in 1643; the girl rocking a baby in an empty house during one of the royalist raids on Nottingham struck dead by the wind of a bullet, which yet left the child in the cradle unharmed. Several women were killed during the siege of Chester, a girl died while carrying earth for the ramparts at Hull, another lost a hand in the siege of Lyme. Two of Lady Winchester's maids were killed in the storming of Basing House, and a clergyman's daughter was knocked on the head as she tried to protect her father from being beaten up.

Then there were the victims: Susan Rodway, the London wife bemoaning the fact that her husband, away at the war, did not consider that she was a lone woman, and praying for his safe return; widows like the young Countess of Sunderland, eight months pregnant with her fourth child when her husband was killed at Newbury; the Verney sisters, marooned at Claydon, fatherless, unprotected and impoverished.

This is not a history of the Civil War. Rather it is an attempt to illustrate how the conflict, as it unfolded, affected the lives of women of all classes and how they coped with unfamiliar and frightening responsibilities, loss and bereavement, divided families, exile and financial ruin. 'Not only the family I am linked to is ruined', wrote Margaret Cavendish, Duchess of Newcastle, born Margaret Lucas, 'but the family from which I sprung, by these unhappy wars; which ruin my mother lived to see, and then died having lived a widow many years . . . She made her house her cloister, for she seldom went abroad, unless to church. But these unhappy wars forced her out, by reason she and her children were loyal to the king. For which they plundered her and my brothers of all their goods, plate, jewels, money, corn, cattle and the like; cut down their woods, pulled down their houses, and sequestered them from their lands and livings.'

Even when the fighting ended, the war was not over for the losing side and wives like Mary Verney, Margaret Newcastle, Isabella Twysden and Ann Fanshawe journeyed tirelessly to and fro, petitioning to get their husbands' property freed from sequestration or their husbands freed from gaol. The strength and stamina of these women is amazing, especially bearing in mind that the relentless cycle of reproduction was hardly interrupted. Ann Fanshawe suffered four miscarriages, including one of triplets, carried fourteen babies to term and saw nine of them die. Lucy Hutchinson miscarried of twins and lost two more children during the war, but still had four sons and four daughters surviving. The queen's ninth and last child was a wartime baby, born at Exeter just before Henrietta Maria was finally driven out of England.

None of the ladies seem to have resented the heavy demands made upon them. Lucy Hutchinson, a woman of brains and strength of character, was content to wait on her husband as his shadow. Brilliana Harley, although often afraid, accepted her situation as an inescapable duty, while continuing to worry about whether her husband, away in London, was eating a proper breakfast.

The degree of love and trust existing between these husbands and wives emerges strongly from their letters and memoirs. Hugh Cholmley was so heartbroken when Elizabeth died that he could not bear to stay in the house where they had lived together. When Ralph Verney was left a widower, he 'bid adieu to all that most men count theire happinesse'. 'Her company made every place a paradice to me', he told his friend William Denton, 'but she being gonn, what good can be expected by your most afflicted and unfortunate servant.' Lucy Hutchinson wrote of her husband that 'never man had a greater passion for a woman, nor a more honourable esteeme of a wife . . . So liberall was he to her and of so generous a temper that he hated the mention of sever'd purses, his estate being so much at her dispose that he never would receive an account of anie thing she expended.' Richard Fanshawe, whose finances were, of necessity, frequently of the hand to mouth variety, was happy to turn the management of his money over to his wife, who could say of her marriage that 'our aims and designs were one, our loves one, and our resentments one. We so studied one the other that we knew each other's mind by our looks.'

For all their courage and devotion the women had little effect on the course of the war or its outcome – not even the queen, for all her efforts. Nor did it have any lasting effect on the position of women in society. As things settled down again, the heroines slipped back into their accustomed subservience, apparently believing with Lucy Hutchinson that their sex, 'through ignorance and weakness of judgement', would always be inferior to the masculine understanding of men.

But although there were atrocities on both sides – the sack of Bolton and the massacre of the camp followers in the royal baggage train after Naseby, for example – much suffering and loss of innocent life, the general conduct of the English Civil War bears no comparison with the sort of barbarity commonplace in the near contemporaneous religious wars in Europe, and perhaps some at least of the credit for that should go to the women of England.

Map showing principal places and battles of the English Civil War

CHAPTER ONE

'Her She-Majesty Generalissima'

I wish to share all your fortune, and participate in
your troubles, as I have done in your happiness,
provided it be with honour, and in your defence.

Henrietta Maria to Charles I

Dover, Tuesday 23 February 1642, and a small crowd had gathered in the
harbour below the castle to see Queen Henrietta Maria and the ten-year-
old Princess Royal prepare to set sail for Holland. King Charles had
accompanied his wife and daughter as far as the water's edge and their
parting was a sorrowful one. The king kissed the Princess Mary, of all his
children the one who most closely resembled him, sighing that he was
afraid he would never see her again, and the Venetian ambassador heard
that husband and wife had clung together 'conversing in sweet discourse
and affectionate embraces'. Both were in tears and many of the
onlookers wept in sympathy. At last the king reluctantly tore himself away.
The queen and princess went on board the *Lion*, the ships weighed
anchor and Charles rode along the shoreline, a lonely little figure waving
his hat in farewell until the sails faded from sight.

The publicly announced purpose of the queen's journey was to deliver
her daughter, married the year before to Prince William of Orange, to
her new family and see the child well settled in. But although the Prince
of Orange had sent out a fleet of fifteen warships to greet and escort his
son's bride, on the English side there had been a noticeable lack of the
sort of elaborate preparation normally associated with such a royal
progress. Only three 'ladies of honour' and two noblemen were to be of
the party, and it was not until 13 February that Sir John Pennington,
Admiral of the Fleet for the Guard of the Narrow Seas, had received a
warrant authorizing him to 'take up sufficient vessels for the transporting
into Holland provisions and baggage, besides horses and coaches, for the
use of the Queen, Princess Mary, their servants and followers'. The
Admiral's secretary did not see how the queen could be ready so soon,
'except she will go without her horses and coaches', and was seriously

shocked by the way in which the travel arrangements were being made. 'Things are done in such post haste that I never heard of the like for the voyage of persons of so great dignity.'[1]

It was being given out that the queen's 'sudden resolution' to leave the country had been caused by Orange insistence that young Mary should be sent over to Holland without further delay, but there was more than a suggestion of panic about the speed of her departure. During the past fifteen months, as the conflict between king and parliament steadily escalated, the Catholic queen had been made the target of a virulent hate campaign accusing her, among other things, of encouraging a revival of popery, of protecting Jesuit and other missionary priests from the consequences of their treasonable activities, of conspiring to bring foreign armies into the realm, and of being in secret communication with the rebellious Irish Catholics. Her position had thus become increasingly unsustainable and by the beginning of 1642 events had brought matters to a crisis, forcing her into something uncomfortably like flight.

There had never been any secret about Henrietta Maria's devotion to her religion, not since she had first arrived from France as a fifteen-year-old bride. On the contrary, she chose deliberately to parade it, regardless of the offence caused to radical Protestant opinion. Her chapel at Somerset House was always open to other Catholics and, indeed, to anyone who cared to come and explore the mysteries of the Old Faith which had acquired a new glamour under the influence of the elegant, vivacious little queen. The radical Protestants, or Puritans, always strongest in London and the south-east, looked on with deepening alarm and resentment as they saw the Catholics growing in numbers and boldness – 'priestes, friars and Jesuites walking at noon day' – while superstition and idolatry flourished at court. But it was not until 1640, when the king's dire need for money to pay for his disastrous Scottish wars forced him to summon parliament after more than a decade of personal rule, that the Puritan tendency gained leadership and formal organization. The assembly known to history as the Long Parliament met at Westminster at the beginning of November and nothing in England was ever the same again. 'The Parliamentarians', reported the Venetian ambassador, 'let it be freely understood that they will not allow the parliament to be dissolved any more but only prorogued, so that it shall meet every year. If this happens no further authority will remain to the king than to be the minister and executor of the will of his people.'[2]

By order of parliament Tuesday 17 November was observed as a day of prayer and fasting, and Puritan preachers everywhere mounted their pulpits to thunder against tyranny and popery, 'stirring up the people to put down the Catholic religion entirely'. Thus encouraged, a hostile crowd gathered outside the queen's chapel on the following Sunday and proceeded to attack members of the congregation with stones and weapons as they emerged after mass.[3] The House of Commons meanwhile had appointed a committee to look into the operation of the penal laws affecting the Catholic minority. This body quickly fastened on to the suspicious number of priests released from prison at the instigation of people in high places, as well as noting the swarms of papists protected by reason of their status as the queen's servants. In December the queen was notified that she must dismiss all the English Catholics in her household, but her majesty, 'justly incensed', retorted that if she was forced to deprive herself of her Catholic servants, she would dismiss the Protestants as well.[4] There was more unpleasantness over the fate of a Jesuit priest named Goodman, condemned to death for treason but reprieved by the king at the queen's request. 'When the parliament and the city learned this they both had recourse to the king, to permit the sentence to be carried out, or else they assured him of the offence his people would take . . . They also threatened the queen with greater ills.' The king hesitated, temporized and then gave way, remitting the case into the care of parliament, so that the Venetian ambassador feared the unfortunate priest would eventually come to the butcher's knife.[5]

Threats against his wife were those which Charles dreaded most, but for the time being the opposition's vengeful attention was concentrated on Thomas Wentworth, Earl of Strafford, a tough, uncompromising Yorkshireman, recently recalled from his post as Lord Lieutenant in Ireland. A ruthlessly efficient administrator and by far the king's most loyal and able servant, 'Black Tom Tyrant' represented a dangerous obstacle to be removed as a matter of urgency. One of parliament's first acts, therefore, had been to secure his arrest on a charge of high treason and in March 1641 he was brought to Westminster Hall to answer a long list of articles of impeachment.

The king and queen attended the trial on a regular basis in a deliberate show of support for the accused and Henrietta, who had not previously taken much interest in politics – she was later to regret that she had not studied English history as a girl – sat listening intently, taking notes and trying to understand what was going on. The queen, who tended to see everything in terms of personalities, had never liked the Earl of Strafford – to be fair, he was not a particularly likeable individual – but having once realized his importance to her husband's cause she was eager to do what she could to help him.

Characteristically enough her idea of being helpful consisted of arranging a series of late night secret rendezvous with some of the 'most wicked' members of the opposition party. According to her own account, these interviews took place in the apartments of one of her ladies-in-waiting who was conveniently absent in the country, and the queen would descend the backstairs, quite alone and carrying a single candle to light the way.[6] But with the possible exception of George Digby, the Earl of Bristol's son, she does not appear to have succeeded in getting any of her visitors to change sides and her persuasive efforts, if they did not actively harm, certainly did nothing to improve Strafford's prospects.

Actively damaging, however, was her encouragement of a scheme being discussed by a group of young army officers and courtiers to occupy London, seize the Tower and free the prisoner, using the remnants of the second expeditionary force sent against the Scots. This enterprising plan, with its promise of action and quick results, made an immediate appeal to Henrietta's restless, impatient nature. Although she might occasionally be driven to make a conciliatory gesture, it never once crossed her mind that the enemy might have a valid point of view. In her eyes all those who, for whatever reason, challenged the king's authority were quite simply rogues, rebels and traitors to be destroyed without compunction by whatever means came nearest to hand. But unfortunately for its begetters, the Army Plot, as it came to be known, owed a good deal more to wishful thinking than to the facts of life. The increased comings and goings of certain military men about the court and the general air of suppressed excitement among the queen's friends did not go unremarked. Inevitably the amateur conspirators lacked cohesion and discretion. Inevitably news of their intentions was leaked and before long had reached the ears of John Pym and other leaders of 'the inflexible party' in the House of Commons.

It was probably no coincidence that the attack on the Earl of Strafford now abruptly changed gear and, while his trial was still proceeding, a bill of attainder against him was introduced into parliament. This obsolete but still deadly weapon merely decreed the guilt of an accused person by the will of the majority and on 21 April the Commons effectively passed sentence by a majority of 204 to 59.

The royal family's attention was temporarily distracted from the rising political storm by the arrival from Holland of the Princess Royal's fifteen-year-old fiancé, and the two children were married very quietly in the chapel at Whitehall on Sunday 2 May. In normal times a royal wedding would have been the occasion for civic banquets, street parties, firework displays and plenty of free wine and beer to drink the health of the happy pair, but in that turbulent spring of 1641 the event passed almost unnoticed outside the palace. Strafford's attainder was now before the House of Lords and on the day following the marriage a large crowd of 'substantial citizens' gathered at Westminster noisily demanding justice and the head of the Lieutenant, 'calling him traitor and enemy to the public liberty'. According to the Venetian ambassador, they refused to be pacified by mere words and threatened violent actions against 'his majesty's own person and all the royal house'.

On 5 May John Pym, choosing his moment, revealed the details of the so-called Army Plot, informing a jittery House of Commons that 'he had great cause to fear, there was at that time as desperate a design and conspiracy against the parliament, as had been in any age; and he was in no doubt, persons of great quality and credit at court had their hands in it.'[7] The army plotters, 'five servants of the queen of the highest standing and favour' and including her close friend Henry Jermyn, fled ingloriously for their lives, while something approaching mass hysteria gripped the usually level-headed Londoners. Strafford had been accused of planning to bring his Irish army over to subdue the English. Now it seemed that the English army, too, was involved and rumours quickly spread that the French, or perhaps the Spanish, were about to land at Portsmouth and that the papists had attacked the House of Commons and set it on fire.

The Lords continued to be surrounded by an angry mob and on 8 May a thinly attended House passed the attainder, only eleven peers dissenting. All that was needed to complete the process was the king's signature and for two nerve-racking days Charles held out against the relentless pressure being exerted on him. The mob was now besieging Whitehall and could clearly be heard baying for justice, 'not without great and insolent threats and expressions, what they would do, if it were not speedily granted'. The palace, a rambling warren of courts, alleys and gardens, would have been impossible to defend if the bloodthirsty rabble outside had once broken in and, as no less a personage than the Archbishop of York pointed out to his majesty, it was no longer a question of whether he should save the Earl of Strafford, but whether he and, most probably, his wife and children should perish with him.[8] On 10 May he signed, and within forty-eight hours Strafford had been beheaded on Tower Hill in the presence of a triumphant crowd more than 100,000 strong.

It was a bitter defeat and a surrender for which Charles never forgave himself. 'The king,' commented the Venetian ambassador, 'thus deprived of authority with the hatred of the people, which is even stronger against the queen . . . suffers the tortures of the deepest affliction.' Henrietta, too, shed tears of mortification and was later to tell her friend Madame de Motteville how she and the king had both foreseen that this death would some day take the life of one and the peace of mind of the other.

The queen had already lost most of her peace of mind. Not only was she widely suspected of responsibility for the recent French invasion scare, but evil-minded gossip accused her of having had an improper relationship with Henry Jermyn, her Master of the Horse. It was true that those not 'blinded by passion' were beginning to discount some of the wilder rumours, but the parliamentary committee set up to enquire into the origins of the Army Plot found the queen to have been deeply implicated in the conspiracy. 'The end of this enquiry', reported the Venetian ambassador, 'remains uncertain, and it keeps the whole Court in a state of anxious anticipation. Meanwhile,' he continued ominously, 'as they are searching ancient documents to find out what was done with other queens in like circumstances, the fear grows that parliament intends to force the queen to clear herself.'[9]

The king was planning to go north that summer to try and reach an accommodation with the Scots and the queen announced that she wished to go abroad for the sake of her health. She would first take the Princess Royal to Holland as requested by the Prince of Orange, and then go on to Spa to take the waters. Suspecting that she meant to stir up trouble in Europe, the Commons at once raised objections and insisted on interrogating her doctor, who failed to convince them that there was anything very much the matter with her majesty, apart from 'an unquiet mind' which they promised to make every effort to soothe if she would agree to stay at home. As for the princess, the members positively could not consent to her joining her husband until she was old enough to be a wife.

Thwarted, Henrietta retreated gloomily to Oatlands, the old Tudor hunting lodge near Weybridge. She was deeply depressed. 'I swear to you that I am almost mad with the sudden change in my fortunes', she wrote to her sister Christine. 'From the highest point of happiness I am fallen into despair . . . Imagine what I feel to see the King's power taken from him, the Catholics persecuted, the priests hanged, the people faithful to us sent away and pursued for their lives because they serve the King. As for myself, I am kept like a prisoner, so that they will not even allow me to follow the King who is going to Scotland, and with no one in the world to whom I can confide my troubles.'[10]

Henrietta found her forced inactivity one of the hardest things she had to bear. As she told her sister, it seemed she could only sit waiting helplessly for the enemy to do their worst. All the same she was not entirely idle, using the summer months working to try to strengthen support for the king in the Lords and especially urging the younger more impressionable members of the peerage to do their duty by attending the House.

Charles returned to London in November to a surprisingly warm welcome from the citizens, but almost simultaneously came the stunning news of rebellion in Ireland and stories of atrocities against the Protestant settlers produced a fresh outburst of anti-Catholic fury. The rumour factory was once more working at full stretch, and this time the queen was accused of being hand-in-glove with the Irish rebel chieftains. The capital was once more in uproar, with excited mobs roaming the precincts of Westminster and Whitehall looking for trouble. There were some violent confrontations between the king's officers and bands of city apprentices on the loose during the Christmas holidays, and for the first time the opprobrious epithets Roundhead and Cavalier were being flung around.[11]

The old year ended in disorder, bitterness and fear. The new year opened with a development long dreaded by both the king and queen. Charles had recently been showing signs of attempting a counter-attack on his tormentors in the Commons and, reported that industrious correspondent the Venetian ambassador: 'After the riot of the apprentices his Majesty decided to form a *corps de garde* at the palace composed of the trained bands here and also to keep near him those officers who volunteered their services.' The hard core of the opposition chose to regard this as a deliberate provocation and 'persuaded them-selves that the king's action and his resentment were due to the advice of the queen. Accordingly they decided to accuse her in parliament of conspiring against the public liberty and of secret intelligence in the rebellion in Ireland.'[12]

If the junta led by John Pym had intended to force a showdown they could not have calculated it more exactly. The king's devotion to and dependence on his wife were well known and, as soon as rumours of her

7

impending impeachment came to his ears, he prepared to launch a pre-
emptive strike, ordering the Attorney General to bring charges of high
treason against Pym and four of his closest associates. The Commons,
predictably, refused to surrender them. On the contrary, they declared
the accusations to be an infamous libel and a breach of privilege, 'thus
casting shame on his Majesty's commands'. Next day, on 4 January, in a
desperate bid to re-establish his authority, the king made his famous
descent on the Commons' chamber, only to find that the birds,
forewarned, had flown.

The queen, waiting at the palace and anxiously watching the clock
until she could contain her excitement and impatience no longer, had
blurted out to her friend and confidante the Countess of Carlisle:
'Rejoice, for at this hour the King, I hope, is master of the state and such-
and-such are doubtless under arrest.' Lucy Carlisle showed no emotion at
this startling announcement but found an excuse to slip away and send a
hasty warning to *her* friend and confidant John Pym, so that Henrietta,
who believed herself to have been the only person with prior knowledge
of the intended *coup*, ever afterwards blamed her own indiscretion for the
fiasco of the Five Members.[13]

In fact, the informant appears to have come from the French embassy,
the ambassador having his own reasons for wanting to keep on good
terms with parliament. But in any case Charles had walked into a
carefully baited trap and had now committed the ultimate folly of
attempting a violent and unlawful act and failing. It was the end of
London for him, and a week later the king and queen with their three
eldest children fled from Whitehall to Hampton Court. On the following
day the five members emerged from their hiding-places in the City and
returned to Westminster in triumph. As the cheering procession passed
under the windows of the deserted royal apartments there were derisive
cries of 'Where is the King and his Cavaliers?'

The king and his family had passed an uncomfortable night at
Hampton Court, which had been quite unprepared for their arrival – so
much so that they had all had to sleep in one bed. They moved on to
Windsor for greater security, but it was now obvious that the queen
would have to leave England as soon as possible. This time the
Commons made no objection because, so the Venetian ambassador
believed, they thought the king would be easier to control with his wife
out of the way. But there were still misgivings about the queen's
unadvertised intentions, and steps had been taken to prevent her from

taking crown property out of the country. Nevertheless, when she went on board the *Lion* at Dover that February day, as well as her own and the king's personal jewellery, Henrietta had in her luggage a number of other important pieces. These included the Grand Sancy, acquired by James I and said to be the most valuable white diamond in Western Europe, another huge diamond known as the Mirror of Portugal which had belonged to Queen Elizabeth, and several gold collars, one set with rubies and pearls belonging to Henry VIII.[14] These were all part of the crown jewels which Henrietta was planning to use to raise money for the approaching armed struggle.

The queen was later to become notorious for her bad luck at sea but this particular voyage was uneventful, apart from the unfortunate loss of one of the baggage vessels which sprang a leak and sank at the mouth of the River Maas, taking with it all her majesty's chapel plate and the wardrobe of her principal lady-in-waiting. Prince William was waiting to welcome the travellers and it was decided that after fifteen hours in the cramped, uncomfortable conditions on board ship, they should go first to the palace at Honselaersdijck to rest and refresh themselves before going on to the Hague.

Among those who came out to greet the Queen of England and her daughter was another queen, Elizabeth of Bohemia, King Charles's elder sister, who had left England at the age of sixteen at the time of her marriage to Frederick, Elector Palatine of the Rhine. In 1619 Frederick had rashly accepted the offer of the throne of Bohemia, only to be ignominiously ejected within a year by the vengeful Habsburgs and stripped of his ancestral lands in what turned out to be the opening shots of the Thirty Years War. The family had been forced to seek sanctuary in Holland, and when he died twelve years later the Elector left his widow and ten surviving children to face a penurious and increasingly debt-ridden future, heavily dependent on the goodwill of their hosts. The various shattering calamities and disappointments she had endured would have destroyed a lesser woman, but Elizabeth was a survivor and, in spite of everything it had thrown at her, she retained her eager zest for life, her 'wild humour to be merry'. Now, as they sat side by side in the Orange state coach, she was doing her best to make friends with her sister-in-law, although she disapproved of Henrietta's Catholicism and thought her influence on Charles unhelpful. 'The queen is against any agreement with parliament but by war, and the king doth nothing but by her approbation.'

The Queen of Bohemia was also accompanied by a daughter – eleven-year-old Sophie, chosen from among her sisters because she was nearest in age to the Princess Mary. Long afterwards when, as Duchess of Hanover, she was writing her memoirs, Sophie vividly recalled her surprise at finding her glamorous aunt from England, 'so beautiful in her picture', to be a thin little woman 'with long lean arms, crooked shoulders, and teeth protruding from her mouth like guns from a fort.'[15] In fact, and Van Dyck's portraits notwithstanding, Henrietta had never been beautiful. But she had all the Frenchwoman's instinctive flair for chic, and in the days when she could describe herself as 'the happiest queen in the world', people noticed only her gaiety and animation, her big sparkling dark eyes, her perfect complexion, her exquisite taste in dress. But she was thirty-two now, and ten years of childbearing and nearly two years of mounting anxiety and nervous strain had taken their toll of the tired little woman being carefully gracious to her husband's sister and remembering to compliment young Sophie on her looks.

The queen was given a polite but not ecstatic reception at the Hague. The situation was not without its social awkwardness, for in normal circumstances the King and Queen of England would not have considered the Prince of Orange's son a fit match for their eldest daughter and it had raised eyebrows in several European courts; but the prince had been prepared to pay handsomely for the privilege of acquiring such a prestigious addition to his family and King Charles, who badly needed the ready cash, had been in no position to refuse a good offer. Now, although the Prince of Orange took delivery of his daughter-in-law with satisfaction and all the deference due to her exalted rank, he had not bargained for having to entertain her mother as well and had done what he could to discourage the queen's visit. More seriously, the oligarchy of Dutch burghers who made up the States General of the United Provinces, of which Holland was the largest and richest, and who wielded the real power of an increasingly important maritime trading nation were less than impressed by the grandeur of the English alliance. Sturdy Calvinist citizens stared suspiciously at her majesty from under their hat brims, sat down uninvited in her presence and sometimes just walked away without bowing or speaking. The High Mightinesses of the States General were predominantly republican in sympathy and, wrote an English resident at the Hague in a letter to his brother, were 'studying all the wayes they can to gratifie and complie with your Parliament; not caring who they displease, so they satisfie them. I verily thinke', continued William Newton, 'the Queen as the matter stands, will not trouble them long heere, and that yee shall have her in England yet a good while before Easter.'[16]

But Henrietta, now installed in comfortable apartments in the New Palace in the Staedt-Straat, had begun to turn her attention to the serious purpose of her journey and showed no signs of being easily dislodged. She was anxious for news from Charles, who had left on his way north after their parting at Dover. He was making for the provincial capital of York, but it was also imperative that he should lose no time in making sure of the town of Hull, which was not only a valuable sea-port but contained a 'great magazine of arms and ammunition' left there after the Scottish wars. 'Hull must absolutely be had,' wrote the queen. It was vital to have an east coast port to which money, military supplies and letters could safely be sent across the North Sea.

Henrietta was worried about the security of the code in which she and Charles were to communicate. 'Be careful how you write in cipher . . . Take good care I beg of you, and put in nothing which is not in my cipher. Once again I remind you to take good care of your pocket, and not let our cipher be stolen.'[17] She was still waiting to know 'assuredly' where the king was when she wrote again. 'I hope this bearer will find you at York . . . and that if you find York well-affected, you will go to Hull, for we must have Hull.' She had heard a disturbing rumour that he was returning to London, but 'I believe nothing of it; and hope that you are more constant in your resolutions; you have already learned to your cost, that want of perseverance in your designs has ruined you.'

It was obvious that Henrietta placed very little reliance on her husband's standing firm without her beside him to stiffen his backbone. If he had indeed gone back to London with some idea of reaching an 'accommodation' with parliament she would, she told him flatly, have to leave him and retire into a convent, for she could never trust herself 'to those persons who would be your directors, nor to you, since you would have broken your promise to me'. She could hardly bring herself to think that he would do such a thing but: 'I confess I am troubled almost to death for fear of the contrary; and I have cause, for if you have broken your resolution, there is nothing but death for me.'[18]

While she was writing this letter, she heard from Charles at Newmarket. This was disappointing, as she had been hoping he would be at York by now, but she was so relieved to find that he had not gone back to London that she did not reproach him, apart from reminding him that delay had never yet been to his advantage. For her part she was losing no time, but had to admit that so far she had no money worth sending. She had been encountering unexpected difficulty in pawning the more valuable pieces of jewellery she had brought with her. It seemed they were just too grand and too expensive for the market at the Hague, added to which irritating doubts were being expressed about the queen's authority to pledge such large and important pieces.

At last, in mid-April, she received the news that the king had finally reached York and found the country 'well-affected', but he had still made no attempt to occupy Hull and Henrietta was furiously impatient with his excuses. 'As to what you write me, that everybody dissuades you . . . from taking it by force, unless the parliament begins, – is it not beginning to put persons into it against your orders? . . . For you having Hull is not beginning any thing violent, it is only against the rascal who refuses it to you.' In the queen's opinion, parliament was simply playing cat and mouse, and at this rate any money she succeeded in raising would be spent while the king waited for them to declare war. Then 'there will be no further means of getting other monies, and thus you will be reduced to do what the Parliament shall please, and I shall be constrained to retire into a convent, or to beg alms.' Poor Henrietta's frustration was almost unbearable, but afraid she might have said too much, she apologized for her 'folly and weakness'. It was surely understandable, for 'my whole hope lies only in your firmness and constancy, and when I hear anything to the contrary, I am mad.'[19]

In her next letter the queen was able to report that 'after much trouble, we have at last procured some money, but only a little as yet, for the fears of the merchants are not yet entirely passed away. It was written from London that I had carried off my jewels secretly, and against your wish, and that if money was lent me upon them, that would be no safety for them.' However, now that she had received a 'power' signed by the king, it was easier to do business. She had had to part with some cherished possessions, such as Charles's pearl buttons. 'You cannot imagine how handsome the buttons were, when they were out of the gold and strung into a chain . . . I assure you that I gave them up with no small regret. Nobody would take them in pledge, but only buy them. You may judge', she wrote bitterly, 'now, when they know that we want money, how they keep their foot on our throat. I could not get for them more than half of what they are worth.' She had already pledged all her own jewellery, including her 'great chain' and a crucifix which had belonged to her mother, but 'with all these I could not get any more money than what I send you'. She had been advised to try and pawn the ruby collar at Antwerp, and was trying to interest the King of Denmark in the largest gold collar. 'This is all that concerns money', she went on, 'but if we put all our jewels in pledge and consume them without doing anything, they would be lost, and we too.' Yet again she urged her husband to 'take a good resolution and pursue it . . . for to begin and then stop is your ruin – experience shows it you.'[20]

Henrietta had repeatedly been told that the Jews of Amsterdam might be willing to lend her money, and early in May the Prince of Orange escorted her there 'to note the marvels of the wealth of the city'. The Amsterdammers were well known for their republican sympathies and disapproval of all royal pretensions, but they gave the Queen of England an elaborate welcome, which included a barge drawn by swans, pageants and 'triumphs' on the water. Unfortunately, the visit was cut short by the death of one of the Orange princesses, so that the queen had no opportunity to open negotiations with the money-lenders.[21]

Back at the Hague and back at her desk writing and enciphering her endless letters to Charles, she returned to the seemingly hopeless task of trying to prod him into action, pointing out that the longer he delayed in seizing Hull, the worse his situation would be. If parliament, which now controlled the navy, were to send a fleet to remove the precious arsenal he would be powerless to prevent it, and 'if before that, you do not get the place, the folly is so great that I do not understand it'. She was afraid, too, that he might be pressured into signing the militia bill, ceding control of the armed forces. Perhaps he had already done so and was back at his old game of yielding everything. Henrietta was beginning to wish she had never left England, for all she had done was to make herself look ridiculous. The whole point of her journey had been to leave the king free to act without fear of danger to her person, but if he was only going to sit at York and do nothing, she might just as well have gone there with him, and she ended by repeating her threat of retiring into a convent, 'for you are no longer capable of protecting any one, not even yourself'.[22]

Before this latest broadside could be despatched, a messenger arrived from England with news of 'all that has passed at Hull'. It was not encouraging. Apparently Charles had sent his second son, the eight-year-old James, Duke of York, and his nephew Charles Louis, eldest son of the Queen of Bohemia, to pay a 'friendly' visit to the town. They had been welcomed, rather reluctantly, by the Governor, Sir John Hotham, and entertained to dinner, but when the king himself arrived a little later at the head of a troop of horse, the gates were shut and he was refused admission.

'You see what you have got by not following your first resolutions,' wrote the queen, with pardonable exasperation. 'Do not delay longer now in consultations, it is action which must do the work at this hour; – it is time.' The Governor of Hull was a traitor who must be taken alive or dead, and Henrietta wished she could have been in James's place. 'I would have flung the rascal over the walls, or he should have done the same to me.' There was no point in further reproaches, but: 'Courage! I have never felt so much: it is a good omen.'[23]

Although she was keeping up a brave front for Charles – 'Go on boldly: God will assist you' – with her old friend and former governess Mamie St Georges she could let down her guard. 'Pray to God for me, for be assured that there is not a more wretched creature in this world than I, separated far from the king my lord, from my children, out of my country, and without hope of returning there, except at imminent peril – abandoned by all the world, unless God assist me, and the good prayers of my friends . . . Recommend me to the good Carmelites of Paris. I would fain, if it were possible, wish myself with them . . . I assure you it is the only thing I think of with pleasure.'[24]

Spring turned into summer and at the beginning of June Henrietta and her daughter went to visit the Prince of Orange and his son with the Dutch army in camp near Utrecht, and were present at a grand military review. The queen was now busy learning her way about the unfamiliar business of acquiring weapons of war, and on 4 June wrote to tell the king that she hoped very soon to be able to send him 'six pieces of cannon, with one hundred barrels of powder, and two hundred pairs of pistols and carabines'. She was also planning to send 'for the present ten thousand pieces [of money]'.[25]

The task of accumulating supplies became all the more necessary when, a few days later, a letter arrived from Charles bringing the not unexpected news that the arms and ammunition stored at Hull had been removed to London by order of parliament. In her reply, Henrietta commented with noble restraint that it would not be easy to find the money to make up for this 'sad loss'. 'I must say', she went on, 'that if you had not delayed this going to Hull so long as you did, I think that you would not have lost your magazine . . . I am ever returning to the old point – lose no time, for that will ruin you.' But, 'believe, my dear heart, that I am moved to speak by no consideration in the world but by that of my affection for you.'[26] The king does not seem to have resented his wife's plain speaking, for in a fragment of a letter written that summer complaining that there had been nothing from her in the 'weekly despatch', he says sadly 'I would rather have thee chide me than be silent'.

Exactly how much money and matériel Henrietta managed to collect while she was in Holland remains somewhat unclear. Writing in July she enumerates thirty thousand guilders received from the Prince of Orange, plus 'one thousand saddles with all appurtenances, five hundred carabines, two hundred firelocks, ten loads of powder', but does not explain whether these were part of or in addition to the earlier list.[27] Nor is it at all clear just how many of these precious supplies ever reached their destination.

Two of the Queen of Bohemia's soldier sons, the Princes Rupert and Maurice, were now preparing to join their uncle and Henrietta proposed to send a shipment of arms over with them. The Palatine princes, sailing in the *Lion*, were driven back by bad weather, but their other ship, the 300-ton *Providence*, managed to reach the Humber. According to the Venetian ambassador, she brought 'cannons, gunpowder, arms, saddles and other munitions of war', but was attacked by ships of the parliamentary fleet which were lying in wait. Fortunately for the king, her master, Captain Strahan, was not only 'full of zeal for the royal service', but a skilful seaman who evaded pursuit by running the *Providence* into one of the small sandy creeks in the estuary, where her cargo was successfully unloaded.[28]

Others were less fortunate, for in a postscript to his next despatch, dated 25 July (NS) Giovanni Giustinian reported: 'News comes at this moment that two ships from Holland appeared off Uls [Hull], sent by the queen with munitions to his Majesty. Falling in with the ships of the fleet they had to surrender, with disadvantage to his Majesty's designs.'[29] There is mention, too, of 'a small Dutch ship, sent . . . towards York by the queen of England with military provisions', which had to turn back 'having escaped from the pursuit of two large Parliament ships'.[30]

But in August two ships did reach the king from Holland, carrying 'munitions, arms, money, and many English captains, who have fought a long time in the armies of the Prince of Orange'. Giustinian does not say so, but these were presumably part of the convoy escorting Rupert and Maurice, who finally landed at Newcastle on 20 August (OS) bringing with them 'money, munitions and arms sent by the queen to his Majesty'. Two more ships are mentioned in the Venetian despatches as 'arriving in the waters of Newcastle' during the autumn, one of them bringing the king 'a thousand sets of horse armour, 3500 muskets and other munitions'; but a third, carrying 'munitions, arms and 140 officers for the army', was forced to put in at Yarmouth, where it was seized by the enemy. 'A serious loss to the royal cause' commented Giovanni Giustinian.[31]

In one of her letters Henrietta speaks of having found a merchant who had assured her that he would deliver arms where she pleased, and there may well have been other anonymous little ships sailing out of the River Maas which managed to run the parliamentary blockade and slip unadvertised into the fishing ports of Bridlington, Scarborough and Newcastle. But the cargoes such vessels could carry would have been pathetically small, and the obstacles presented by wind and weather and hostile fleets must often have appeared insurmountable. Altogether it was a disheartening business and the queen often felt quite crushed by her various afflictions and anxieties. 'If you knew my unhappiness as it really is, you would pity me still more,' she told her sister. She was suffering acutely from migraine – 'I have almost always pains in the eyes, and my sight even is not so good as it was.' She didn't know whether this was caused by the air of Holland, by too much crying, or the strain of all the writing she was having to do.[32] She was worried about her children. The Prince of Wales and the Duke of York were with their father, but the two youngest, Elizabeth and Henry, who was not much more than a baby, had been left behind at St James's when the family fled to Hampton Court and were now in the hands of the parliament. This was bad enough, but worst of all was her nagging fear that the king might yet be persuaded into agreeing to some dishonourable 'accommodation' with parliament, and find himself pardoning his enemies and forsaking his friends. 'You should take good care what you grant', she wrote urgently, 'for you are lost for ever if you abandon your servants . . . If you abandon your servants, it will be worse than your crown . . .'. It would be the end of everything and she would have to 'retire to some place, like a good country lady, where I can pray to God to take care of you, as he has assured me he will'.[33]

In spite of these trials and tribulations – her uneasiness about what was going on at home, her headaches and her continuing problems with tight-fisted Dutch pawnbrokers and money-grubbing arms dealers – Henrietta struggled valiantly on with her self-appointed task, sustained always by her angry, protective love for Charles – 'there is nothing in the world, no trouble, which shall hinder me from serving you and loving you above everything in the world' – and her unshakeable conviction of the justice of their cause. 'Justice suffers with us. Always take care that we have her on our side: she is a good army.'[34]

Henrietta was not, in fact, quite so friendless as she sometimes made out. The Prince of Orange had done what he could for his uninvited and often importunate guest. He had allowed several exiled royalists such as Henry Jermyn, the Lords Goring and Digby and the former Secretary of State Francis Windebank, to join her at the Hague in spite of the ban imposed on them by the States General. He had also turned a blind eye, in defiance of the States' disapproval, to the shipment of arms from Dutch ports and had given a number of his more experienced officers leave to go and join King Charles. He was less eager to part with money, although he did offer himself as guarantor for the loans being made on the queen's jewels, even for 'the great collar' which, for some reason, no one would touch. Henrietta thought it must have some malediction on it.[35]

The prince's helpfulness to his embattled in-laws had not gone unnoticed in London and in August, to Henrietta's fury, 'the rebels under the name of Parliament' had the impudence to send an envoy of their own to the Hague. The queen immediately registered a violent objection to his presence and the envoy, Walter Strickland, was not given official recognition but, the States 'have sent to the rogue in private to know what his commission was'. This appears to have been to protest to their High Mightinesses over the assistance being rendered to the king, coupled with a warning that if nothing was done to put a stop to it, the English fleet would be obliged to regard all Dutch ships passing through the Channel as potential enemies. Henrietta told Charles that she thought her best course would be to issue a statement setting out 'the things which the Parliament has done against you, and that you have done for Parliament', in order to show their malice and try to undeceive the Hollanders. She was so weary, having been talking all day, and in such a passion about the envoy, that she was afraid her letter did not make much sense and Charles would have to get someone to help him decipher it. 'If I do not turn mad', she wrote, 'I shall be a great miracle.'[36]

The queen did not turn mad, but she was desperately hurt when rumours began to reach her from England that the king was dissatisfied with her efforts. She had been trying so hard to serve him and had been pathetically pleased by some of 'the pretty things' he had put in his letters, 'for you know I like to be praised'. But now it appeared she was being censured for not trying hard enough, which was especially unfair considering that 'if everybody had done their duty, as I have', Charles would not have been reduced to his present condition. Henrietta was certainly not prepared to accept blame from the armchair critics surrounding her husband – 'base souls, as are many of those near you' – and wrote him a long, self-justificatory letter listing the 'one thousand muskets, and as many pikes and swords', the two or three thousand pistols, another three thousand muskets and the thousand saddles so laboriously assembled and shipped during the past three months. The fact that many of them had failed to arrive was admittedly disappointing, but she could not be held responsible for adverse winds, nor was it her fault that the navy had gone over to the parliament, or that Hull had been allowed to remain in enemy hands. As for money, Charles knew the problems she had had in raising cash on their jewels, but she had sent him every sou left over from her expenditure on arms. She was still hoping to be able to negotiate further loans, although 'these people here are so Parliamentarian that it is with great trouble we can get anything from them'. It was no use trying to hurry the Dutch – 'the more they are hurried the less they do'.[37]

By this time – mid-September – the queen's anxieties had grown, for on 22 August the king had finally raised his standard at Nottingham and England had slid confusedly, almost insensibly, into civil war. Communication was now more difficult than ever. Henrietta heard nothing from Charles for six weeks and news was reaching her only in disconnected snippets from anonymous sources. 'There is a poor man arrived here, who has come to seek birds, who says he left the place where you are a fortnight ago. He has comforted me much by his relations, simple though they be.' Less reassuring was the 'poor woman', whom the queen had once employed for intelligence gathering in England and who now came to her in Holland with a tale of having overheard some parliamentarian captains discussing a plot to seize the king.[38] Holland, of course, was rife with rumours that the king had been defeated – 'for battles, there is not a day in the week in which you do not lose one' – that he had been killed or captured, that the Prince of Wales was a prisoner, that the Palatine princes had been killed – there were men who claimed to have seen and touched their dead bodies. 'Such are the pastimes of this country and their tidings,' remarked Henrietta bitterly.[39]

She was now talking wistfully of coming home, but much as she longed to see Charles again – 'the only pleasure left for me in this world: for, without you, I should not wish to remain in it an hour' – she felt in duty bound to let him know that her brother, the King of France, had offered her asylum and a warm welcome. 'Wherefore consider well', she wrote, 'whether you would wish me to go there or not.' There were several contingencies to be taken into account before deciding. 'Women cannot follow an army without great inconveniences, even for you. You may be sure too that the rebels will do all they can to prevent me from joining you, and to take me, believing that they will thus make a better bargain with you. If you were to chance to lose a battle, where would the poor women be? If by misfortune you were taken, I, being abroad, might yet serve you, whilst were I with you, all would be lost . . . For my own part', she went on, 'you may imagine that my inclination leads me for England, but I entreat you not to think of that which will please me most . . . for I can bear much when your service is concerned . . . Only let me have a speedy and direct answer, because the season is advancing, and I do not wish to stay in this country.'[40]

The answer, or at least an assurance that Charles wanted her with him whatever the risks involved, appears to have been brought by the king's cousin, the Duke of Richmond, who visited the Hague at Michaelmas, for in her next letter Henrietta speaks of preparing for her journey as quickly as possible. Richmond was also able to remove a number of misunderstandings and to tell her of the king's courage and constant resolution against all the assaults made upon him. This cheered her up so much that she even ventured a little joke at the expense of the hell-fire Puritans. 'I'll go pray for the man of sin that has married the popish brat of France, as the preacher said in London.'[41]

The queen had been planning, she said, to sail for home 'by All Saints' Day, according to the style of England' – that is 1 November (OS) – but the weeks passed and still she lingered. By this time the battle of Edgehill, the first major engagement of the war, had been fought and, strictly speaking, drawn, although the king is credited with a narrow victory, as it was the Earl of Essex, commanding the parliamentarian forces, who withdrew, leaving the road to Oxford undefended. This offered a rare opportunity for a swift advance on the capital and the Venetian Secretary at the Hague thought the queen was waiting in the hope of being able to go straight to London with her court.[42] If so it was a vain hope. The king had advanced through Oxford and Reading, but Essex was before him, and by the time the royal army reached the western approaches to

London the city was roused and ready. In the tense confrontation which took place among the orchards and market gardens of Turnham Green, Chiswick and Hammersmith on 13 November it was the king who turned away, and by the end of the month he was back at Oxford settling into winter quarters.

The queen had been in correspondence with the Earl of Newcastle, royalist commander in the north, regarding her impending arrival in his territory, but York was now being threatened by Captain Hotham, son of the rascally Governor of Hull, and the earl had been forced to fall back to Durham. 'I have received letters from the Earl of Newcastle', wrote Henrietta at the beginning of December, 'by which he begs me not to come yet, for he is constrained to march into Yorkshire. Hotham is playing the devil. So that I shall wait the issue of his march. . . .'[43]

As always she found waiting the hardest part. She had a shocking cold and badly needed the air of England to cure it. However, as she repeatedly assured the king, she was not wasting her time. She had not given up hope of securing a loan from the merchants of the Dutch East India Company, but the usual endless delays meant that the business would probably not be concluded before she left Holland – 'this country is too trying to the patience of persons who, like me, scarcely have any'. She was also continuing tirelessly to badger and cajole the other European princes, pointing out that it was in their own interests to show solidarity with a fellow sovereign under attack from his own subjects. She had very little hope of France, where they still suspected the King of England of pro-Spanish sympathies, but Denmark looked more promising. King Christian was, after all, Charles's uncle and the Danish ambassador had made some large, if rather vague offers of help during a recent visit to the Hague. She herself could do no more. Her jewels were all in pawn by this time and she was virtually penniless. 'Adieu my dear heart', she wrote in the first week of the New Year, 'I am going to take my supper, and as it has cost money I must not let it be spoiled.'[44]

The Earl of Newcastle having regained control of the situation around York, only a contrary wind now hindered the queen's setting out and on 19 January she was writing what she hoped would be her last letter from Holland. A final consignment of arms and ammunition had been loaded on to the waiting transports and the Dutch were providing an escort of eight warships. According to the Venetians, they were so anxious to see her off the premises that they were doing everything possible 'to render her departure comfortable and splendid'.

The Queen of Bohemia, too, would not be sorry to say goodbye to her sister-in-law. Although they had remained on civil terms, Elizabeth had never been at ease in Henrietta's company. 'I find by all the queen's and her people's discourse that they do not desire an agreement betwixt his majesty and the parliament, but that all be done by force, and rail abominably at the parliament. I hear all and say nothing', she told her friend, the diplomat Sir Thomas Roe.[45] Elizabeth was in a particularly awkward predicament with regard to parliament, being dependent on its continued goodwill for the payment of her English pension and quite literally could not afford to alienate the source of 'those necessary supplies'. She was therefore obliged to write conciliatory letters to the Speaker of the honourable House of Commons and deny that she had ever encouraged her sons to fight for the king.

At long last, and to the enormous relief of all concerned, Henrietta took the road to Scheveningen, a short distance up the coast from the Hague, and on 2 February her fleet of eleven vessels put to sea. It was a voyage likely to be fraught with danger, for the parliamentary ships based at Yarmouth had been ordered to be on the look-out for the arrival of the queen and her popish army, and to be ready to open fire without ceremony. But whatever her other faults, Henrietta did not lack physical courage. She feared none but God, and 'as to the rebels, neither their writings nor their threats shall ever make me do anything . . . much less shall they frighten me, – God being my guide and my safeguard'.

On this occasion, however, it was the forces of nature rather than those of her earthly enemies which proved the greater danger. A fierce north-easterly gale blew up, and the queen and her escort were battered by one of the worst storms seen in the North Sea for many years. For nine hideous days and nights the hapless passengers remained tied to their cots in the chaotic darkness, noise and stench below decks, tended only by one of the Capuchin friars accompanying the queen, an ex-Knight of Malta who, being 'habituated to a naval life', was the only member of the party not suffering from the miseries of seasickness. All expected death at any moment and the Catholics present were frantically confessing their sins at the tops of their voices, any feelings of shame overcome by fear of imminent extinction. Henrietta herself is said to have quelled the general panic by reminding her companions that no queen of England had ever yet been drowned, but all the same she made a vow to go on a pilgrimage to Our Lady of Liesse if she were spared, and was later to tell the king that she had never expected to see him again.

Two ships managed to reach Newcastle and two more went down in the raging seas with the loss of 18 men and 23 horses, but the rest staggered back to port at Scheveningen and the queen and the others on board the *Princess Royal* were carried ashore in varying degrees of prostration. Their clothes, stiff and sodden with sea water, vomit and excreta, had to be peeled off them and burnt, while the priest who gave thanks for their deliverance at the water's edge was unable to stand unsupported.[46]

Sensible men, like the Venetian Secretary resident at the Hague, thought the queen would now wait until the spring, or at least for better weather, but Henrietta, bruised, exhausted, seasick and 'stupified' from lack of sleep, had no intention of waiting. Nor was she impressed by those who did nothing 'but preach to me on the dangers I am incurring, and a strange conjunction of planets which will happen when I am at sea'. God had already saved her from one great danger and she did not expect Him to abandon her now.

She had to wait for ten days while the ships were repaired and refitted, using the time to convert a loan from the King of Denmark into coin and acquire an additional supply of ammunition. At the last moment there was a hitch, when an unwise Dutch bureaucrat tried to arrest one of her transports on the pretext that the queen had not applied for a licence for the shipment of the munitions it carried. The queen disputed this hotly. The munitions were for her own defence during her passage to England, and she addressed a furious protest to the States General over this quite intolerable injustice and affront. The States hurriedly gave way, two parliamentary ships lurking in ambush at the mouth of the Maas were warned off, and the fleet set sail once more on or about 22 February.

This time the queen's faith in the providence of the Almighty proved fully justified. The sea remained calm and the voyage passed without incident, although it was known that half-a-dozen parliamentary ships were patrolling the waters off Newcastle in order to prevent her landing. Here again the luck held, for a late change of wind direction enabled the Dutch commander of the convoy to veer away to the south-west, making landfall in Bridlington Bay on the Yorkshire coast below Flamborough Head.

After waiting on board ship until a contingent of Lord Newcastle's forces could arrive from York, Henrietta went ashore and was put up in a thatched cottage on the quayside of the little fishing village of Bridlington. But her adventures were not over yet. 'That night', she wrote to Charles, 'four of the Parliament ships arrived at Burlington [sic] without our knowledge, and in the morning about 4 o'clock, the alarm was given that we should send down to the harbour to secure our ammunition boats, which had not yet been able to be unloaded; but, about an hour after, these four ships began to fire so briskly, that we were all obliged to rise in haste, and leave the village to them: at least the women, for the soldiers remained very resolutely to defend the ammunition . . . One of these ships had done me the favour to flank my house, which fronted the pier, and before I could get out of bed, the balls were whistling upon me in such style that you may easily believe I loved not such music.'

Dressed 'just as it happened' Henrietta and her ladies were hustled out into the street, when the queen suddenly realized that her pet dog had been left behind. Mitte was apparently an ugly beast but much loved by her mistress, who insisted on running back to fetch her. The ladies now went on foot to some distance from the village, to seek shelter in a ditch, 'like those at Newmarket' according to the queen. 'But before we could reach it', her account goes on, 'the balls were singing round us in fine style, and a serjeant was killed twenty paces from me. We placed ourselves then under this shelter, during two hours that they were firing upon us, and the balls passing always over our heads, and sometimes covering us with dust.' At last the Dutch Admiral van Tromp sent a message to the 'parliament ships' to say that if they did not stop, he would fire on them as enemies. Henrietta thought he had left this a bit late, 'but he excuses himself on account of a fog which he says there was'. At any rate, the bombardment now ceased and as the tide went out the larger ships were obliged to retreat out of range. The queen then returned defiantly to her lodgings, 'not choosing that they should have the vanity to say that they had made me quit the village', and she ended what she assured the king was a 'very exact' relation of all that had passed with the information that 'after this, I am going to eat a little, having taken nothing today but three eggs and slept very little'.[47]

News of the queen's safe return was variously received. Sir Thomas Roe hoped that she had come 'as an angel and mediatrix of peace' and the king was naturally 'looking for her with tender affection'. But the new Venetian ambassador reported that some of his majesty's more prudent servants, who favoured a negotiated settlement with parliament, were not pleased, fearing that 'she may by her influence do considerable mischief in the successful conduct of affairs'.[48] Ferdinando, Lord Fairfax, parliamentary general in the north, wrote to offer her his protection if she would only refuse the attendance of those who had been declared by the highest authority to be enemies of the state. He also expressed the hope that by the powerful influence of the queen's presence and mediation with his majesty, 'this kingdom (that hath tasted nothing but war and misery since your departure) shall now be restored to the happy condition of peace'.[49]

Henrietta always maintained that she wanted peace more than anyone and with most reason, but since she regarded the dissolution of the 'perpetual parliament' as an essential precondition for any kind of settlement, her chances of success as a mediatrix did not look promising. Parliament itself harboured no illusions about the violence of the queen's resentment towards it – a feeling it fully reciprocated – and, according to the Venetian ambassador, feared that 'her ardent French temper' would now inspire the king to more vigorous action. On hearing of her arrival, the Commons voted to send a message desiring her majesty's 'reparty to London, where she should be royally and lovingly entertained', but warning that if she refused this invitation, the parliamentary forces would do all they could, by open force of arms, to hinder her proceedings and oppose her march.[50]

Henrietta was delayed for several days in the neighbourhood of Bridlington by the difficulty of finding waggons to transport the precious ammunition she had brought from Holland, and in the end it was decided to leave half Newcastle's men to protect the baggage train, while the other half escorted the queen to York. 'We have to do with enemies who are very vigilant', she told Charles, 'therefore we must be on our guard.' The danger that she might be snatched by the enemy was real enough – John Pym had reportedly hinted to certain members of the Lords who were pressing him for peace that if they would only have a little patience, 'they should see them get so good a pawn into their hands, that they might make their own conditions'.[51]

Happily, though, no hostage-takers were lying in wait on the road to York and by the second week of March Henrietta was safely installed in Sir Arthur Ingram's house, receiving visits from the local gentry and conferring about Scottish affairs with the Duke of Hamilton and James Graham, Marquis of Montrose. She did not plan to stay long in the north – 'I am in the greatest impatience in the world to join you' she had written to Charles from Bridlington – but communications between Oxford and York were proving almost as difficult as those between Oxford and the Hague. Letters were intercepted and misunderstandings inevitably arose. The queen was particularly worried by disturbing rumours filtering through about the negotiations currently being conducted with a delegation of parliamentary commissioners and was, as usual, afraid that Charles might allow himself to be persuaded into agreeing to some damaging concessions. 'If you make a peace, and disband your army, before there is an end of this perpetual parliament,' she wrote on 30 March, 'I am absolutely resolved to go into France, not being willing to fall again into the hands of those people, being well assured, that if the power remain with them, that it will not be well for me in England.' And again, a week later: 'Never allow your army to be disbanded, till it [the parliament] is ended, and never let there be a peace till that be put an end to . . . remember that you are lost if you consent to a peace, unless that be first abolished.'[52]

The king had not, in fact, been prepared to accept the terms offered and parliament recalled its commissioners on 14 April. But that was not quite the end of it. Much as they detested the queen and everything she stood for, the House of Commons never underestimated the importance of her influence, believing that 'without her encouragement and aid the king would never have put himself in a position to resist'. His intercepted letters had revealed that he was consulting her over the proposed ceasefire and made it all too plain 'that nothing is to be done in that or other matters without her consent'. A discreet approach was therefore made to see if she would be willing 'to listen to a peace' and advise the king to reopen negotiations, promising that 'the army of Essex' (which had just occupied Reading) should not advance further until a reply had been received. 'I thought it fitting to show a desire for peace,' wrote Henrietta demurely on 5 May, while at the same time taking advantage of the proffered truce to get an urgently needed consignment of gunpowder through to Oxford.[53]

It was surely not entirely coincidental that a couple of weeks later the Commons finally carried out their long-standing threat to impeach her. Having agreed, after long and serious debate, that the queen was as liable to the censure of the law as any subject in the kingdom, the question was raised whether her pawning of the crown jewels in Holland, her buying arms and ammunition to assist the war against the parliament, and 'her actual performances with her popish army' amounted to high treason – a question 'which was unanimously resolved by the whole house for the affirmative'.

The Venetian ambassador was deeply shocked and could not bring himself to prophesy where 'this audacious presumption of subjects' might end. 'The only thing clear', he wrote, 'is the extreme feeling against the royal house and a line of conduct that indicates that the end of these affairs will not be reached without a change of the government or the total destruction of the kingdom.'[54] The queen herself was not greatly concerned. She had long ago accepted that her battle with parliament was a fight to the death, but assured the Duke of Hamilton in a letter written at the end of May that she forgave the rebels from her heart for what they were doing against her.

From Henrietta's point of view, the most annoying thing the rebels were doing against her that spring was to delay her reunion with Charles, for they controlled a wide swathe of territory lying across the road to the south. Back in March the king had sent Prince Rupert, now rapidly acquiring a formidable reputation as a cavalry general, to clear a passage for his wife. Rupert had taken Birmingham, a busy little Puritan town which made swords for the parliament, and laid siege to Lichfield, which fell to him on 21 April, but the loss of Reading and consequent threat to Oxford had led to his hasty recall before the end of the month.

The royalists held most of the country north of the Humber, but Hull remained in parliamentary hands, and Fairfax and his son Thomas were a force to be reckoned with in the south and west of Yorkshire. In spite of her eagerness to join the king, Henrietta had become deeply involved with the northern campaign and her letters were beginning to read more and more like despatches from the front. 'The rebels have quitted Tadcaster, upon our sending forces to Wetherby', she told Charles on 30 March, 'but they are returned with twelve hundred men; we send more forces to drive them out.' And on 9 April: 'Our army is gone to Leeds, and at this time are beating down the town.'

A fortnight later the queen reported in more detail on the situation at Leeds, where Thomas Fairfax had now retreated. A council of war was called to decide 'whether the town should be forced by an assault, or rather by a siege'. The veterans, 'all the old officers from Holland', were of the opinion 'that an assault would be too dangerous . . . and also that a siege was impossible, as we were not enough to make lines of circumvallation, the town being of very large circumference, and the weather also being bad.' The 'fresh commanders', led by George Goring, were all for an assault, 'and I was with them', wrote the queen, but the voice of experience won the day, and the army withdrew to nearby Wakefield.[55]

Henrietta's plans were now being held up by the absence of Lord Newcastle. 'He is gone to bury his wife, who has died, and is not yet returned; and without him I can resolve on nothing . . . He gives me to hope that he will be here tomorrow, but he has already written me that twice . . .'[56] William Cavendish, first Earl of Newcastle, was a great nobleman of immense wealth and local influence. A model of old-world courtesy and an acknowledged expert in every branch of the art of equestrianism, he had been perfectly suited to his former office of Governor to the Prince of Wales, but he was quite unfamiliar with the brutish demands of modern warfare and although certainly not lacking in courage, it was sometimes hard to shake him out of his leisurely peacetime habits. 'This army is called the queen's army', wrote Henrietta in one of her frequent moments of exasperation, 'but I have little power over it, and I assure you that if I had, all would go on better than it does.' When at last they were together again, she went on, Charles would say she was a good little creature and very patient; 'but I declare to you that being patient is killing me'.[57]

Still complaining of headaches and eyestrain – 'my sight is much weakened with writing' – the queen was nevertheless still tirelessly writing letters: to Charles, to the Duke of Hamilton, to Montrose; to France – where her brother had just died; to Holland – where she was exploring the possibilities of a marriage between the Prince of Wales and the Orange Princess Henriette; and to Denmark – where she believed she might be able to make a contract with King Christian by offering a delayed promise to cede him the Orkney Islands in exchange for present military aid, though of course this optimistic plan must be kept secret from the Scots, who would be bound to take offence.[58]

With Leeds and Hull still in enemy hands, the northern commanders were understandably reluctant to spare any of their forces to escort the queen on her way south, but on 18 May Henrietta was telling the king that 'our army is now to go to Leeds, Bradford and Halifax, which is only twenty miles from Manchester'. If Leeds were taken, Manchester, another Puritan stronghold and a wealthy town 'capable of arming six hundred men', would be the next objective and then 'all Lancashire is yours . . . When that is done, all these counties on this side will be cleared, so that only garrisons in some places will suffice; and after that, the army may march where you will, all being clear behind them.'

As far as her journey was concerned, it had been agreed that Newcastle would give her a regiment of foot, with six companies of horse and one park of artillery. One way and another, she hoped to make up the number to 1,000 foot and 1,500 horse at least, 'and well armed I promise you'. However, to clinch the bargain with Newcastle she had been obliged to give up some of the arms she had brought from Holland, 'so that I cannot bring the proportion which I expected, but believe that what I have done is well worth the arms: for, instead of an army which you should have had out of the north, you will have one in the north, and a little one which will go to you, and Lancashire regained, which would have been lost . . . I pray God that you may think this all right. It is all that I desire, or else I should not take the pains I do.'[59]

But before the queen could set out, the royalist cause in Yorkshire suffered a nasty surprise, when on 24 May Thomas Fairfax broke out of Leeds and made a night attack on Wakefield, 'in which we have lost five hundred or six hundred men nearly, which is no small loss I assure you'. Newcastle was now begging her majesty to stay until he had taken Leeds, and to let him have what was left of the store of muskets and pistols she had been keeping for the king. It was not an easy decision to make, but thinking that if she refused and 'some new accident happened' she would get the blame, Henrietta felt obliged to acquiesce – on condition that the soldiers she was arming would be allowed to march with her when she went south. This was promised, 'and thus we lose neither time nor arms; instead of arms I shall bring armed men'. She herself now wanted to wait to see the fall of Leeds and asked the king's permission to stay. 'Although I am dying to join you, I am so enraged to go away without having beaten these rascals, that if you permit me, I will do that, and then will go to join you.'[60] But Charles, still threatened by the presence of the Earl of Essex in the Thames Valley, was not prepared to wait any longer and insisted that the queen – and her army – must leave at once. He also wanted Newcastle and his army, an order which caused furious consternation in the north and which the queen calmly ignored. 'I do not send it to you, since I have taken a resolution with you that you remain,' she told his lordship.

Henrietta finally left York on 4 June with an escort of 4,500 horse and foot, reaching Newark on the River Trent by the 18th. She stayed there for two weeks, gathering more support and waiting in some hope that the Hothams might change sides and surrender Hull. 'Young Hotham having been put in prison by order of Parliament, is escaped, and hath sent to me that he would cast himself into my arms, and that Hull and Lincoln shall be rendered.' Unfortunately, though, young Hotham was recaptured and Hull remained in parliamentary hands.

The queen despatched her last situation report to Charles from Newark on 27 June: 'At this present, I think it fit to let you know the state in which we march.' She was leaving 2,000 foot, the wherewithal to arm five hundred more and twenty companies of horse for the defence of Nottinghamshire and Lincolnshire; but 'I carry with me three thousand foot, thirty companies of horse and dragoons, six pieces of cannon and two mortars'. Harry Jermyn was in overall command – George Goring had been taken prisoner at Wakefield – while 'her she-majesty generalissima and extremely diligent' had a hundred and fifty baggage waggons to govern in case of an attack.[61]

The journey proceeded in easy stages by way of Ashby-de-la-Zouch, Croxall, Walsall and King's Norton to Stratford-upon-Avon, and had taken on almost a holiday air. Henrietta was later to tell her friend Madame de Motteville how, having got a fine army together, she had put herself at the head of her troops and marched towards the king, always on horseback, *sans nulle délicatesse de femme,* and living among the soldiers as she imagined the great Alexander must have lived with his; how she had picnicked with them outside in the sunshine, using no ceremony but treating them like brothers, and how they had all loved her in return.[62]

The generalissima's martial progress had not, of course, gone unnoticed. A certain parliamentary colonel, one Oliver Cromwell, was urging that every effort should be made to intercept her, and Henrietta herself had asked for care to be taken 'that no troop of Essex's army incommode us'.[63] The Earl of Essex, who had been immobilized at Reading by an outbreak of typhus and was seriously inconvenienced by lack of money to pay his men, was now advancing northwards to Thame, twelve miles east of Oxford; but on 17/18 June, Prince Rupert staged one of his brilliant cavalry forays which culminated in a short but bloody encounter in the cornfields at Chalgrove between Abingdon and Thame, where John Hampden, hero of the Ship Money affair and most sympathetic of the parliamentary leaders, was mortally wounded.

Having achieved his object of scattering and unsettling the enemy and frightening Essex away from Oxford, Rupert was now free to meet the queen at Stratford, where she spent the night at New Place as the guest of Shakespeare's daughter Susanna Hall, and to escort her on the last few miles to the village of Kineton below Edgehill where, on 13 July, she was finally reunited with the king and the two princes, Charles and James. The royal couple slept that first night at Sir Thomas Pope's house at

Wroxton and went on next day to Woodstock. They entered Oxford to a rousing welcome and were further cheered by the news that the Earl of Newcastle had beaten the Fairfaxes handsomely at Adwalton Moor, while in the West Country the royalist cavalry had routed Sir William Waller at Roundway Down.

Henrietta's adventure had lasted for fifteen months and, despite her many protestations to the contrary, the impression somehow remains that she had rather enjoyed the challenge and excitement of it all. The absence of any systematic or official records makes it difficult to evaluate just what she had accomplished in practical terms, but even if her efforts had not been enough to have any real effect on the outcome of the war, they still represent an extraordinary achievement for a woman whose previous experience had been confined within the carefully ordered limits of one of the most civilized courts of Europe. The doll-like figure of the curled and bejewelled queen immortalized by Van Dyck, looking as if her only possible function was to be ornamental, had proved herself quite capable of striking bargains with hard-faced pawnbrokers and arms dealers. She had been undaunted by the prospect of shipwreck and shown cool courage under fire. Henrietta had made plenty of mistakes in the past and would make more in the future, but no one could now doubt her valiant spirit.

CHAPTER TWO

Heroic Englishwomen

My dear husband hath entrusted me with his house and
children . . . and I do not know it is his pleasure that
I should entertain soldiers in his house.

Brilliana Harley to Sir William Vavasour

As the queen got ready to set out on her triumphant march south from
Newark at the head of her 'fine army', another woman was about to
experience the war at first hand. On 30 June the Fairfaxes, père et fils,
had confronted Newcastle's advancing army at Adwalton Moor on the
outskirts of Bradford. Although heavily outnumbered they held their own
against repeated cavalry charges, their musketeers, stationed in the
shelter of the hedges on the edge of the moor, being able to offer 'sharp
entertainment', while the left wing engaged the royalist foot and gained
ground of them. 'The resolution our soldiers shewed in the Left Wing,
made the Enemy think of retreating,' commented Thomas Fairfax.
'Orders were given for it; and some marched off the Field.' But, 'whilst
they were in this wavering condition, one Colonel Skirton, a wild and
desperate man, desired his General to let him charge once more, with a
Stand of Pikes. With which he brake in upon our men.' As the
parliamentary line broke, fresh royalist troops poured into the gap and
another cavalry charge threatened to cut off the retreat, so that the
Yorkshiremen 'being herewith discouraged, began to flee; and so were
soon routed.'[1]

Newcastle now prepared to lay siege to Bradford, but Thomas Fairfax,
who had been fortunate and skilful enough to extricate his own small
force of cavalry from the melée more or less intact, managed to get back
into the town that night to rejoin his father, his wife and small daughter.
Fairfax senior then departed in the direction of Leeds, leaving Thomas to
try to hold Bradford. It quickly became clear that this was not going to be
practicable. The royalist cannon, popularly known as 'the Queen's pocket
pistols', were able to command the whole town from their position on the
nearby hills and 'shot furiously' on the inhabitants. The garrison, too,

was acutely short of ammunition and after beating off two attempts to storm its defences, was reduced to one barrel of powder and no match.

Soon after midnight on 2 July, therefore, Sir Thomas summoned his officers to a conference at which it was agreed that they would have to force a way out through the encircling enemy, 'presently, before it was day', and join the retreat to Leeds. 'Here', says Sir Thomas, 'I must not forget to mention my Wife, who ran great hazards with us in this retreat as any others; and with as little expression of fear: not from any zeal or delight, I must needs say, in the War; but through a willing and patient suffering of this undesirable condition.'[2]

Anne Fairfax already knew a good deal about war – her father, Horace Vere, having been England's leading career soldier. A veteran of the Dutch campaigns of the 1590s, Sir Horace had also commanded the meagre expeditionary force grudgingly despatched by King James to assist the unhappy Elector Palatine in 1620. Anne herself had spent some of her early life in the Netherlands, and the Earl of Clarendon was always inclined to blame her upbringing among the Calvinistic republican Dutch for her lack of proper reverence for the Church of England and her regrettable concurrence in her husband's rebellion. Whether or not this was so, Lady Fairfax was known to be a strong, independent-minded woman who wielded considerable influence over her husband and who insisted on sharing the dangers of his campaigns. Certainly she was in the front line with him on 2 July, riding pillion behind one of the officers in the little group of cavalry waiting tensely to make a break for it in the pre-dawn twilight.

'I sent two or three Horsemen to discover what they could of the Enemy', wrote Sir Thomas, 'which presently returned, and told us, There was a Guard of Horse close by us. Before I had gone forty paces, the day beginning to break, I saw them on the hill above us; being about 300 Horse.' Fairfax himself led the charge and got through with half a dozen companions; but 'the rest of our Horse, being close by, the Enemy fell upon them, taking most of them prisoners; amongst whom my Wife was, the Officer behind whom she was [on horseback] being taken.'

Sir Thomas, a helpless witness to this calamity, was forced to carry on to Leeds, where he found 'all in great distraction'. A Council of War had just decided that the whole of the West Riding would have to be abandoned, which meant a further retreat of some sixty miles to Hull for the tired and discouraged parliamentary troops. At Selby, where there was a ferry over the Ouse, they were intercepted by a royalist force from the garrison at nearby Cawood, and although Fairfax senior managed to get across the river, his son was driven south of the Humber and through the Lincolnshire Levels. This proved 'a very troublesome and dangerous passage: having oft interruptions from the Enemy; sometimes in our front, sometimes in our rear'.

Sir Thomas, who had been shot and wounded in the wrist at Selby, had now been in the saddle for the best part of two days 'without any rest or refreshment' and, to add to his afflictions, he was beginning to be seriously worried about his five-year-old daughter. Little Mary Fairfax had been got safely out of Bradford, and 'being carried before her maid, endured all this retreat on horseback'; but now she kept falling into swoons of exhaustion and seemed to her anxious father 'ready to expire her last breath'. As they approached Barton-upon-Humber, nearly opposite Hull, he caught sight of a likely looking house not far away and sent the child with her nursemaid to take shelter there, meaning to send for her next day, although he confessed that at the time he had 'little hopes of seeing her any more alive'.

Fairfax, with the remnant of his cavalry, now no more than 100 strong, finally crossed over the estuary to Hull some time in the evening of 3 July, 'our men faint and tired: and I myself having lost all, even to my shirt'. His clothes torn and bloodstained, his body full of pain and his mind full of trouble, Sir Thomas felt moved to compare his present plight to Job's condition, 'when he said, "Naked came I out of my mother's womb, and naked shall I return thither. The Lord gave, and the Lord hath taken away. Blessed be the name of the Lord."' But happily for all concerned, the Lord, 'who is a God of Mercy and Consolation', proved to be listening to prayer. Mary Fairfax was retrieved on the following day, apparently 'pretty well recovered of her long and tedious journey', and shortly afterwards the Earl of Newcastle, always the perfect gentleman, returned Lady Fairfax in his own coach complete with a mounted escort. 'Which generosity', observed Sir Thomas, 'gained more than any reputation he could have gotten in detaining a Lady prisoner upon such terms.'[3]

Outside their own immediate circles, the exploits of heroic souls like the queen and Anne Fairfax, who deliberately sought to put themselves forward into danger, still tended to be regarded as freakish and slightly shocking by a society which had not yet begun to question the universally accepted dogma that, whatever the circumstances, a respectable woman's place was in the home. Unfortunately, though, it was rapidly becoming obvious that the home was not necessarily a more retired or safer place than the field of battle. Lady Arundell of Wardour Castle in Wiltshire was far from being the only respectable woman to make this alarming discovery, but she does have the distinction of being one of the first.

The West Country was generally considered to be royalist in sympathy, but there were exceptions. Plymouth and Lyme were held by the Parliament, as were the important strategic centres of Gloucester and Bristol. Early in February 1643 Prince Rupert had captured Cirencester, key to the wealthy Cotswold district, and parliament had countered by appointing Sir William Waller as Sergeant-Major-General of the Western Association, which took in the counties of Wiltshire, Somerset and Gloucester. Waller, like many other officers on both sides of the conflict, had acquired his military experience fighting in Bohemia and the Palatinate and had the reputation of being an energetic and successful commander. He arrived at Bristol in March and drove the royalists out of Malmesbury, leaving Sir Edward Hungerford in charge, before going on to make his presence felt in the Severn Valley and South Wales.

To Waller's annoyance, Sir Edward, who commanded the parliament's forces in Wiltshire, presently left his post to go off to Bath, in order, so he said, to collect more ammunition and money to pay his soldiers who were, it seemed, 'generally discontented that they had not pillage'. Towards the end of April he was back in Wiltshire carrying out a series of marauding expeditions against his royalist neighbours, in the course of which he and his men broke into the park at Longleat and killed some of Sir James Thynne's fallow deer. Then, on Tuesday 2 May, he appeared at the gates of Wardour Castle in the valley of the River Nadder between Shaftesbury and Salisbury, the property of Thomas, 2nd Baron Arundell, a well-known Catholic gentleman and scion of the ancient Cornish family of Arundell of Lanherne.

A brief reconnaissance having revealed that Wardour, a fourteenth-century building extensively modernized and remodelled in the 1570s, was unexpectedly strong and 'those that were in it resolute not to yield it unless by force', Hungerford proceeded to call up reinforcements from his second-in-command, one Colonel William Strode of Street. With their numbers increased to an estimated 1,300, the attackers felt brave enough to send a trumpeter forward with a summons to surrender. 'The reason pretended was, because the castle being a receptacle of cavaliers and malignants, both Houses of Parliament had ordered it to be searched for men and arms; and withal by the same trumpeter declared, that if they found either money or plate, they would seize on it for the use of the Parliament.'[4]

In fact, Wardour just then was chiefly a receptacle of women and children: namely Lady Arundell, her daughter-in-law Cecily and three young grandchildren. Like many another loyal gentleman, Lord Arundell was away from home that spring, having ridden off to join the king at Oxford, taking a troop of horse raised from his own tenantry and leaving his wife with only a skeleton staff quite literally to hold the fort. Blanche Arundell, daughter of Edward Somerset, 4th Earl of Worcester, was an aristocrat in her own right and could claim royal Plantagenet descent from Thomas of Woodstock through her mother, Lady Frances Hastings. Born in the early 1580s, she had grown up close to the court in the last two decades of the Elizabethan era. Her father, although 'a stiff Papist', was counted a good subject and after the fall of the Earl of Essex held the prestigious office of Master of the Horse. Two of her sisters were maids of honour and in June 1600 her brother was married to Anne Russell in a grand wedding which was the social event of the season. Young Blanche, wearing a skirt of cloth of silver and mantle of carnation taffeta, was one of the eight ladies who danced in 'a memorable masque' given before the queen as part of the celebrations, and she may well appear in the famous Procession to Blackfriars picture, showing Elizabeth carried in a litter on the shoulders of her courtiers, which is generally believed to commemorate the great Russell–Somerset marriage.[5]

With that kind of background, Lady Arundell, now in her sixtieth year, was not easily intimidated. She might have no more than a score or so of able-bodied men at her disposal, but she knew her duty and absolutely refused to deliver up the castle; she had a command from her lord to keep it, and she would obey his command.

There are two accounts of the siege of Wardour, which lasted for six days. According to Edmund Ludlow, a parliamentary officer who arrived at the castle towards the end of the week, the besiegers had been battering it with two small pieces of artillery and done very little damage, 'save only to a chimney-piece, by a shot entring at a window: but', he went on, 'there being a vault on each side of the castle, for the conveying away of filth, two or three barrels of powder were put into one of them, and being fired, blew up some part of it; which with the grazing of a bullet upon the face of one of the servants, and the threatening of the besiegers to spring the other mine, and then to storm it, if it was not surrendered before an hour-glass, which they had turn'd up, was run out, so terrified the ladies therein, whereof there was a great number, that they agreed to surrender it.'[6]

A more detailed report, published in the royalist newsletter *Mercurius Rusticus*, says that two mines were sprung. 'The first in a vault, through which beer and wood and other necessaries were brought into the castle: this did not much hurt, it being without the foundation of the castle. The second was conveyed into the small vaults; which, by reason of the intercourse between the several passages to every office, and almost every room in the castle, did much shake and endanger the whole fabrick.'[7]

The besiegers, it seems, had offered quarter to the women and children but not the men in the castle, an offer which was promptly rejected: 'The ladies both infinitely scorning to sacrifice the lives of their friends and servants to redeem their own from the cruelty of the rebels.' But, of course, there could be only one outcome of the siege of Wardour. After six days and nights of 'continual watching and labour' the small handful of defenders were becoming exhausted – so exhausted, in fact, that they were falling asleep at their posts, and 'it might have been a doubt which they would first have laded their musquets withal, either powder before bullet, or bullet before powder, had not the maidservants (valiant beyond their sex) assisted them and done that service for them'.

On Monday 8 May, the besiegers brought up petards – explosive devices designed to be attached to a gate or wall to blow a hole through it – and applied them to the garden doors. Realizing that this was the end, for once breached these doors would give free passage into the castle, Lady Arundell asked to parley with the enemy. The parliamentary propaganda machine apparently spread a story that she offered Edward Hungerford £60,000 to go away, but he virtuously refused. *Mercurius Rusticus* did not believe it for a moment, 'for if they in the castle offered so liberally how came the rebels to agree upon articles of surrender so far beneath that overture?'

Certainly the articles of surrender were surprisingly generous, stipulating that the ladies and all others in the castle should have quarter; that the ladies and servants should carry away all their wearing apparel and that all the furniture and goods in the house should be safe from plunder – a careful inventory was to be taken and copies held by the interested parties.

In the event, only the first of these articles was observed. Everyone's life was spared, although, again according to *Mercurius Rusticus*, 'they had slain in the defence at least sixty of the rebels'. But the rebels were more interested in pillage than revenge and the looting began immediately. Half-packed trunks and boxes were seized, and the ladies and their servants bundled out of the castle with nothing but the clothes they stood up in. The castle itself was ruthlessly stripped of its valuables and anything which could not be removed was destroyed by the soldiers, including a carved chimney piece valued at £2,000 which they attacked and 'utterly defaced' with their pole-axes. This orgy of wanton vandalism spread to the park and gardens. Outbuildings were burnt, fences torn up and deer either killed or set loose. Fine mature trees were cut down to be sold for a fraction of their worth, orchards grubbed up, fishponds drained, horses and livestock driven away and, observed *Mercurius Rusticus* bitterly, 'having left nothing either in air or water, they dig under the earth'. Wardour Castle's water supply was brought from two miles away by a lead conduit, and 'intending rather mischief to the king's friends than profit to themselves, they cut up the pipe and sold it, as these men's wives in North Wiltshire do bone-lace, at sixpence a yard . . . They that have the unhappy occasion to sum up these losses, value them at no less than one hundred thousand pounds.'

Meanwhile, Blanche Arundell, together with Cecily and the three children, had been taken to Shaftesbury, where she suffered the added mortification of seeing five cartloads of her best furniture being driven off in triumph towards Dorchester. After a few days it was decided to transfer the captives to the greater security of Bath, but as the town was known to be infected with plague and smallpox, both ladies resisted fiercely. Lady Arundell took to her bed and refused to move unless taken by force, causing the enemy, afraid lest 'so great inhumanity might incense the people against them', to have second thoughts. Instead, they took her two grandsons, Thomas aged nine and his seven-year-old brother, away to Dorchester, 'a place no less dangerous for the infection of schism and rebellion than Bath for the plague and the smallpox . . . The complaints of the mother, the pitiful cry of the children prevail not with them', raged *Mercurius Rusticus*, 'like ravenous wolves they seize on the prey.'[8]

And the family's misfortunes were not over yet. On 19 May, barely ten days after the loss of her home, Blanche Arundell's husband died at Oxford and at the end of the month she was left to travel to Salisbury to seek the protection of the Marquis of Hertford, the king's Lieutenant-General for the Western Counties. Hertford was on his way to a rendezvous with Ralph Hopton's forces advancing up from Cornwall, but he found time to arrange and pay for lodgings for the widow, who 'had not a bed to lie on, nor means to provide herself a house or furniture'.

Then came news that her son Henry, now 3rd baron, had been shot in the thigh at the bloody fight on Lansdown Hill above Bath, where the Cornish hero Sir Bevil Grenville was killed. But Henry Arundell recovered from his wound and, temporarily at least, also recovered Wardour Castle. After the victory at Roundway Down near Devizes on 13 July 1643, which virtually destroyed Waller's army, the whole of the West Country came under royalist control, and by the end of the year Wardour was once more under siege. The garrison, commanded by Edmund Ludlow, held out stubbornly until the following March when, with his men losing heart and the building now so badly damaged as to be in danger of collapsing round him, besides 'not having provision sufficient for one day left, nor any hopes of relief', Ludlow finally agreed to surrender. The besiegers treated him with marked consideration, especially Lord Arundell whose civility was such that Ludlow was moved to dig up the family plate – which had somehow escaped notice the previous year and which he had buried in the cellars – and restore it to its rightful owner.[9]

Edmund Ludlow was taken a prisoner to Oxford, where Arundell tried to arrange his exchange for his own two sons, who were still in the hands of the parliament, but, according to Ludlow, this was refused by the king, who regarded two small children a poor exchange for an experienced fighting man of Ludlow's quality. Ludlow got his exchange after three weeks, thanks to the good offices of the Earl of Essex, but Lord Arundell had to wait until May 1644 before reclaiming his sons, and even then Edward Hungerford had the gall to demand compensation for the cost of keeping them.

The Arundell estates, like those of other so-called delinquents, were sequestered at the end of the first Civil War and administered on behalf of the parliament by a panel of local commissioners, who had discretionary powers to authorize the payment of one-fifth of the revenues for the maintenance of the wife and children of the delinquent owner. The Dorset Committee for Sequestrations allowed Cecily Arundell her fifth in August 1646, and she received all the rents of her husband's Dorset manors up to the value of £220 for one year ending on Lady Day 1647. The same grant was extended for a year from Michaelmas 1648 and she was also allowed all the rent grain for the year, but was ordered to pay a third of a third to her mother-in-law, Blanche, Dowager Lady Arundell.[10]

In 1652 many of the Arundell estates were sold to Humphrey Weld of Lulworth, to be redeemed at the Restoration by Henry Arundell for

£35,000. But Blanche did not live to see that happy day. She died at Winchester in October 1649 and was buried beside her husband in the parish church of the village of Tisbury, two miles from Wardour. The family did not attempt to restore the old castle. A smaller house was built over part of the site after 1660. Then, a century later, a smart new mansion, designed by the architect James Paine, began to rise on higher ground about two-and-a-half miles away, and the ruins of Wardour Old Castle (now in the care of English Heritage) were left with their memories.[11]

While Blanche Arundell was bravely defying the enemy at Wardour, Mary Bankes, another wife and mother, was facing a similar ordeal in another castle not so many miles away. The parliamentary party was strong on the south coast in the spring of 1643 and from Portsmouth to the east to Plymouth in the west its forces controlled Southampton and the Isle of Wight, Poole, Wareham, Melcombe and Weymouth, Portland and Lyme, so that by the beginning of May only Corfe Castle on the Isle of Purbeck still held out for the king.

Corfe, 'so ancient as without date', had dominated the surrounding landscape since Saxon times and over the succeeding centuries had been used intermittently as a prison, hunting lodge and occasional residence by members of the royal family. Henry VII granted it to his mother, Lady Margaret Beaufort, although she appears to have visited it only once, and the later Tudors took little interest in the place, except as a supplementary source of income for deserving friends and relations – Henry VIII granted the castle, lordship and manor of Corfe to his bastard son and Edward VI passed it on to his uncle and guardian, the Lord Protector Somerset. Finally, Queen Elizabeth, never noted for over generosity, sold it with all its liberties and privileges and demesne lands to her friend and Lord Chancellor, Sir Christopher Hatton, for the curiously complicated sum of £4,761 18s 7¼d. Hatton died a bachelor and Corfe was inherited by his nephew William, who had married a Cecil heiress. There were no children and after William Hatton's death his widow married the lawyer Edward Coke. Widowed again in 1634, Lady Coke, or Lady Hatton as she was more generally known, sold the castle to another lawyer, Sir John Bankes.

A medieval fortress sprawling over a five acre site on a steep rocky hill crowned by an eighty-foot-high Norman keep, the so-called King's Tower, with its battlements and twelve-foot-thick walls, seems an eccentric choice of country seat for a rising professional man with a young family, and it would be interesting to know if Sir John had consulted his wife about his purchase. Most likely, though, he simply regarded it as an investment, for as well as the manorial rights which went with ownership of the castle he had acquired a considerable acreage of land on the Isle of Purbeck, where the chalk downs made fine pasture for sheep and the stone quarries yielded valuable building material – 'marbre de Corf' had been much sought after for centuries.

As it happened, John Bankes can have had very little leisure to enjoy his new grandeur, for in the years following the acquisition of Corfe his legal career prospered. Appointed Attorney General in 1634, he prosecuted in several high-profile cases brought against members of the Puritan tendency – notably William Prynne the pamphleteer and John Hampden of Ship Money fame – and in 1641 Sir John, described by Clarendon as 'a Grave and a Learned Man in the Profession of the Law', became Chief Justice of the Common Pleas. Like many other thoughtful men with much to lose, he viewed the rapid deterioration of the political situation with the deepest misgiving. 'I have studied all meanes which way matters may be brought to a good conclusion between the king and the houses [of Parliament]', he wrote to a friend in May 1642, 'all high wayes and wayes of force will be distructive; and if we should have civill warrs, it would make us a miserable people.'[12] Nevertheless, although sometimes disapproving, he remained steadfastly loyal to the king, whom he had joined at York and would later follow to Oxford.

After her husband's departure from Westminster for the north in the spring of 1642, Lady Bankes, 'a vertuous and prudent lady', retreated to Corfe with her children and servants, 'there to shelter themselves from the storm which she saw coming'. It certainly seemed a wise move, for Corfe, which had never yet fallen to an enemy, should surely offer a safe refuge. The living quarters had been 'much repaired and amended' in Sir Christopher Hatton's time and John Bankes was a rich man, more than capable of providing his family with everything necessary for their comfort, so that life in the castle, even in winter, could be made quite cosy. Hangings of fine tapestry, scarlet and green gilded leather and blue silk damask were used to disguise the harshness of the stone walls in the gallery and great chamber, and kept the worst of the draughts out of my lady's bedroom. There was a quilted silk carpet for the table in the withdrawing room, window cushions of wrought satin and crimson velvet, a rich ebony cabinet with gilded fixtures, Turkey and Persian carpets, a large suite of crimson velvet chairs and stools with cushions to match, and furniture – that is, curtains, quilts and counterpanes – for all the beds.[13]

The household remained undisturbed throughout the autumn and winter of 1642 but Corfe was far too important a strategic feature to be ignored for long, and its capture would represent a conspicuous triumph. It also presented a conspicuous challenge to any would-be assailant. According to *Mercurius Rusticus*, the structure was so strong, the ascent so steep, the walls so 'massie' and thick, that it was 'one of the impregnablest forts of the kingdome'. The local parliamentary commanders, Sir Walter Earle and Sir Thomas Trenchard, therefore came to the conclusion that they would stand a better chance of gaining their objective by low cunning than by open hostility, and planned to try to take advantage of a conveniently approaching annual festivity. By 'ancient usage' the mayor and the so-called 'barons' of Corfe, together with the local gentry, gathered at the castle on May Day each year to course a stag – an event which was performed with great solemnity and attracted large crowds of onlookers. But on May Day 1643 these crowds were to be joined by some troops of horse from Dorchester and elsewhere who had come to the Isle of Purbeck 'intending to find other game than to hunt the stagge, their businesse being suddenly to surprise the gentlemen in the hunting and to take the castle'. Unfortunately for the success of this ingenious plan news of their coming leaked out, 'disperst the hunters, and spoyled the sport for that day'. It also caused the prudent Lady Bankes to order her gates to be watched and kept shut against all comers. When some of the troopers, balked of their prey, approached the castle 'under a pretence to see it', they were refused access, at which 'the common soldiers used threatning language, casting out words implying some intentions to take the castle, but the commanders (who better knew how to conceale their resolutions) utterly disavowed any such thought, denying that they had such commission'. Lady Bankes, 'very wisely and like herself', did not believe them and called in a guard of her tenants and friends to help her protect her home. This, however, 'rendred her suspected abroad', and from then on she was kept under close surveillance by the enemy. 'Whatsoever she sends out, or sends for in, is suspected; her ordinary provisions for her family are by some multiplyed, and reported to be more than double what indeed they were, as if she had now an intention to victuall and man the castle against the forces of the two Houses of Parliament.'

The next move by the parliamentary committee at Poole was to demand the surrender of the four small cannon which were the only armament now remaining in the castle, alleging that the islanders had 'conceived strange jealousies' because the pieces had been seen to be mounted on their carriages. Lady Bankes replied by begging the commissioners to allow her to keep these few 'small peeces' for her own defence and, in order to take away suspicion, had the guns taken off their carriages again. A promise was then received that they might stay, but not long afterwards a party of forty seamen from Poole arrived at the castle without warning very early in the morning to demand that the cannon should after all be given up. Early as it was, her ladyship went down to the gatehouse in person asking to see their warrant. This was produced, signed by several of the commissioners but, although there were only five men inside the castle just then, Mary Bankes evidently felt the time had come for a show of defiance. She therefore ordered these five, assisted by her maidservants, to put the guns back on to their carriages, and 'lading one of them they gave fire, which small thunder so affrighted the seamen that they all quitted the place and ran away'. As soon as they had gone, her ladyship summoned help by beat of drum and some fifty of her neighbours hurried to answer her call. This provoked a flurry of threats to burn the houses of anyone who came to her assistance which, in turn, brought their wives up to the castle, where 'they weepe, and wring their hands, and with clamorous oratory perswade their husbands to come home, and not by saving others expose their own houses to spoyle and ruine'.

The parliamentary authorities had succeeded in intercepting a consignment of two hundredweight of powder, ordered 'against a siege', and went on to issue a proclamation at Wareham, the nearest market town, forbidding the sale of beer, beef or other provisions to the Lady Bankes. They also instituted a system of strict watches to ensure that no messengers passed in or out of the castle. 'Being thus distressed . . . and being but slenderly furnished for a siege', her ladyship was obliged to agree to a compromise, handing over her precious cannon, of which, says *Mercurius Rusticus*, the biggest only carried a three pound bullet, in return for an undertaking that she would from now on be left 'to enjoy the castle and armes in it in peace and quietnesse'.[14]

Unlike Blanche Arundell, Mary Bankes was no great aristocrat. Born Mary Hawtrey, the only daughter and heiress of Sir Ralph Hawtrey, of Ruislip in Middlesex, a gentleman of ancient but otherwise not particularly distinguished family, we have no details of her life before 1642, but there seems no reason to suppose that it differed from that of any other well-to-do, upper-middle-class married woman of the time. It would have been a life bounded by family concerns and subject to the relentless physical demands of more or less perpetual pregnancy (Mary Bankes bore thirteen children); a life of household cares, religious observance and home-grown amusements lived quietly in the background, uneventful and unsurprising, until the war thrust her forward to take her modest place in history – a place more than earned by her qualities of courage, determination and good judgement.

This last was demonstrated by her apparent surrender in the matter of the Corfe Castle cannon, 'for the rebells, being now possessed of their guns, presumed the castle to be theirs . . . Nowe it was no more but aske and have; hereupon they grew remisse in their watches, negligent in their observations, not heeding what was brought in, nor taking care, as before, to intercept supplies.' Mary Bankes, who knew better than to trust any of the enemy's promises, hastened to make use of the opportunity which their overconfidence had given her and, 'as much as the time would permit, furnish't the castle with provisions of all sorts' – provisions which included a hundredweight and a half of powder and a quantity of match.

There was an old soldier named Captain Bond in the castle but as soon as she heard that Lord Hertford and Prince Maurice were approaching Blandford, Lady Bankes sent an urgent request for some officers to come and take charge of the defence. Accordingly, a Captain Laurence, son of Sir Edward Laurence of Creech Grange, was despatched to take command. Robert Laurence arrived with about eighty men, but unfortunately he came without a commission and therefore had no power to requisition further supplies until it was too late.

The first direct attack on Corfe was made early in June by a force of between two and three hundred horse and foot and 'two peeces of ordnance' which were fired off from the surrounding hills. The enemy then torched four houses in the town and summoned the castle to surrender, but 'receiving a deniall, for that time they left it'. Not for long though. On 14 June the accounts of Richard Bury, County Treasurer, record a payment made for loading and unloading great guns from Portsmouth to Corfe Castle, and on 23 June Sir Walter Earle, accompanied by Captains William Sydenham, Henry Jervis and George Skutt 'with a body betweene five and six hundred, came and possessed themselves of the towne, taking the opportunity of a misty morning that they might find no resistance from the castle'. They brought with them a demi-cannon, a culverin and two sakers, or six-pounders. With these and their small shot, 'they played on the castle on all quarters of it . . . making their battery strongest where they thought the castle weakest'.

Artillery firing iron or stone missiles could make little or no impression on the massive walls of Corfe Castle and, attempts to corrupt the garrison by underhand methods having failed, a primitive form of siege engine was brought into use. This contraption, known as a Sow, was a sort of shed on wheels, made of strong boards lined with wool 'to dead the shot' and intended to give cover to an assault party. This particular Sow had cost £2 3s 4d plus 6s for three truckle wheels, but she was not a success and 'cast nine of her farrow, for the musketiers from the castle were so good marksmen at their legs, the only part of their bodies left without defence, that nine ran away as well as their broken and battered legs would give them leave'. The Sow's companion, christened the Boare, seeing her discomfiture, 'durst not advance'.

The besiegers, 'without fear of prophanation', had made their headquarters in the church at Corfe, where they broke up the organ to use the pipes as cases for powder and shot, and took the lead from the roof to make bullets. The royalist *Mercurius Rusticus* went on to assert that while Walter Earle and the other commanders were prodigal of the blood of their common soldiers, 'they were sparing enough of their own'. It seemed that the valiant Sir Walter never willingly exposed himself to hazard, for having suffered a chance graze from a musket ball, he dressed up in a bearskin coat for extra protection and was to be seen creeping on all fours on the side of the hill 'to keep himselfe out of danger'.

The long summer days passed slowly. June turned into July and the besieging force was still 'as farre from hopes of taking the castle as the first day they came thither'. Meanwhile the garrison was getting bolder, making sorties into the surrounding fields to fetch in a herd of cows, and shouting rude words from the safety of the walls. Finally, towards the end of the month, a detachment of 150 mariners arrived from the parliamentary naval base at Portsmouth, bringing with them several cartloads of supplies, including petards, granadoes and scaling ladders 'to assault the castle by scaladoe'. A reward of twenty pounds was offered to the first man to scale the walls but Walter Earle's 'common souldiers', many of whom had been taken out of the local gaols, a traditional source of cannon fodder, proved disappointingly reluctant to be the first to risk a bullet through the head. Their officers had therefore to resort to another time-honoured custom 'which was to make them drunke, knowing that drunkennesse makes some men fight like lyons, that being sober would runne away like hares'. A firkin of 'hot waters', costing £1 12s was provided for this purpose and it was decreed that when twenty men had entered the castle they would give a watch-word to the rest. The word was 'Old Wat', which *Mercurius Rusticus* considered ill-chosen by Sir Wat. Earle, 'for if I be not deceived, the hunters that beat bushes for the fearfull timorous hare, call him Old Wat'.

The assailants, now hopefully pot valiant, were divided into two groups, one of which was to storm the middle ward defended by Captain Laurence and the main garrison. The other would make for the upper ward, 'which the Lady Bankes (to her eternal honour be it spoken) with her daughters, women and five souldiers, undertooke to make good against the rebels, and did bravely performe what she undertooke; for by heaving over stones and hot embers, they repelled the rebels and kept them from climbing their ladders, thence to throw in that wild-fire, which every rebell had ready in his hand.'

The assault had failed and now news was coming in of the royalists' successes in the West Country. Bristol, the second most important sea-port in the realm, had fallen to Prince Rupert on 26 July and, even closer to home, Dorchester surrendered on 2 August. Two days later the last of the besiegers had fled from Corfe, abandoning their artillery, ammunition and about a hundred horses, which were seized joyfully by the soldiers of the garrison. 'Thus,' recorded *Mercurius Rusticus*, 'after six weeks strict siege, this castle, the desire of the rebels and the key of those parts, by the loyalty and brave resolution of this honourable Lady, the valour of Captaine Laurence and some eighty souldiers (by the losse only of two men), was delivered from the bloody intentions of these mercelesse rebels on the 4th of August, 1643.'[15]

During the next few weeks Portland, Weymouth and Melcombe were all occupied by royalist troops commanded by the Earl of Carnarvon and Lady Bankes was able to turn her attention to tidying up the mess and helping her neighbours whose houses had been damaged or destroyed. But life at the castle would never be normal again. In December 1644 John Bankes died at Oxford, by which time the tide had begun to turn against the king. Corfe was once more becoming an isolated outpost and in July 1645 the Speaker of the House of Commons issued a warrant addressed 'to all Courts-of-Guard, officers of Ports and Forts' requiring them to 'permit the bearer, Mary, Lady Bankes, with her two daughters and four servants quietly to pass either by coach or horseback to London'.[16]

The castle finally fell on 27 February 1646 after a long blockade and then only by the treachery of an officer in the garrison who, 'being weary of the King's service, let the enemy know, that, if he might have a protection, he would deliver the place to the Parliament'. This was done by tricking Colonel Anketil, the then governor, into admitting a party of about fifty soldiers, believing them to be reinforcements. Some were local men who knew every part of the castle and were able to seize the strategic towers and platforms under cover of darkness. When daylight came and the besieging force prepared to attack, the garrison, realizing they had been betrayed, were forced to ask for a parley. It was all quite civilized. It was agreed that everyone's life should be spared and that 'those who were of the town should return quietly to their houses'.[17]

A week later the House of Commons passed a motion ordering Corfe Castle to be 'slighted' and the work of destruction began with the help of large quantities of gunpowder. 'Thus this ancient and magnificent fabric was reduced to a heap of ruins and remains a lasting monument of the dreadful effects of anarchy and rebellion and the rage of Civil War.' The ruins were allowed to be 'the noblest and grandest in the kingdom' and the Reverend John Hutchins, rector of Holy Trinity, Wareham, writing his scholarly account of the *History and Antiquities of the County of Dorset* some hundred years later, observed that 'the vast fragments of the King's Tower, the round towers, leaning as if ready to fall, the broken walls and vast pieces of them tumbled down into the vale below, form such a scene of havock and desolation as strike every curious spectator with horror and concern.'[18]

Before the demolition crews moved in the castle had been systematically plundered, the building stripped of its valuable lead and timber, the best of the contents stowed in packs and trunks and taken up to London to be sold. John Bankes's estates had, of course, been sequestered and his widow was now obliged to petition the Dorset Committee of Sequestration for permission 'to enjoy the jointure settled on her before the delinquency of her husband'. The Committee found themselves in some difficulty over this request and in June 1646 applied to their superiors in London for guidance in deciding the case of Lady Bankes, explaining that 'we, finding her active in the defence of Corfe Castle against the Parliament during her coverture, have not granted her desire; but conceive we ought to continue the sequestration until we shall receive some satisfaction from your Lordships whether her act during coverture includes her within the ordinance, or whether your Lordships be not informed of any delinquency in her since her husband's decease – from which time the greatest part of her residence hath been near London, as we are informed.'[19]

The matter was not finally settled until the following February, when the sequestration order was lifted on the payment of substantial fines by the family. After the Restoration Ralph Bankes, eldest son and heir of Sir John, made a determined effort to recover some of the property looted from Corfe; but although he traced several sets of fine hangings and other furnishings valued at £1,000 to a broker named Stone in the Barbican, and had a very good idea of where most of the rest had gone, all he ever seems to have got back was one red velvet chair and some damask tablecloths and napkins. The long list of household effects carefully endorsed in his mother's handwriting 'about things lost in the castle', the trunks full of monogrammed sheets and table linen, the six large down and five feather beds with bolsters, the four pairs of down pillows and quilts and five pairs of fine long blankets, the several trunks of 'wearing clothes and wearing linenn', the 'crimson satten petticoat, with stomacher and sleeves lined with silver laces', the trunk 'with all sorts of fine child-bed linen, as sheets and pilow-cases and mantles' had gone for ever, together with the pewter, brass and iron utensils, the tables and stools and 'all else belonging to a house; with many armes in the magazine and hall of Sir John Bankes owne, all there, to the value of above 4001., pilledg'd by the souldiers'.[20]

The castle, too, had gone for ever. Even if it had been possible to make it habitable again, no gentleman in the England of the Restoration – especially one who had travelled in France and Italy as Ralph Bankes had done during the Commonwealth – would consider living in such out-dated surroundings, and Sir Ralph, who had been knighted in 1660, set about building himself a luxurious modern house at Kingston Lacy near Wimborne.

The new family home was finished in 1663 but Mary Bankes did not live to see it. She died rather suddenly in the spring of 1661 and was buried among her ancestors in St Martin's Church at Ruislip, where her son presently erected a white marble tablet on the south wall of the chancel dedicated to the memory of that virtuous and prudent lady, 'who having had the honor to have borne with a constancy and courage above her sex a noble proporcion of the late calamities, and the happiness to have outlived them so far as to have seene the restitution of the government with great peace of mind laid down her most desired life, the 11th day of April 1661'.[21]

Although the great majority of Civil War siege heroines were royalist, there were exceptions, perhaps the best remembered being Brilliana

Harley of Brampton Bryan. Her unusual Christian name appears to have been a somewhat fanciful adaptation of Brill – one of the Dutch 'cautionary towns' occupied by the English as security for the loans made to the States of Holland and Zeeland during their revolt against Spanish rule – where her father, Sir Edward Conway, was Governor and where she herself was born, most probably in 1598. Like her cousin Anne Fairfax, Brilliana spent some of her childhood years in the Netherlands and, also like her cousin, was noted for her radical religious opinions. The Conways were back in England by 1606 and although nothing is known of Brilliana's life until her marriage in 1623, her many surviving letters make it plain that she had been well-educated and had developed into a thoughtful, genuinely pious young woman. She would have been about twenty-four when she married Robert Harley as his third wife – late for a first marriage but it seems that her father, despite a successful career in government service, had found it a struggle to raise the cash for dowries for Brilliana and her three sisters.

Harley was in his mid-forties and anxious for an heir, which neither of his previous wives had been able to give him, but Brilliana was to be more fortunate in this vital department. Three sons, Edward, Robert and Thomas appeared at two yearly intervals from 1624 to 1628, followed by four daughters born between 1629 and 1634. Apart from this unusually happy child-bearing record – only the youngest girl, Elizabeth, failed to survive – the marriage was a success story from the beginning, with a strong bond of affection and mutual respect uniting husband and wife. The fact that both were committed members of the Puritan or Presbyterian persuasion would certainly have helped to ensure the 'conjunction of minds, of affections, of wills' generally felt to be necessary for a good marriage, but it also meant that in the troubled 1640s the couple were often apart. Robert Harley had first entered the House of Commons in 1604 and was returned to Parliament as a knight of the shire in 1624, 1626 and 1628. He sat in the so-called Short Parliament of 1640 and in November of that year became one of the most hard-working members of the Long Parliament. His considerable experience and zeal for the cause earned him a place on numerous committees and while parliamentary business kept him in London, his wife remained at home at Brampton Castle with the younger children.

The Harleys were an old-established gentry family who had been settled at Brampton Bryan in north Herefordshire not far from the Welsh border since the early fourteenth century, but in a solidly royalist county the political and religious sympathies of Sir Robert and his lady inevitably set them apart from their neighbours. As early as June 1642 Brilliana was reporting that the country people were grown very insolent. They had set up a maypole at Ludlow with 'a thing like a head upon it . . . and gathered a great many about it and shot at it in derision of Roundheads'. Brilliana herself was not immune from insult and told her husband that 'they are grown exceeding rude in these parts. Every Thursday some of Ludlow, as they go through the town [Brampton] wish all the puritans of Brampton hanged and as I was walking one day in the garden . . . they looked upon me and wished all the puritans and Roundheads at Brampton hanged, and when they were gone a little further they cursed you and all your children and thus they do every week as they go through the town.'[22]

It was not pleasant to feel herself among enemies, and Brilliana had more than once begged her husband to agree to her coming to join him – 'Let me earnestly desire you to consider well whether it is safe for me and my children to be at Brampton.' Sir Robert, however, remained firm in his insistence that she should stay where she was and, like a good wife, she obeyed. 'Since you think Brampton a safe place for me, I will think so too', she wrote submissively, 'and I would not for anything do that which might make the world believe our hopes did begin to fail in our God.'[23] All the same, she still felt very uneasy and told her much-loved eldest son Ned, now also in London, that 'since your father thinks Herefordshire as safe as any other country, I will think so too; but when I considered how long I had been from him, and how this country was affected, my desire to see your father and my care to be in a place of safety, made me earnestly desire to come up to London. But since it is not your father's will, I will lay aside that desire.'[24]

Robert Harley may quite genuinely have believed that his wife would be safer in Herefordshire than in London and, busy as he was, he may have found it more convenient to have the family out of the way at Brampton. There was, too, the purely practical consideration that in present circumstances it could not be thought wise to leave the house and estate unoccupied. This had also occurred to Brilliana, who wrote to Ned in July: 'At first when I saw how outrageously this country carried themselves against your father, my anger was so up, and my sorrow, that I had hardly patience to stay; but now, I have well considered, that if I go away I shall leave all that your father has to the prey of our enemies, which they would be glad of; so that, and please God, I purpose to stay as long as it is possible, if I live . . . I cannot make a better use of my life, next to serving my God, than do what good I can for you.' 'I thank God I am not afraid', she declared stoutly in another letter. 'It is the Lord's cause we have stood for, and I trust, though our iniquities testify against us, yet the Lord will work for His own name sake, and that He will now shew the men of the world that it is hard fighting against heaven.'[25]

Throughout that anxious summer, when, as another parliamentarian lady was to recall, 'before the flame of the warre broke out in the top of the chimnies, the smoake ascended in every country', Brilliana found herself increasingly preoccupied with matters not normally within the experience of a God-fearing housewife. 'I hope your father will give me full directions how I may best have my house guarded, if need be; if he will give the directions, I hope I shall follow it.' She had already begun to take precautions against a possible attack and on 15 July received 'the box with 20 bandoliers, but the boxes with the muskets and rests the carrier has left to come in a waggon to Worcester; he promises I shall have them shortly.' Later in the month she was still waiting for the muskets to arrive, but had taken delivery of a hamper containing a supply of powder and match – that is, cord specially treated to smoulder and ignite the powder in a matchlock musket. Having been told 'that none can make shot but those whose trade it is', she made the plumber write to Worcester for '50 weight of shot'. She was sending to Worcester, she told Ned, because she did not want it to be known locally.[26]

Brilliana continued to be distressed by the hostility of her neighbours – 'your father they are grown to hate. I pray God forgive them.' She was also afraid of treachery within her own household and sent one 'roguish boy' up to London with a letter, because 'I dare not keep him in my house, and as little do I dare to let him go in this country, lest he join with the company of volunteers, or some other such crew'. She did not want him back and suggested hopefully to Ned that he might be persuaded to go to sea, or 'take some other imployment'.[27]

On top of everything else, she was now beginning to be worried about money. She was already having problems in collecting her rents from the estate tenants and had had to lay out 'an extraordinary sum of money' for repairs to the roof at Brampton. The plumbers working on the leads demanded an exorbitant five shillings a day, and there were carpenters and masons to be paid as well. So when Sir Robert wrote to say that she was to pack up the family plate and have it sent to him in London to be sold for the parliamentary war effort, Brilliana felt bound to register a protest, telling Ned she thought it would be more sensible to borrow money for the cause than surrender the plate: 'for we do not know what straits we may be put to, and therefore I think it is better to borrow whilst one may and keep the plate for a time of need'. But Robert Harley would not be deflected and on 9 July Brilliana despatched a hamper containing a voider, or tray, eighteen plates and a salt by the Leominster carrier. A week later another instalment went off via Ludlow in a trunk carefully sewn up in canvas and addressed to Mr Smith at the Old Bailey.[28]

In the midst of all her other preoccupations, Brilliana never forgot her obligations as a wife and mother, sending Ned a regular supply of clean shirts and handkerchiefs, and 'I pray you send me one of your socks, to make you new ones by'; worrying about her husband's health: 'I fear your father in this great business will neglect himself; therefore, dear Ned, put him in mind to eat something in a morning', and sending him homemade cakes and pies and, on one occasion, a runlet, or cask, of good Herefordshire cider.[29]

Robert Harley and Ned were both at Brampton for a while in the autumn of 1642, but by December Brilliana was alone again and missing them horribly. 'I never was in such sorrows, as I have been since you left me.' She still clung to a faint hope that she might even now be able to get away herself, and in a letter written on Christmas Day, asked Ned to talk to his father and see whether he thought 'it be best for me to go from Brampton or by God's help to stand it out'. She would, of course, 'be willing to do what he would have me do'.[30]

The New Year came in and the outlook remained bleak. Hereford was occupied by royalist troops and Brilliana told Ned that she knew he would be grieved to hear she was being used 'with all the malice that can be'. The fowler was not allowed to bring her any game. Her rents were no longer being paid. The young horses had all been commandeered and none of her servants dared go as far as the town. 'And dear Ned, if God were not merciful to me, I should be in a very miserable condition. I am threatened every day to be beset with soldiers. My hope is, the Lord will not deliver me nor mine into their hands; for surely they would use all cruelty towards me, for I am told that they desire not to leave your father neither root nor branch. Dear Ned, desire the prayers of the godly for us at Brampton . . . I know not whether this will come to your hand or no, but this I know, that I long to hear from you, and I pray God bless you.'[31]

Early in February Lord Herbert, the royalist commander, held a council of war at which it was agreed that the Sheriff of Radnorshire with his trained bands and some of the Herefordshire men would be mustered to capture Brampton and, so Brilliana heard, to blow it up. The plan fell through, partly because the Welsh militia refused to cross the border into England and partly because Herbert's men had been diverted to attack Gloucester. 'Now they say, they will starve me out of my house,' wrote Brilliana bitterly in her next letter to Ned; 'they have taken away all your father's rents, and they say they will drive away the cattle, and then I shall have nothing to live upon; for all their aim is to enforce me to let those men I have go, that then they might seize upon my house and cut our throats by a few rogues, and then say, they knew not who did it.'[32]

At the end of the month Lady Harley received a formal summons from the Governor of Hereford, the sonorously named Fitzwilliam Coningsby, requiring her 'to deliver up to his Majesty's use the fort and castle of Brampton Bryan, with all arms, munitions, and all other warlike provisions about or in the said fort and castle under the pain to be taken and proceeded against both by law and martial force as persons guilty of high treason'. Brilliana responded by declaring that the only arms she possessed were 'no more than to defend my house', and went on to point out that, since the king had many times promised to maintain the laws and liberties of the realm, 'by which I have as good right to what is mine as anyone', she did not know 'upon what ground the refusal of giving you what is mine (by the laws of the land), will prove me, or anyone that is with me, traitors.'[33]

The arrival in the west of Sir William Waller, followed by his successful incursions into South Wales and brief occupation of Hereford itself – 'God has mightily been seen in Herefordshire' – temporarily relieved the pressure on Brampton, although Brilliana now had the added anxiety of knowing that Ned and her second son, Robin, were fighting in Waller's army. Ned's horse was killed under him at Roundway Down, but his mother thankfully acknowledged the great mercy of her God which had preserved him unhurt 'in so sharp a fight'. 'My heart is with you', she had written in the weeks before the battle, 'and I know you believe it; for my life is bound up with yours. . . .' 'I hope the Lord will in mercy give you to me again, for you are both a Joseph and a Benjamin to me.'

The defeat at Roundway Down was a severe blow to the parliamentary cause and bad news for the family at Brampton. The royalists were back in Hereford in triumph and raising fresh troops, and Brilliana knew she must 'look for new on-sets, but I hope I shall look to my rock of defence the Lord my God, from whom is deliverance'. Nevertheless, on the principle that the Lord helps those who help themselves, she had asked

Colonel Massey, commanding the garrison at Gloucester, 'to send me an able soldier, that might regulate the men I have, and he has sent me one that was a sergeant, an honest man and I think an able soldier'. She was also trying to do her bit by encouraging volunteers to join Ned's regiment and had promised to 'endeavour to see whether any will contribute to buy a horse', but came up against the problem familiar to fund-raisers in every age, finding that 'those that have hearts have not means, and they that have means have not hearts'.[34]

By 24 July Prince Rupert and Lord Hertford's Western Army were at the gates of Bristol, and William Vavasour, the newly appointed Governor of Hereford, decided the time had come to deal with the troublesome nest of Roundheads at Brampton Bryan. So, on Wednesday 26 July, the moment which Brilliana Harley had been dreading for more than a year arrived at last when, at about two o'clock in the afternoon, two or three troops of horse, closely followed by two or three hundred foot soldiers, appeared before the castle and proceeded to block all access to the outside world.

Several of the officers deploying in the village of Brampton Bryan that summer afternoon were connected to the Harleys by ties of blood or marriage and were undoubtedly aware of the social awkwardness of their situation. It is, after all, embarrassing to find yourself preparing to mount an armed attack on the wife of a neighbour with whom you have in the past been on friendly terms, with whom you have often sat on the bench or ridden out hunting, and who has entertained you as a guest in the house you now propose to take from him by force.

Some of this embarrassment was reflected in the wording of the summons delivered to Lady Harley that same evening in the names of Henry Lingen, High Sheriff of the county, Sir William Pye of Mynde Park and William Smallman JP. Their relations with her ladyship made them careful to prevent if possible any further inconvenience to her, but since Sir William Vavasour had been commanded by his majesty to reduce Brampton Castle, her ladyship would do well to consider her position. 'Bristol is taken by Prince Rupert and he is now before Gloucester,' they continued. 'His Majesty's forces are successful everywhere, so that your ladyship cannot hope for any relief, and upon these terms if your ladyship should be obstinate, we cannot promise and expect those conditions for you that are fit for your quality . . . neither any quarter for those that are with you, who further must look for all extremity upon their families and substance.'[35]

Brilliana responded by remarking that the relationship to her which the gentlemen had been pleased to mention might have prompted them 'to another piece of service than this that you are now come upon'. As for William Vavasour's drawing his forces before her house by the king's command: 'I dare not, I cannot, I must not believe it, since it has pleased our most gracious King to make many solemn promises that he would maintain the laws and liberties of this kingdom. I cannot then think he would give a command to take away anything from his loyal subjects, and much less to take away my house. If Sir William Vavasour will do so, I must endeavour to keep what is mine as well as I can, in which I have the law of nature, of reason and of the land on my side, and you none to take it from me.'[36]

During the next two days some sporadic musket fire was exchanged and the besiegers took possession of the parish church which stood within sixty or seventy paces of the castle gates. They also drove off the household's flock of sheep and their 'fat beefs'. On the evening of 28 July William Vavasour replied to Brilliana's letter and 'denial' more in sorrow than in anger. Her defiance was useless, 'for we will never suffer the King's power to be affronted by so small a part of the county . . . I shall deal fairly with you, madam,' he went on. 'I am your servant, and to one so noble and virtuous am desirous to keep off all insolences that the liberty of the soldiers, provoked to it by your obstinacies may throw upon you; yet if you remain still wilful, what you may suffer is brought upon you by yourself, I having by this timely notice discharged those respects due to your sex and honour.'[37]

Fourteenth-century Brampton Castle was no Corfe, nor could it for a moment be compared to border fortresses such as Ludlow or Chepstow. It was, however, acknowledged to be a strong place, with a gatehouse flanked by two round towers and protected by a double portcullis in full working order. Inside, conditions were uncomfortable. As well as a garrison of some fifty musketeers and their 'gentlemen commanders', a considerable number of non-combatants were crowded into the castle's living quarters: Lady Harley with her three youngest children, Thomas, Dorothy and Margaret, aged fifteen, thirteen and twelve; her friend Lady Colebourn; Nathaniel Wright, the family doctor, his wife and his apothecary, and Samuel Moore, son of the Member of Parliament for Bishop's Castle, plus servants and other miscellaneous hangers-on. It was, however, observed 'that although there were of men women and children above a hundred all immured up in a close house, and in the dog days, yet there was not one feeble or sick person amongst us.'[38]

Brilliana was continuing to protest her loyalty. 'You and all the world are deceived', she told William Vavasour somewhat disingenuously, 'if you think there is any drop of disloyal blood in my heart, and none can less cherish our gracious King's enemies than myself.' She also protested vigorously over the theft of her livestock. Her rents had already been stopped for almost a year, and now even the beasts on which she and her children must depend for food had been taken by the soldiers. In fact, she believed the pathos of her situation to be without parallel: 'That one of my condition, who have my husband from me, and so wanting much comfort, should be besieged, and so my life and the lives of my little children sought after, with that of my whole family without any cause given on my part.'[39]

But when Sir William offered to guarantee the safety of the household if her ladyship would order her people to lay down their arms and allow him to send in a guard of his own men, her ladyship would have none of it. 'I should become a prisoner in my own house, which I cannot yield to, for so I should speak myself guilty; and thus much more I must say, my dear husband hath entrusted me with his house and children, and therefore I cannot dispose of his house but according to his pleasure, and I do not know it is his pleasure that I should entertain soldiers in his house.' Brilliana reminded William Vavasour that her father had been 'in a particular manner' his majesty's servant and was now demanding to be granted 'the liberty to send to Sir William Pelham [her brother-in-law] who is with the King, that by his means I may obtain a pass by which I may go safely to some other place of more safety than my own house.'[40]

She was, of course, playing desperately for time and contrived to keep up the exchange with Vavasour for a full week. But on 3 August 'the greatest part of the town was consumed and burnt' and the enemy torched the castle's mills and outbuildings. They had also mounted a cannon in the church steeple and began a bombardment 'which only shattered the battlements but did no execution'. According to the account of Captain Priam Davies, one of those present throughout the siege, 'none of us were daunted either by the enemy, or by the malignants of the country, who stood upon hills about us, giving great shouts whenever the ordnance played'. This continued even on Sunday, when 'they made eight shots against us before morning sermon, then left off that day as if they had been ashamed'.[41]

Both sides accused the other of atrocities. The royalists were said to have murdered a blind man 'because upon demand he said he was for

the King and Parliament', while Vavasour complained that shots from the
castle had killed a little boy. Captain Davies was to boast that the garrison
had slain about sixty of the enemy, but casualties inside the castle appear
to have been surprisingly light. On 7 August a bullet shattered part of a
wall, which injured Lady Colebourn, who lost an eye, and Mrs Wright, the
doctor's wife. Later in the siege the cook died, presumably from
septicaemia, as the result of a bullet wound in the arm.

The royalists had now brought up more artillery and their
bombardment continued intermittently for the next fortnight, 'the
enemy . . . cursing the Roundheads, calling us Essex's bastards, Waller's
bastards, Harley's bastards, rogues, thieves, traitors, and all to reduce us
to the obedience of the king'. They had dug trenches and thrown up
great earthworks in the gardens of the castle, so close that the soldiers'
bad language was clearly audible from within and, remarked Priam
Davies primly, 'annoyed us more than their poisoned bullets'.[42]

On 23 August a drummer announced the arrival of a messenger from
the king. This was Sir John Scudamore, also a kinsman of the Harleys,
who was admitted to the castle by means of a rope ladder to deliver a
letter from his majesty to Lady Harley. The king, now camped before
Gloucester, was ready to believe that her ladyship's defiance was due to
evil counsel rather than ill-affection to himself, and being anxious to
avoid unnecessary bloodshed and having due regard to her 'sex and
condition', was graciously pleased to offer her a free pardon in return for
her surrender.

Brilliana now demanded to be allowed to address a petition to his
majesty. After complaining bitterly about the various wrongs being daily
inflicted on her, 'whereas your poor subject did never offend your
Majesty, or ever take up arms against your Majesty', she went on to pray
that he would not require her to give up that 'which by the law of the
land is mine'. If she was forced to leave her house, then 'my humble
desire is that you will in your clemency allow unto me some maintenance
for me and mine and fit time to remove myself and family by your
protection to pass to some other place where we may find subsistence,
that we perish not'.

Brilliana had wanted to send her petition by one of her own people,
who would be able to plead her cause with the king, but this was refused
and she had to entrust it to Sir John Scudamore, who returned a week
later with a letter written by Secretary of State Lord Falkland. Although
his majesty was not at all satisfied with Lady Harley's excuses and

protestations, he was still prepared to give her the benefit of the doubt and so far to reflect with pity upon her sex and condition as to renew his offer of a full pardon and licence for everyone at Brampton 'to depart out of the castle whither and with what arms and ammunition – ordnance only excepted – they shall please themselves, and to assure them of a convoy accordingly'. Alternatively, and provided his forces were immediately received into the castle, the king would be content to allow her ladyship and her family to remain 'until she have provided herself of another habitation'. Scudamore added a verbal message that he was empowered to grant her ladyship 'what other conditions she could in reason demand'.[43]

Brilliana had throughout skilfully exploited her connections as well as her sex, and it was plain from the quite generous terms still being offered that everyone was anxious to avoid the embarrassment of having to proceed to extreme measures against such a well-respected lady of her social standing. But the lady herself was not yet ready to give in and managed to spin out the correspondence with Scudamore for almost another week. Every day counted now, for on 7 September a whisper reached the castle that William Waller and the Earl of Essex were marching to the relief of Gloucester, and the royalists were already beginning to remove their 'great guns'. The following day they took the church bells, 'and as they were carrying them out of town', wrote Priam Davies, 'we sent some of his Majesty's good subjects to old Nick for their sacrilege'. On Saturday the 9th, 'we continued with small shot most of the day', but that night 'we had secret intelligence that the Lord General [Essex] was with a very great army near Gloucester, that the Cavaliers had raised their siege to give him battle and that all the King's forces were called together for that purpose . . . and that the Cavaliers about us would be gone. This, indeed, was the day of our deliverance, a day to be remembered and never to be forgotten throughout our generations.'[44]

The siege by 'these bloody villains' had lasted for seven weeks and, as Priam Davies recorded, the sufferings of the garrison had been great. 'All our bread was ground with a hand mill, our provisions very scarce, the roof of the castle so battered that there was not one dry room in it; our substance without plundered and all our friends fled.' Davies had nothing but praise for the noble Lady Harley, who had borne it all with admirable patience and who now faced the task of restoring some sort of order and replenishing her stock of provisions. This was made harder by the open defiance and obstruction of tenants, many of whom had not paid their rents for years and who now refused either to help level the earthworks round the castle, or to 'let us have provisions nor any of the conveniences of life which they could hinder us from'. Confronted with such 'barbarism', Brilliana was obliged to resort to force, sending out foraging parties 'against those that had been most active against us; whereby our necessities were in a short time supplied'.

Encouraged by the news that Gloucester had now been relieved and aware that some at least of the enemy had not retreated very far, Brilliana moved on to the offensive. 'This noble lady', says Davies, 'who commanded in chief, I may truly say with such a masculine bravery, both for religion, resolution, wisdom and warlike policy, that her equal I never yet saw, commanded that a party of about forty should go and beat up their quarters in Knighton, a market town in Radnorshire, four miles off, where Colonel Lingen's troop, her late antagonist, was quartered. This was so performed that we brought some prisoners, arms and horses without the loss of one man.'[45]

For all her brave display of masculine resolution, Brilliana longed to get away from Brampton but still could not decide where her duty lay. In a letter to Ned dated 24 September, she begged him to 'let me know your mind whether I had best stay or remove'. At the same time she was writing to her husband, who was now advising her to leave, that 'God has made me (though an unworthy one) an instrument to keep possession of your house, that it has not fallen into the hands of spoilers, and to keep together a handful of such as fear the Lord . . . In this work I have not thought my life dear, nor shall I.'[46]

She wrote again to Ned on 9 October: 'How much I long to see you I cannot express . . . and if it pleased the Lord, I wish you were at Brampton. I am now again threatened; there are some soldiers come to Leominster and 3 troops of horse to Hereford with Sir William Vavasour, and they say they mean to visit Brampton again; but I hope the Lord will deliver me . . . I have taken a very great cold, which has made me very ill these 2 or 3 days, but I hope the Lord will be merciful to me, in giving me health, for it is an ill time to be sick in. My dear Ned, I pray God bless you and give me the comfort of seeing you . . .'[47]

Sadly this consolation was denied her. Whether or not the unremitting strain and anxiety of the past two years was a contributory cause is impossible to say for certain, but Brilliana's health had begun to break down and towards the end of the month 'this honourable lady, of whom the world was not worthy . . . suddenly and unexpectedly fell sick of an apoplexy with a defluxion of the lungs'. She lingered for three days, looking death in the face 'without dread and the Lord Jesus with joy and comfort, to whom she resigned her soul'. She died on 31 October, leaving 'the saddest garrison in the three kingdoms', and Priam Davies was not able to express 'the extremity of grief and sorrow that this sudden deprivation and discouragement produced'. If the enemy had returned at that moment, 'we had been able to make very little resistance but volleys of sighs and tears'.[48] In fact, the castle was not threatened again until the following spring when, in spite of being deprived of their beloved 'head and governess' whose commands had carried them into the cannon's mouth, the garrison, now under the command of Nathaniel Wright, held out for three weeks before surrendering to William Vavasour on the Wednesday of Easter week 1644.

So, after all Brilliana's valiant efforts, Brampton had finally fallen into the hands of spoilers. The castle itself was left in ruins, its parks and warrens laid waste and Sir Robert Harley's losses were estimated at £13,000. The lives of the defenders were spared, although there had been a nasty moment two hours after the surrender when, according to Priam Davies, an order arrived from Prince Rupert 'to put us all to the sword, especially Dr. Wright, our Lieutenant-Colonel'. Fortunately, William Vavasour 'that had more of a gentleman and soldier in him, protested against it, by whose means, through God's mercy, we were preserved'.[49] On the following day they were all, including the Harley children, taken as prisoners to Ludlow, where the inhabitants 'baited us like bears and demanded where our God was'. The young Harleys, however, appear to have been kindly treated. The order for their release came through on 18 June, when they were transferred into the charge of John Scudamore and soon afterwards reunited with their father.

Robert Harley and Ned continued to serve the parliamentary cause, but they both opposed the trial of the king and, as staunch Presbyterians, both became victims of Colonel Pride's celebrated purge of the House of Commons. Sir Robert died in 1656, but Ned lived on to see the Restoration and the Glorious Revolution, representing either Radnor or the county of Hereford in all of Charles II's parliaments and the first parliament of William and Mary before retiring to Brampton, where he died in 1700. His son, another Robert Harley, was to carry on the family tradition of public service, rising to high office and the peerage under Queen Anne and becoming one of the first career politicians to whom the title of prime minister was applied.

The fame of Brilliana Harley spread through the kingdom, earning the 'admiration and applause even of her enemies', but there were other parliamentary heroines, such as Mrs Purefoy of Caldecot Manor in Warwickshire, who held Prince Rupert and a detachment of five hundred troopers at bay for several hours in the opening weeks of the war. Her husband being away, the house was defended only by a Mr Abbott and eight serving men, 'but the heroic spirit of an Englishwoman infused a strength and courage . . . that set odds at defiance'.

Mrs Purefoy having refused to admit him, Rupert ordered an assault and the gate of the outer courtyard was soon forced, but a well-directed volley of musket fire from the defenders killed three officers and several troopers in the first few minutes. The attack was renewed with heavy loss to the cavaliers, who had only their pistols and possibly a few carbines against an enemy firing with deadly accuracy from behind the protection of stone walls. There were only twelve muskets in the house, 'but the ladies and their maidservants loaded as fast as they were discharged, melting down the pewter plates for bullets when the ammunition began to fail'. After a while Rupert was forced to withdraw his men under shelter; 'but finding a strong wind blowing from the farm-yard, he fired the barns, and advancing under cover of the smoke, assailed the very doors. Then at last the brave lady came forth, and claimed protection for the lives of her little garrison. When the prince ascertained their number, his anger was changed to admiration; he complimented Mr Abbott on his gallant defence, and offered him a good command in his regiment, which was declined. The prince then respectfully saluted Mrs Purefoy and drew off his troops; nor did he allow a man of the garrison or any property whatever to be injured.'[50]

Another lady who defied Prince Rupert was Mistress Elizabeth Leigh of Rushall Hall near Walsall who, in April 1643, 'valiantly defended her house with the only help of her men and maides . . . and at length came off bravely with quarter and credit'.[51] Rushall was a prize worth taking. A 'House built about with a Wall and a Gate-House of Stone, all embattled Castle-wise', it occupied a strategic position on the road to Coventry and London and was immediately garrisoned for the king under Colonel Lane of Bentley – the same Colonel Lane whose sister Jane was later to play so vital a part in the Stuart story.

In those early days of the war there was still some room for chivalry, but it has to be said that not every parliamentarian lady received as much consideration for her 'sex and condition' as did Brilliana Harley or

Mrs Purefoy. Eleanor, Lady Drake of Ashe on the Devon–Dorset border was unceremoniously turned out of house and home by Lord Paulett, the royalist commander at Axminster, whose Irish soldiers 'stripped the good lady, who, almost naked, and without a shoe to her foot but what she afterwards begged, fled to Lyme for safety'.[52] Or so at least the good lady herself later declared when claiming compensation from Paulett. But then Lady Drake was a forceful personality with a vivid turn of phrase – perhaps suitably for the mother-in-law of the first Sir Winston Churchill.

CHAPTER THREE

'As His Shaddow'

I thought myself a queen, and my husband so glorious
a crown that I more valued myself to be call'd by
his name than borne a princess.

Ann, Lady Fanshawe

In the late summer of 1643 the royalists were riding high. The king was now master of the west. From Cornwall to Dorset and Wiltshire only a few isolated pockets of resistance remained and the whole of Wales, apart from a corner of Pembrokeshire, was 'at his devotion'. The Earl of Newcastle still controlled Yorkshire and more of Nottingham and Lincolnshire than Parliament did, while Parliament was no stronger in the north-west than it had been at the beginning of the year, at least according to Lord Clarendon.

Parliamentary morale was low, and in the first week of August the peace party in the Lords felt brave enough to draw up a set of propositions for a negotiated settlement which the Commons agreed to consider. This brought an immediate reaction from the City and the pulpits. The Lord Mayor organized a petition protesting against any talk of peace and the usual rumours about hordes of Irish papists poised to invade began to circulate. On 7 August a crowd about 5,000 strong came flocking to Westminster shouting 'No peace! No peace!' and the Commons voted to reject the Lords' propositions.

Counter-demonstrations followed, culminating on 9 August when a mob of women, clamouring for peace, swarmed into Palace Yard. They hammered on the door of the Commons chamber, yelling 'Give us those traitors that were against peace!' and 'Give us that dog Pym!' When the militia men on guard tried to disperse them by firing powder, the women responded with stones and brickbats, so that in the end a troop of horse had to be called in to restore order. Sir Simonds D'Ewes, the parliamentary diarist, disapproved. 'No man can excuse the indiscreet violence of these women', he wrote, 'but the remedy used against them by the procurement of John Pym and some others, who were enemies to all kind of peace, was most cruel and barbarous; for, not content to have them suppressed by the ordinary foot guard, which had been sufficient, there were divers horsemen called down, who hunted the said women up and down the back Palace Yard, and wounded them with their swords and pistols with no less inhumanity than if they had been brute beasts, of which wounds some of the poor women afterwards died.' Estimates of the casualty numbers varied widely. Ten were killed and more than a hundred injured, according to the Venetian ambassador. Other accounts say two men killed and a few women injured, but one unlucky maidservant, 'that had nothing to do in the tumult', was shot dead by a trooper – by accident, he afterwards claimed – as she crossed St Margaret's churchyard on her way to draw water.[1]

The incident was quickly taken up by the propaganda machines on both sides of the political divide. To one, the protesters were respectable wives wearing white ribbons in their hats, who came with their children in their arms to cry for peace; to the other, a mere rabble of whores, bawds, oyster-wives, and dirty tattered sluts, 'the very scum of the scum of the Suburbs'. It was even suggested that the whole affair had been got up by the royalists and that there had been men disguised in its ranks.

It is not impossible that there was an element of 'rentacrowd' in the women's protest but, although most Londoners were solidly parliamentarian in sympathy, an undercurrent of discontent and disillusion certainly existed. The general disruption of trade and communications had led to high prices and shortages (fuel was in particularly short supply) and those ordinary housewives uninterested in the finer points of the conflict, especially those left to cope on their own in the gloomy wartime city, were understandably bewildered and resentful. The individual complaints of such women were, for obvious reasons, seldom recorded, but Susan Rodway's often quoted letter to her 'most dear and loving husband', a trained soldier away serving in Colonel Warren's Westminster 'Red' militia regiment, surely speaks for very many of them. 'I pray you to come whome [home], ife youe cane cum saffly [safely]. I doo marfull that I cannot heere from you ass well other naybores [neighbours] do. I do desiere to heere from you as soone as youe cane. I pray youe to send me word when youe doo thenke youe shalt returne. You doe not consider I ame a loen woemane; I thought you woald never leve me thuse long togeder, so I rest evere praying for your savese [safest] returne . . .' Poor Susan may have had a very long wait, for it seems only too probable that her husband was killed in one of the first assaults on the Marquis of Winchester's stronghold at Basing House.[2]

There was, of course, never any question of peace in 1643, and John Pym, now mortally ill with the cancer which would kill him before the end of the year, was working against time to negotiate the treaty with the Presbyterian Scots which would ultimately decide the outcome of the Great Rebellion. Meanwhile, early in September, parliament received some much-needed encouragement when the arrival of the Earl of Essex had forced Rupert and the king to raise the siege of Gloucester.

Although at the time this seemed no more than a disappointing setback, the royalist failure at 'that unfortunate obstinate town' has often since been pinpointed as the moment in the war when the tide turned, and the king himself was seen to be in a despondent mood. There is a local tradition that as his army marched in the rain to camp on Painswick Hill, Charles stopped to rest, sitting on a stone by the roadside. When one of his young sons, 'weary of their present life', asked him if they were going home, he replied sadly, 'I have no home to go to'.[3]

At Gloucester, as at most sieges, the women had taken an active part in the defence of the town, 'lining the walls and repairing the breaches'. It was not unusual for women of the labouring class, well accustomed to hard manual work and every bit as tough as the men, to join in the digging and building of fortifications, but when London had been threatened the previous year women and girls of every class had turned out to help, and

> Raised rampiers with their own soft hands
> To put the enemy to stands;
> From Ladies down to oyster-wenches
> Labour'd like pioneers in trenches,
> Fell to their pick-axes and tools,
> And help'd the men to dig like moles.

The Lady Mayoress herself, together with such patriotic 'lady-volunteer engineers' as Lady Waller, Lady Middlesex, wife of the self-made millionaire Lionel Cranfield, and Lady Foster, wife of the Chief Justice of the King's Bench, were all said to have 'resorted daily to the works, not as spectators but assisters in it.'[4]

At Bristol, where Mary Smith had carried provisions to the men on the out-works, she, with Joan Batten and the suitably named Dorothy Hazzard (a parson's wife, incidentally) and 'divers other women, and maydes, with the help of some men, did with Woolsackes and earth, stop up Froome gate . . . being the onely passage by which the Enemy must enter'. Two hundred women are also supposed to have gone to the Governor, Colonel Fiennes, offering excitedly to put themselves and their children in the mouth of the enemy cannon to 'keepe off the shot from the Souldiers', and in the recriminations which followed Fiennes's surrender it was being said that the very women had shown more resolution in defence of the town.[5]

By contrast, in Gloucester, where the garrison was commanded by the young, energetic Edward Massey, morale remained high. John Corbet, citizen and preacher of God's word, recalled that 'no great complainings were heard in our streets . . . the usuall outcryes of women were not then heard, the weaknesse of whose sexe was not overcome by the terrible engines of warre'; while the town clerk commended 'the cheerfull readinesse of yong and old of both sexes . . . to labour in the further fortification of our citie. Nay, our maids and others wrought daily without the works in the little mead, in fetching in turfe in the very faces of our enemies.'[6]

Up in Yorkshire, where Hull was currently under siege by the Earl of Newcastle's army, a maidservant was killed while carrying earth for the fortifications – an upsetting event which temporarily discouraged her companions. But afterwards 'all the women, even those of the best rank, strangers and others, willingly helped forward the workes'. Indeed, the parliamentarian tract declared enthusiastically, 'we can boast of our Troops of Virgins, who shewed so much diligence, that many of our fortifications may deservedly be called the Virgins Workes'.[7]

When Lyme, on the Dorset coast, came under siege by Prince Maurice Palatine with a force of about 6,000 men in April 1644, the royalists did not expect to encounter any very great difficulty. In fact, they confidently expected to be able to reduce this 'little vile fishing town' between breakfast and dinnertime. But the inhabitants of Lyme, inflamed by the hell-fire sermons of their numerous 'puritanical lecturers', resisted with such courage and tenacity that, after two months, Maurice was finally forced to admit defeat and withdraw to Exeter 'with some loss of reputation'.

A few of the better-off women had been evacuated by sea, but the great majority stayed to fight and share the danger with their menfolk. The parliamentary lawyer and commentator Bulstrode Whitelocke records that the besieged 'beat back the enemy at three assaults and forced them to leave behind them their scaling ladders', as well as taking more than a hundred prisoners, three great guns and Prince Maurice's own colours. 'In these assaults they relate that the women of the town would come into the thickest of the danger, to bring powder, bullet, and provisions to the men, encouraging them upon the works.'[8]

The heroism of the women of Lyme, who also acted as fire-watchers and look-outs, was commemorated in a long piece of doggerel verse, written by several hands and entitled *Joanereidos, or Feminine Valor discovered in Western Women at the Siege of Lyme*:

> The Roman Capitoll by Geese was kept
> They wake't, poore foules, when the dull Souldiers slept.
> Alas! who now keepes Lime? poore femall Cattell
> Who wake all night, labour all day in Battell,
> Geese, as a man may call them, who doe hisse
> Against the opposers of our Countries blisse.
> And by their seasonable noyse discover
> Our Foes, when they the Workes are climing over.[9]

Casualties were heavy on both sides throughout the siege, and at one time the town's water supply was said to have been coloured with blood. At about noon on Saturday 1 June the attackers had fired burning arrows dipped in tar or pitch into the west end of the town, and since the weather was hot and dry two streets of little thatched houses were soon alight. According to the diary kept by Mr Edward Drake of Colyton, if it had not been for a south wind which helped to blow the flames northwards and away from the town, the whole might have been destroyed; especially as 'the enemy this while was not idle but played with their small shot amongst the fire very hotly to the intent the fire might not be quenched by any within the Town that should endeavour it'. But it took more than small shot to intimidate the men and women of Lyme, and being well provided with water and 'wet hydes', they were able to contain the damage. The enemy bombardment continued and a shot from a piece of ordnance killed two and caused a number of injuries, including one woman carrying a pail of water who lost both arms, and a maid whose hand was struck off. When this girl was asked how she would now manage to earn a living, she replied: 'Truly I am glad with all my heart I had a hand to lose for Jesus Christ for Whose Cause I am as willing and ready to lose not only my other hand but my life also.' This was considered to be 'a sweet and most saint-like speech indeed'.[10]

There was, however, nothing sweet or saint-like about some other members of the sisterhood. A gruesome story is told concerning the fate of a poor old Irishwoman, presumably a camp-follower of one of the Irish regiments under Maurice's command, who got left behind in the retreat. Wandering about in search of her friends, she was set upon by a group of women, who drove her through the streets to the seaside, stripped and robbed her and almost tore her to pieces, before, so tradition says, rolling her into the sea to drown in a hogshead stuck with nails.[11]

It was not only parliamentarian women who helped to defend their towns. After William Waller's attack on royalist Worcester was driven off in the summer of 1643, 'the ordinary sort of women to the number of 400' turned out armed with spades, shovels and mattocks and within a very few days, by 'their own industry and free service', had levelled the fortifications left by the enemy, 'to prevent Sir William Waller's approach near if he should return suddenly against them'. They also 'and with their own hands sleighted the worke that had sheltered his Musketeirs, and the day after very orderly levelled all the ditches in and about the Town; which will make them so famous, that no honest maid of that Corporation shall hereafter want a good husband.'[12]

The English Civil War was a curiously domestic affair. Locally raised troops were always reluctant to serve outside their own familiar counties or neighbourhoods and would often take their wives and sweethearts along with them. Where it was felt they could be useful by nursing the wounded or freeing the men from menial chores, these women were encouraged and would, from time to time, dress in men's clothes for convenience and protective colouring; although when the king got to hear about it, he was deeply shocked at such defiance of 'Nature and Religion', and issued orders that any woman who presumed to counterfeit her sex by wearing man's apparel should be subject to the 'severest punishment which Law and our displeasure shall inflict'.[13]

Some women not only dressed as men, but fought beside them on the battlefield. It is impossible to say with any kind of accuracy how widespread this practice was – for obvious reasons the 'She-Souldiers' did not advertise themselves – but it seems fair to assume that it was a pretty haphazard sort of business, to fill a gap in the ranks, to help out in an emergency, or even perhaps just for the hell of it. Certainly documented accounts of women acting as regular soldiers are very few and far between. The Scots were reported to have made use of females to swell their numbers when they marched on Newcastle in 1644, 'and their women (good Ladyes) stood with blew caps among the men'. When Shelford near Nottingham was taken for the Parliament in 1645, one of the royalist prisoners is said to have been a woman corporal, and a popular ballad of 1655 told the story of a woman who had served for some years in her husband's regiment under the name of Mr Clarke.[14]

After Gloucester, both armies had turned east, a movement which soon developed into a race, for if the royalists could get between the Earl of Essex and the capital and inflict on him the sort of defeat suffered by William Waller at Roundway Down, the way to London would be open. But there were those in the king's army with little stomach for the coming battle, among them Viscount Falkland, that 'passionate promoter of all endeavours of peace betwixt the king and parliament', who had become increasingly depressed of late, foreseeing nothing but 'much misery' for his country. Another reluctant member of the king's entourage was Henry, 3rd Baron Spencer of Wormleighton in Warwickshire and recently married to Dorothy Sidney, eldest daughter of the Earl of Leicester.

Lady Dorothy came of a long line of courtiers, soldiers, diplomats and administrators who had served their country nobly throughout the Elizabethan age and was herself a very lovely girl – the Sacharissa so eloquently and hopelessly adored by the poet Edmund Waller:

> Go, lovely Rose!
> Tell her that wastes her time and me
> That now she knows
> When I resemble her to thee
> How sweet and fair she seems to be.

Dorothy Sidney also possessed charm and intelligence, being admired by her contemporaries for her 'wit and discretion' as much as for her good looks, and long remembered by those who knew her as the ideal type of great lady.

Much careful thought had naturally been devoted to the choice of husband for this paragon of grace and beauty, and several possible suitors had been considered by the family, including Lord William Russell, the Earl of Bedford's heir, the young Earl of Devonshire and Lord Lovelace. But William Russell had already set his heart on Lady Anne Carr, the Devonshires were curiously lukewarm, and Lord Lovelace was rejected by Dorothy and her mother on the grounds of his addiction to bad company, drunkenness and debauchery. Nothing but the best was good enough for Doll, and Lady Leicester wrote to her husband: 'My dear

Hart, let not these cross accidents trouble you, for we do not know what God has provided for her.' As it turned out, God provided Henry Spencer, who combined all the qualities of character, rank and fortune demanded by Lady Dorothy and her anxious parents. As well as being an exceedingly rich young man, he was handsome, thoughtful and serious-minded beyond his years, showed no signs of any addiction to debauchery and altogether seemed a 'most happy match' for the exquisite Sacharissa.

They were married on 20 July 1639 in the idyllic surroundings of the bride's home at Penshurst Place in Kent and spent the first two years of their married life with the Leicesters in Paris, where the earl held the post of ambassador to Louis XIII. There, in the summer of 1640, Dorothy gave birth to her first child, a girl also christened Dorothy. A son, Robert, followed a year later and a third child, another girl, was born in 1642, but by that time the family had returned to England ready to face the approaching crisis.

Henry Spencer was no courtier and his political sympathies were inclined to be radical, but he was soon alienated by the violence of the parliamentary party, declaring that no power on earth would ever induce him to draw his sword against the king. During his brief career in the House of Lords he joined the group of loyal peers, led by Lord Falkland, who were still vainly trying to heal the breach and, when the moment of decision arrived in the summer of 1642, young Lord Spencer was among the thirty-two peers who rode to join Charles at York. All the same, he plainly hated the whole business, dreading the consequences of a royalist victory almost as much as those of a parliamentary one but, as he wrote to Dorothy from Shrewsbury in September: 'Unless a man were resolved to fight on the Parliament side, which for my part I had rather be hanged, it will be said without doubt that a man is afraid to fight. If there could be an expedient found to solve the punctilio of honour, I would not continue here an hour. The discontent that I, and many other honest men, receive daily is beyond expression.'[15]

A month later Spencer was present on the field at Edgehill, having entertained Prince Rupert at Wormleighton on the eve of the battle. In the lull in the fighting which followed he was able to get leave of absence to see his family at Penshurst, where his second daughter, Penelope, had just been born; but by the spring of 1643 he was back with the king at Oxford and in June was created Earl of Sunderland in consideration, so it is believed, of a large loan to the royal exchequer.

The new earl had hoped to be able to send for Dorothy and the children to join him, but before this could be arranged the army was off to lay siege to Gloucester. He wrote on 25 August: 'My dearest Hart, Just as I was coming out of the trenches on Wednesday, I received your letter of the 20th of this instant, which gave me so much satisfaction that it put all the inconveniences of this siege out of my thoughts. At that instant, if I had followed my own inclinations, I had returned an answer to yours; writing to you and hearing from you, being the most pleasant entertainment that I am capable of in any place.' He was quartered, he told her, in one of the many little private cottages scattered about the country, and its solitariness made a welcome change from the noise of the trenches, the 'tin-tamarre of guns and drums', and the distressing sights and sounds of dead and wounded men. It also made him reflect 'how infinitely more happy' he would be quietly enjoying her company at his home at Althorp, than being 'troubled with the noises and engaged in the actions of the Court'.[16]

One more of his letters survives, written from Oxford on 16 September, in which he sends his blessing to 'Popet', his three-year-old daughter, tells Dorothy he has such a bad cold that he does nothing but sneeze, and signs himself 'most passionately and perfectly yours'.[17]

Four days later the armies clashed at Newbury and in the confused and bloody fighting which followed, 'the loss on the King's side was in weight much more considerable and penetrating; for whilst some obscure, unheard of, colonel or officer was missing on the enemy's side, as some citizen's wife bewailed the loss of her husband, there were above twenty officers of the field and persons of honour and public name slain upon the place'. Among those persons of honour slain at Newbury was Viscount Falkland, who had courted death as the only solution to his problems – riding 'more gallantly than advisedly' into a hail of enemy bullets. Another noble casualty was Henry Spencer, Earl of Sunderland, 'a lord of a great fortune, tender years (being not above three and twenty years of age), and an early judgement; who, having no command in the army, attended upon the King's person under the obligation of honour; and putting himself that day into the King's troop a volunteer, was taken away by a cannon bullet'.[18]

One of Lord Leicester's servants brought the news to Penshurst, where Dorothy was waiting for the birth of her fourth child and very near her time. The earl had given orders that his letter was to be delivered to Mr Sudbury, who seems to have been tutor to one of the Sidney boys and who was charged with the task of first breaking the sad tidings to Lady Leicester. Unfortunately, the messenger had been seen arriving and the fact that he had asked to speak privately to Sudbury had roused Dorothy's suspicions. 'I found my Lady Sunderland in soe great an apprehension that some ill accident had befallen some of her friends, that it was not possible for me to suppress it from her soe long as till I had delivered your Lordship's letters to my Lady,' wrote Sudbury apologetically to his employer. 'Her Ladyship was soe full of expectation, that . . . she would not suffer me to go to my Lady till I would tell her what it was that made a footman from your Lordship come after so unusual a manner.' The harassed tutor tried to change the subject, saying that he was afraid Lord Falkland had been killed; but 'this would not satisfy her Ladyship, in soe much that after some discourse of the miseries of these times, and how much it concerned all who had friends engaged in these wars to be ever armed against the worst news they can apprehend, I was forced to let her know that my Lord Sunderland was also hurt. This put her into a great passion of grief, and soon after into some fits of the mother. Her griefe, I perceived, was the greater because she feared I had not told her all . . . and I had noe way to divert her from it.'

Sudbury now managed to escape and go to Lady Leicester, who was waiting for him in a frenzy of anxiety and 'notwithstanding all I could say to her, through the extremity of her sorrow she fell into a swoone'. But, he observed briskly, 'we soone recovered her out of that, and made her Ladyship understand how much she was concerned to put on all possible courage and resolution, and to goe and comfort my Lady Sunderland'. Mother and daughter clung together in the first agony of bereavement. 'I shall not need to tell your Lordship that neither of their Ladyships took much rest that night,' wrote Sudbury. 'But this I can now affirme of them both, that it hath pleased God to give them patience, and I hope it will not be long before He sends them comfort likewise.'[19]

A week later Lord Leicester was writing a tender letter of fatherly counsel to his 'deare Doll'. 'I know it is no purpose to advise you not to grieve, that is not my intention, for such a loss as yours cannot be received indifferently by a nature so tender and so sensible as yours.' But all the same she must not give way too completely and allow sorrow to damage her health. 'You offend him whom you loved if you hurt that person whom he loved. Remember how apprehensive he was of your dangers, and how sorry for anything that troubled you.' Then there were the children, 'those pledges of your mutual friendship and affection which he hath left with you'. She would be betraying a sacred trust if she failed to take proper care of them and for their sake must moderate her grief. 'They all have need of you, and one especially, whose life as yet doth absolutely depend on yours. I know you lived happily, and so nobody but yourself could measure the contentment of it. I rejoyced at it, and did thank God for making me one of the means of procuring it for you. That now is past, and I will not flatter you so much as to say I think you can ever be so happy in this life again; but this comfort you owe me, that I may see you bear this change and your misfortunes patiently.'[20]

Dorothy's baby, another son, was born at the beginning of October. He was baptised at Penshurst and christened Henry after his father, but in March 1649 Lord Leicester recorded sadly in his diary: 'The sweet little boy, Henry Spencer, my grandchilde, five years old from October last, died at Leicester House.'

The Countess of Sunderland was, of course, only one of very many Civil War widows. Her grief, though better documented, was doubtless no more deeply felt than that of the anonymous citizen's wife bewailing the loss of her husband and Dorothy was more fortunate than some in being surrounded by a loving and supportive family. She stayed on with her parents until the end of the war and then went back to live on the Spencer family estate at Althorp which, ironically enough, had escaped a heavy delinquency fine thanks to the influence of her parliamentarian brothers Philip and Algernon.

Ideally, a widow, like a true mourning turtle dove, was supposed to remain faithful for ever to the memory of her dead spouse, although in fact this was exceptional at a time when the average life expectancy for both men and women was only about thirty-five years. Widows needed a protector for themselves and their children, and a wealthy widow was always a much sought-after matrimonial prize. Widowers, too, needed a housekeeper or mother for their children and second, third or even fourth marriages not infrequently took place with almost indecent haste, in spite of the freely expressed disapproval of moralist society. Dorothy Sunderland waited nine years before she remarried and her second husband, Robert Smythe, or Smith, a family connection and neighbour of the Sidneys in Kent, was conceded to be 'a very fine gentleman' who more than deserved his good fortune. Nevertheless, there was still a distinct feeling among Sacharissa's friends that she had rather let the side down. Lady Sunderland, as she continued to be known, lived on into the 1680s, surviving by more than forty years the handsome young lord who had given his life to satisfy a 'punctilio of honour' in the maze of muddy lanes and hedgerows south of Newbury on that long ago September day.

For all the gallantry, the sacrifice and the carnage, nothing had been achieved by the battle. 'It is just as at Edgehill,' commented Elizabeth of Bohemia, 'both sides say they have the victory.' However, at Newbury parliament may be said to have won on points, since the royalists left the field first, dismayed by their heavy casualties and down to their last few barrels of powder. The campaigning season was drawing to a close and the second year of the war ended in apparent stalemate. The Earl of Essex returned to London, where he was given a hero's welcome, and the king once more withdrew to Oxford which had become his de facto capital – the little town crowded with soldiers as well as courtiers, where recruits drilled in the college quadrangles and troops of cavalry clattered noisily through the streets on their way to and from the outlying garrisons of Banbury, Abingdon and Wallingford.

The life of the university had been violently disrupted by the royalist invasion, as students deserted their studies in droves to join the colours and few freshmen came up to take their place. Fodder for the horses was now being stored in the Law and Logic Schools, New College had become a magazine and Magdalen College Grove an artillery park. Tailors cut and stitched uniforms in the Music and Astronomy Schools and a mint had been set up at New Inn Hall. The king had taken over Christ Church as his headquarters, the queen occupied the Warden's Lodgings at Merton and other colleges were used to accommodate the lords and ladies, the army commanders, court officials and royal servants with their wives and families, while the hordes of lesser folk who had come to offer their services or to seek sanctuary squeezed themselves in wherever they could find a corner.

It was to Oxford that eighteen-year-old Ann Harrison and her sister Margaret came in 1643 to join their father, Sir John Harrison, the former customs-farmer and one of the richest men in England. Ann had been carefully brought up and instructed in all the accomplishments proper for a young lady, learning French and singing, to dance and play the lute and virginals, as well as all sorts of fine needlework, though, as she admitted in her Memoirs, she had much preferred riding and other active pastimes, being 'that which we graver people call a hoyting girl'. Her mother had died when she was fifteen, and young Ann had had to put away 'those little childnesses' and take over the management of her father's London house in Bishopsgate Street where, until the outbreak of war, life had continued to follow the comfortable well-ordered pattern of all such prosperous professional families.

At the beginning of 1642 John Harrison and his son William were both sitting members of the House of Commons, but as soon as the king raised his standard William hurried off to Nottingham to join up, and in 1643 Sir John, who had already contributed a large sum of money to the royal cause, was arrested by order of his former colleagues and threatened with transportation to the West Indian colonies. He managed to escape, 'under pretence to fetch some writings they demanded in his hands concerning the publick revenue', but his house was ransacked and his whole estate sequestered, so that when his daughters arrived in Oxford they were horribly shocked by the change in their circumstances.

'We, that had till that hour lived in great plenty and great order, found ourselves like fishes out of the water', wrote Ann; 'for from as good houses as any gentleman in England had we came to a baker's house in an obscure street, and from roomes well furnished to lye in a very bad bed in a garrett, to one dish of meat and that not the best ordered; no mony, for we were as poor as Job, nor clothes more than a man or two brought in their cloak bags. We had the perpetuall discourse of losing and gaining of towns and men; at the windows the sad spectacle of war, sometimes plague, sometimes sicknesses of other kind, by reason of so many people being packt together, as I believe there never was before of that quality.' Everyone was in want, although 'most bore it with a martyrlike cheerfulness'. For her own part, Ann began to think 'we should all like Abraham live in tents all the days of our lives'.

The family was to know sorrow as well as want, for William Harrison died that year as the result of a fall from his horse, shot under him during a skirmish with the Earl of Essex's cavalry. 'He was a very good and gallant young man', wrote his sister sadly, 'and they are the very words the King say'd of him when he was told of his death.'

Ann was married to Sir Richard Fanshawe in Wolvercote Church on 18 May 1644. It was a very quiet ceremony with only family and a few close friends present, 'my dear father (who by my mother's desire gave me her wedding ring, with which I was married), and my sister Margarett . . . Sir Edward Hide, afterwards Lord Chancellor, and Sir Geoffrey Palmer, the King's Atturny'.

Richard Fanshawe, a career diplomat in his mid-thirties, had just been appointed Secretary for War to the thirteen-year-old Prince of Wales, with a promise of further promotion from the king 'so soon as occasion offered'. But, remembered Ann, 'his fortunes and my promised portion, which was made 10000 pounds, were both at that time in expectation, and we might truely be called marchant adventurers, for the stock we sett up our trading with did not amount to 20 pounds betwixt us'. However, as she told her only surviving son for whom, years later, her Memoirs were written, 'our stock bought pens, ink, and paper, which was your father's trade, and by it I assure you we liv'd better than those that were born to 12000 pounds a year as long as he had his liberty'.[21] They were to have an amazing series of adventures in their life together and never had a settled home, but it was an ideally happy marriage and a good partnership. 'I thought myself a queen, and my husband so glorious a crown that I more valued myself to be call'd by his name than borne a princess, for I knew him very wise and very good, and his soule doated on me.'[22]

By the time of the Fanshawe wedding the Oxford scene was changing. During the previous summer it had still been possible to maintain some semblance of normal court life. The queen's return had brought an influx of fashionable visitors, and she and her friends were entertained with theatricals got up by the students in the romantic setting of the college gardens, while the king played tennis and went hunting. There was music and dancing and gay little supper parties, and ladies, 'half-dressed like angels', amused themselves by teasing and scandalizing the elderly dons. But beneath all the surface jollity, back-biting, suspicion and intrigue were rife. Henrietta's determination to re-establish her position as the king's chief mentor and confidante was not surprisingly causing considerable resentment among those who had enjoyed unrestricted access to the inner circle during her absence, and for her part the queen quickly became jealous of her husband's reliance on Prince Rupert. Nephew or no nephew, she did not trust him. In any case, he was too young and self-willed to be taken seriously, and she blamed him for encouraging Charles's foray into the West Country which had left Oxford – and herself – uncomfortably exposed to attack. 'The king is gone himself in person to Gloucester', she wrote crossly to the Earl of Newcastle, 'which gives no small dissatisfaction to everybody here, and with reason, too, to see him take such sudden counsel.'[23]

The queen continued to take a close proprietorial interest in Newcastle's operations in the north which, she felt, were not sufficiently appreciated at court. 'The truth is that they envy your army.' But early in 1644 there were alarming developments in his lordship's sphere of influence as the Scottish alliance, brokered by John Pym in the last months of his life, began to show results. In January the first Scottish regiments crossed the Border and in February they were laying siege to the town of Newcastle. Henrietta felt reasonably confident that her old friend and comrade-in-arms would be able to deal with the invaders and see that they did not get the chance to eat Yorkshire oatcakes as she put it, but she was obliged to add an urgent postscript to a letter dated 15 March. 'Since my letter was written, we have tidings that Sir Thomas Fairfax is marching towards you, to join the Scotch. Therefore lose no time and do not allow yourself to trifle, for if the Scotch pass the river Tees, I fear that there will be no more remedy.'[24] A week or two later his lordship took offence at some fancied slight in a message from Oxford, and the queen wrote again in soothing mode. 'Do not imagine that we design to do or to believe anything to your prejudice. And if you accuse me of scolding you by this letter, remember what I told you when I was at York, that I only scold my friends, and not those whom I do not care about.'[25]

This was her last letter from Oxford, for Henrietta was now in no condition to take any further active part in affairs. She had been unwell during the winter with severe rheumatic pains and on 9 February told her sister Christine that she was pregnant again. She not only felt ill but desperately afraid. In Edward Hyde's opinion it was the queen's being with child 'which wrought upon her majesty's mind very much, and disposed her to so many fears and apprehensions', but it was true that Oxford, overcrowded and full of disease, was hardly a suitable place for a royal lying-in. It would also be very difficult to defend, and the news of William Waller's victory over a royalist force at Alresford in Hampshire on 29 March seemed to confirm her majesty's many fears and apprehensions. 'She heard every day of the great forces raised and in readiness by the Parliament . . . and that they resolved as soon as the season was ripe, which was at hand, to march all to Oxford. She could not endure to think of being besieged there and, in conclusion, resolved not to stay there but to go into the west; from whence, in any distress, she might be able to embark for France.' Hyde clearly continued to believe that the queen's alarm was little more than a pregnant woman's natural fidgets, and the king 'heartily wished that she could be diverted'. However, 'the perplexity of her mind was so great, and her fears so vehement . . . that all civility and reason obliged every body to submit.'[26]

In justice to the queen, a good deal of her panic was undoubtedly due to her conviction that there was nothing Charles would not have done, no concession however damaging he would not have made, had she been taken prisoner, especially in her present condition. She left Oxford on 17 April with an escort of cavalry and accompanied by her husband and sons as far as Abingdon, where there was another sorrowful parting. She rested briefly at Bath and on 9 May the Venetian Secretary in London reported that 'the queen, though unwell, has gone to Bristol on her way to Exeter . . . She had to pass near Gloucester, whose garrison, casting aside all respect, captured a part of her baggage and would have taken the queen herself if she had not had a good escort.'[27]

On this occasion Gerolamo Agostini's information was as unreliable as his geography. It was true that Henrietta had originally planned to go on to Bristol but she had changed her mind and instead turned south-west for Exeter via Bridgwater. As it happened, though, Edward Massey, still in command at Gloucester, had just been having an encounter with another strong-willed lady. Early in May he had marched on Lydney in the Forest of Dean, headquarters of Sir John Winter whose iron foundries supplied the king's army with cannon, and which, together with other royalist outposts in the area, were becoming a serious nuisance to the Gloucester garrison. John Winter was away from home, but his wife proved to have 'a courage answerable to the undertakings of her husband'. Summoned by Colonel Massey to surrender her house, and threatened with fire and sword if she resisted, her reply came straight from the shoulder: 'Sir, Mr Winter's unalterable allegiance to his king and sovereign, and his particular interest in this place, hath by his majesty's commission put it into this condition, which cannot be pernicious to any, but to such as oppose the one, and invade the other; wherefore rest assured that we are, by God's assistance, resolved to maintain it, all extremities notwithstanding. This much in Mr Winter's absence you shall receive from Mary Winter.' Massey, having reconnoitred the Winters' defensive provisions and finding them too strong for the force he had with him, contented himself with burning three of the iron mills before retreating, his hopes disappointed 'by the resolution of a female'.[28]

The queen, meanwhile, had reached Exeter and moved into Bedford House, the Russell family's West Country seat. She was by this time feeling very ill indeed and on 3 May wrote to Sir Theodore Mayerne, the eminent physician who had attended the royal family in happier days, begging him to come to her, 'having always in my recollection the care you have taken of me in my necessities'. It was a long way for an old man in such troubled times, but the king's famously urgent plea – 'Mayerne, for the love of me, go to my wife' – could not well be refused, and

Sir Theodore set out for Exeter, taking his colleague Matthew Lister with him for support and a second opinion.[29]

The authorities in London had given permission for the doctors' journey, but were less receptive to a request for a midwife with a coach and six and three menservants. Fortunately, the queen regent of France came to the rescue, sending Madame Peronne, the French royal family's own sage femme who had attended Henrietta's previous confinements, a supply of baby clothes and a generous present of money. Anne of Austria had also invited her afflicted sister-in-law to come to France if she thought the air would do her good, although the Venetians heard that the French government, as represented by the chief minister Cardinal Mazarin, was less than enthusiastic at the prospect of having to grant asylum to the queen of England, foreseeing that she would be a source of endless expense and embarrassment.[30]

Mazarin, it seemed, was at one with the English parliamentarians, who would not have been inconsolable if Henrietta were to be unlucky enough to die in childbirth – an eventuality which she herself thought only too probable. Writing to Charles what would surely be her last letter before she was brought to bed, 'since I am now more than fifteen days in my ninth month', and perhaps the last letter he would ever receive from her, she told him that her state of weakness 'caused by the cruel pains I have suffered since I left you, which have been too severe to be experienced or understood by any but those who have suffered them, makes me believe that it is time for me to think of another world'.[31]

In spite of all this (Mayerne, as usual, believed that most of her symptoms were of hysterical origin), Henrietta's baby, her ninth child and fifth daughter, arrived safely on 16 June – 'a lovely princess' according to the French envoy M. de Sabran, who visited the queen a week after her delivery. The infant appeared healthy, but the mother's condition was continuing to give serious cause for concern. Henrietta had hoped that she would feel better after her accouchement, but instead she was worse than ever, 'with a seizure of paralysis in the legs and all over the body' and such a constriction round the heart that she thought she would suffocate. 'At times I am like a person poisoned,' she told the king. 'I can scarcely stir and am doubled up.' There was no feeling in one of her arms and her limbs were colder than ice. The disease had even risen to her head, and she could no longer see out of one eye. On top of everything else, to make her misery complete, she was once more being threatened by the enemy.[32] The Earl of Essex had come

Henrietta Maria in 1639 – the exquisitely ornamental little queen immortalised by Van Dyck. (The Royal Collection © 1998 Her Majesty Queen Elizabeth II)

Henrietta Maria arrives in Holland on her fund-raising expedition of 1642. (Ashmolean Museum, University of Oxford)

Henrietta Maria's landing at Bridlington on the coast of Yorkshire in February 1643. (The Royal Collection © 1998 Her Majesty Queen Elizabeth II)

Above: The cottage on the quayside at Bridlington where the queen is reputed to have lodged, and which she had to leave in a hurry when the town was bombarded by the parliamentary navy. (Bridlington Museum)

Blanche Arundell of Wardour Castle, whose home was captured and pillaged by a parliamentarian force in May 1643, leaving her with 'not a bed to lie on, nor means to provide herself a house or furniture'. (Christie's Images)

Corfe Castle, 'so ancient as without date', dominating the landscape in 1643. (Cambridge University Library)

Corfe in 1660, after it had been 'slighted' by order of parliament. (Cambridge University Library)

Mary Bankes who, with her daughters, maids and five soldiers, heaved stones and hot embers over the battlements of Corfe Castle to repel an assault by the parliamentarians. (Cambridge University Library)

Brilliana Harley, the parliamentarian heroine who successfully defended Brampton Bryan, the family home, against the royalists, displaying 'a masculine bravery, both for religion, resolution, wisdom and warlike policy'. (Reproduced by kind permission of Edward Harley, Esq.)

Edward Harley, Brilliana's much-loved eldest son. The 'dear Ned' to whom she wrote regularly while anticipating a royalist attack. (Reproduced by kind permission of Edward Harley, Esq.)

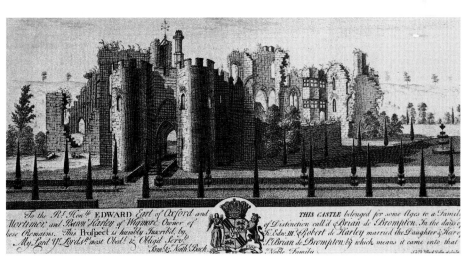

Brampton Bryan Castle, which finally surrendered to the royalist forces in Easter week of 1644. (Hereford and Worcester County Libraries)

Women among the citizens digging the defences of Gloucester.

west again with the intention of relieving the siege of Lyme, and his army was now advancing on Exeter.

De Sabran, whose instructions were to try to persuade the queen to remain in England, had approached the parliamentary general to ask him to give her a safe conduct to Bath, where she could take the waters and recover her health, only to be told 'that the air of London would be even more healthy for her majesty'.[33] But Henrietta had no intention of remaining anywhere within reach of men like Essex; ill and exhausted though she was, she had already made up her mind that she must leave the country as soon as possible. 'I shall show you by this last action', she wrote to Charles, 'that nothing is so much in my thoughts as what concerns your preservation.' Her own life mattered little in comparison, 'for as your affairs stand, they would be in danger if you come to help me, and I know that your affection would make you risk everything for that'.[34]

She set out for the coast with only three companions. 'The Queen is this day gone towards Falmouth, intending to embark herself for France', wrote Henry Jermyn from Exeter on 30 June. 'The reason of this resolution is the apprehension of a siege here of which there hath been and is very much appearance, though no certainty.' It seemed that it had not been possible for her majesty to overcome her dread of being 'shut up' in a siege, although Jermyn thought she was exposing herself 'to more dangers than those she could have undergone in this city in respect of her health and of the sea, if she persist in the desire of passing it'.[35]

Certainly the journey down to Cornwall was slow, painful and not without incident. According to later French accounts, the queen had been forced to lie hidden for two days in a wayside hut a few miles from Exeter, listening to bands of rebel soldiers passing by on the road and boasting 'that they would carry the head of Henrietta to London as they should receive from the parliament a reward for it of 50,000 crowns'.[36] But Henrietta, her party now increased by Henry Jermyn, her faithful dwarf Geoffrey Hudson and several more ladies, went on to reach Truro, where, on 9 July, she wrote a farewell letter to Charles – 'if the wind is favourable, I shall set off tomorrow' – and reminding him that 'I am giving you the strongest proof of love that I can give; I am hazarding my life, that I may not incommode your affairs. Adieu, my dear heart. If I die, believe that you will lose a person who has never been other than entirely yours.'[37]

A sympathetic gentleman, who had seen her as she left Exeter, told his wife that 'here is the woefullest spectacle my eyes ever yet beheld on; the most worn and pitiful creature in the world, the poor queen, shifting for one hour's life longer', and even Theodore Mayerne had prophesied that she would not live for more than another three weeks.[38] But the queen was once again to prove her extraordinary resilience. Although it was known that a squadron of the parliamentary navy was lying in wait, she sailed from Falmouth with a small Flemish fleet which had been anchored in the estuary. The parliament's ships, 'three of the best sailors we had', gave chase, but as most of the Flemings were able to use oars to increase their speed, the English, being 'more heavy far in burden', could not get the advantage of them. They still came close enough to 'bestow a hundred cannon shot' on their quarry, but the aim was high and scored no more than one hit. As the Channel Islands came in sight the Flemings gained the wind, drawing away from their pursuers, and when some French ships appeared on the horizon the English turned back; though it was later claimed that they had almost captured the queen and that she had had 'no other courtesy from England, but cannon balls to convey her to France'.[39]

Henrietta had ordered the captain of her vessel to fire his powder magazine and destroy the ship rather than allow her to be taken by the enemy – a heroic gesture which drew shrieks of protest from her companions and which she herself later regretted as having been an act of selfishness. Even now the ordeal was not over, for the weather turned nasty and landing on the coast of Brittany the queen had to clamber over rocks and climb a steep cliff path to reach the rough shelter of a cluster of fishermen's huts. After some initial hostility on the part of the surprised fishermen, the daughter of Henri IV was given a warm welcome and the local gentry hurried to greet 'this princess who appeared more like the distressed heroine of a romance than a real queen', and escort her to more suitable accommodation.[40]

A posse of doctors now began to arrive from Paris to attend the exalted invalid and it was decided that she should go to the royal spa at Bourbon to take the waters. An abscess in her breast was lanced, which relieved the fever she had been suffering from since her arrival in France, and after an intensive course of treatment at the baths her general condition began slowly to improve. The exact nature of the queen's illness in 1644 remains a matter of conjecture and has been variously diagnosed as rheumatic fever, puerperal sepsis and tuberculosis, but as she was to live for another twenty-five years this last suggestion seems a bit surprising.

By the end of September she was considered to be well enough to set out on the first stage of the journey to Paris and in November was able to write to Charles: 'Thank God I begin to feel like myself again, and my health is much better, though not yet quite good. Nevertheless, I hope that in spring I shall recover it entirely, provided that I have the hope of seeing you again soon; for without that there is neither medicine nor air that can cure me.'[41]

Henrietta had been greatly encouraged by all the kindness and sympathy she had received from her countrymen, 'from the greatest to the least', and as her health improved she embarked once more on her tireless campaign to draw international attention to her husband's predicament. 'There is nothing so certain as that I do take all pains I can imagine to procure you assistance.' Once again she spent hours at her desk writing or dictating letters to anyone and everyone who might be cajoled or badgered into helping; but over the long months and years to come she was forced into facing the bitter truth that, while she herself was treated with the sympathetic respect due to a wronged and insulted princess, in the inner circles of European power there was precious little sympathy or respect for a king who had allowed his own subjects to bully him into killing his most valuable servant, to oust him from his capital and seize control of his navy.

In England during the first half of 1644 the fortunes of war continued to veer back and forth between the armies. Exeter did not, as the queen had feared, come under siege. On the contrary, the king, who had defeated William Waller at the village of Cropredy not far from Edgehill at the end of June, entered the city himself on 25 July to make the acquaintance of his youngest 'and as they say prettiest daughter', who had been baptised in the cathedral with the names Henrietta Anne.

Charles did not linger in Exeter but continued to advance westward into Cornwall, driving the Earl of Essex before him. This was satisfactory as far as it went, but the West Country, Cornwall especially, had always been royalist, just as the south-east and East Anglia was parliamentarian. It was in the disputed territory of the Midlands and the north that 'the grand quarrel' would be settled.

So far the Westminster parliament had been seriously disappointed by its Scottish allies. The Scots had not yet taken Newcastle and their quarters at Corbridge had been successfully raided by royalist cavalry commanded by Marmaduke Langdale. But further south the veteran Scottish professional soldier Sir John Meldrum was besieging royalist

Newark, a vital fortress town situated where the Great North Road crossed the River Trent and which 'being lost, would cut off all possible communication between Oxford and York'. Fortunately for the king, Prince Rupert was then at Chester, arranging for the reception of the Irish reinforcements on which Charles was placing great hopes. Responding to an urgent message from his uncle, he had come hurrying to the rescue and on 21 March, in a brilliant feat of generalship, outwitted and outflanked the enemy. After some bitter fighting Meldrum was forced to sue for terms and Rupert seized 'above four thousand arms, eleven pieces of brass cannon, two mortar pieces, and above fifty barrels of powder'.[42]

News that Newark had been saved was greeted with relief and rejoicing at Oxford, but nearby parliamentary Nottingham strengthened its defences and waited in nervous anticipation of attack, unaware that Rupert was in no position to exploit his success. As usual he was needed in several places at once, and having seen Meldrum safely off the premises he was away again back in the direction of Shrewsbury.

The garrison in Nottingham Castle was commanded by Colonel John Hutchinson, the pattern of an austere and incorruptible Puritan officer, whose wife Lucy has left a vivid account of life in the wartime Midlands city. Born in January 1620 in the Tower of London, where her father Sir Allen Apsley was the Lieutenant, Lucy was a highly intelligent if somewhat priggish little girl, fortunate in having parents who 'applied all their cares and spar'd no cost to improve me in my education'. A Frenchwoman had been chosen for her nurse, so that she learned to speak French and English together; and 'by that time I was foure yeares old I read English perfectly, and having a greate memory, I was carried to sermons, and while I was very young could remember and repeate them so exactly, and being caress'd, the love of praise tickled me and made me attend more heedfully'.

In the fragment of autobiography attached to her Life of her husband, she recalled that by the time she was seven years old she had no fewer than eight tutors for languages, music, dancing, writing and needlework. But, to her mother's distress, young Lucy was not interested in acquiring ladylike accomplishments. 'As for musick and dancing I profited very little in them . . . and for my needle, I absolutely hated it.' A voracious reader, she was only happy when she had her nose in a book, although her mother, worried that too much book learning would prejudice her health (and her marriage prospects), tried unsuccessfully to moderate her enthusiasm. 'Every moment I could steale from my play', wrote Lucy, 'I would employ in any booke I could find, when my own were lockt up from me. After dinner and supper I still had an hower allow'd me to play, and then I would steale into some hole or other to read.' She learned Latin from her father's chaplain 'and was so apt that I outstript my brothers who were at schoole . . . Play among other children I despis'd, and when I was forc'd to entertaine such as came to visitt me, I tir'd them with more grave instructions than their mothers, and pluckt all their babies [dolls] to pieces, and kept the children in such awe that they were glad when I entertain'd myselfe with elder company.'

Lucy was certainly more at ease with older people, listening eagerly to the serious grown-up talk at her father's table or in her mother's drawing-room. Convinced that 'the knowledge of God was the most excellent study', she used to exhort a captive audience of her mother's maids to turn their idle chatter to 'good subjects', but at the same time was not above taking a sympathetic interest in their love affairs. 'There was none of them but had many lovers and some particular friend belov'd above the rest.'[43]

John Hutchinson, Lucy's own particular friend beloved above the rest, was the son of Sir Thomas Hutchinson of Owthorpe in Nottinghamshire, who had come to London to study law and was immediately attracted to a young lady who read Latin – her reputation for being reserved and studious serving only to increase the ardour of one who was from his childhood 'so serious and so rationall in all his considerations'. As for Lucy, her carefully cultivated air of indifference was swiftly abandoned in the company of such a delightfully like-minded admirer, and romance blossomed in 'that sweet season of the spring'.

Lucy discreetly passes over the little 'amorous relations' of their courtship, for those were to be forgotten as the vanities of youth. 'There is only this to be recorded,' she wrote, 'that never was there a passion more ardent and less idolatrous; he loved her better than his life, with unexpressible tendernesse and kindnesse.' She, for her part, loved him with an unswerving, uncritical devotion all the years of their life together, and 'soe, as his shadow, she waited on him every where, till he was taken into that region of light which admitts of none, and then she vanisht into nothing.' They were married in July 1638 at St Andrew's Church in Holborn, when she was eighteen and he approaching his twenty-third birthday. Four months later he nearly lost her when she miscarried of twins, but in September of the following year she was safely delivered of another set of twins, both boys, who survived into adult life.[44]

In October 1641 the young Hutchinsons returned to Nottinghamshire to live at Owthorpe, where they were for a few months happy and peaceful in their own house, 'till the kingdome began to blaze out with the long conceived flame of civill warre'.[45] John Hutchinson, having satisfied himself of the righteousness of the parliamentary cause, was soon heavily involved in the controversial business of defacing and removing the images and superstitious paintings in the local churches, and as a result became branded by the ill-affected 'with the name of Puritane', to the disgust of his passionately royalist cousins, the Byrons of Newstead.

According to Lucy, most of the gentry of the county were disaffected (that is, royalist in sympathy), while most of the 'middle sort', the substantial freeholders, and other commons not dependent on the malignant nobility and gentry, adhered to the parliament. John Hutchinson, therefore, stood out as a natural leader of the 'middle sort' and in August 1642, on the eve of the outbreak of war, he and his brother George, supported by a determined band of citizens, succeeded in foiling an attempt by the Sheriff and Lord Lieutenant of Nottingham to 'borrow' for the king's use the powder magazine belonging to the county militia.[46]

According to his wife, Mr Hutchinson would have been happy to have remained quietly at home, but 'his affections to the Parliament being taken notice of, he became an object of envie to the other party'. Just as the royal standard was about to be raised at Nottingham Castle, word was brought to Owthorpe that the High Sheriff had returned to break open the lock of the ammunition store and although he hurried to the rescue, this time John Hutchinson could not prevent its seizure. 'Some of the king's soldiers were already come to towne', wrote Lucy, 'and were plund'ring all the honest men of their Armes; and as one of them had taken a muskett, seeing Mr. Hutchinson goe by, he wisht it loaden for his sake, and sayd he hoped the day would shortly come when all such roundheads would be faire markes for them.'

This prompted Lucy to make a digression, explaining that 'when Puritanisme grew into a faction, the zealotts distinguisht themselves, both men and woemen, by several affectations of habitt, lookes and words'. These 'affected habitts' included cutting their hair close round their heads, and from this custom 'that name of roundhead became the scornefull terme given to the whole Parliament party'. It was, though, 'very ill applied to Mr. Hutchinson, who having a very fine thicksett head of haire naturally kept it cleane and handsome without any affectation, so that it was a greate ornament to him'.[47]

John Hutchinson now proceeded to fall foul of the king's quarter-master, who procured a warrant for his arrest, so that he was obliged to retreat into Leicestershire. He sent for his wife, then 'big with child', to come and join him, but no sooner had she done so than a letter arrived warning him that the warrant to seize his person had been forwarded to the Sheriff of Leicester. John therefore decided to go on next day to Northampton, but at five o'clock that evening the sound of trumpets announced the arrival in the town of a troop of royalist cavalry, so that 'he stay'd not to see them, but went out at the other end as they came in'. Fortunately for Lucy, who was 'something afflicted to be so left alone in a strange place', the troop proved to be commanded by her own brother, who was billeted in the house next door to her until he and his men were ordered away a few days ahead of the rest of the king's horse quartered in the neighbourhood.

Not long afterwards, Lucy received a visit from a Captain Welch, an acquaintance of her brother's, who remarked that it was a pity she should have a husband so unworthy of her 'as to enter into any faction which should make him not dare to be seene with her'. This annoyed Lucy so much that, believing all the royalist troops had now left the district, she decided to play a trick on the impudent young man, telling him he was mistaken, 'she had not a husband that would at any time hide himself, or that durst not show his face wherever any honest man durst appeare. "And to confirme you", sayd she, "he shall now come to you".' With that she called to her brother-in-law, George Hutchinson, who was in the house with her, and who 'upon a private hint, own'd the name of husband she gave him.'

Captain Welch seems to have been rather taken aback, but after saying that if Mr Hutchinson had been in any other place than his wife's parlour he would have been obliged to take him prisoner, he went sulkily away, leaving Lucy and George to enjoy a good laugh at his expense. But they laughed too soon, for the cavaliers had not gone far and before long Captain Welch was back with a troop of dragoons to arrest Mr George in the name of Mr John Hutchinson. Ignoring their attempts to explain that it was all a mistake, that this was George and John was still in Northampton, he insisted on carrying George away, partly at least it seems 'to revenge himself on Mrs. Hutchinson, at whom he was vex'd for having deluded him'. This naturally put poor Lucy into a great 'affright and distemper . . . which when the women about her saw, they rail'd at him for his treachery and baseness, but to no avail'.

Even when George was brought before Prince Rupert, where several of his Byron cousins positively identified him as the younger brother, he was not immediately set free and Lucy, aghast at the unforeseen consequences of her 'imprudence', hurriedly sent a message to Viscount Grandison, her cousin on her mother's side then serving in the king's army, begging him to intervene. The Hutchinsons and their kin were a classic example of a family 'by the sword divided'.

The whole rather foolish imbroglio was eventually sorted out. George was released, in spite of having refused to give an undertaking not to take up arms for the parliament, and he, Lucy and John were all back at Owthorpe in October, just as the battle of Edgehill was being fought. Lucy had, in the mean time, been brought to bed of her first daughter but, sadly, the infant 'by reason of the mother's and the nurse's griefs and frights in those troublesome times, was so weake a child that it liv'd not foure years, dying afterwards in Nottingham Castle'.[48]

By the beginning of 1643 both the Hutchinson brothers had taken up arms for parliament and on 3 January John was commissioned as Lieutenant Colonel, resigning up his life and all other interests to God's disposal and the defence of Nottingham. 'The preservation of this Towne was a speciall service to the Parliament,' wrote Lucy, and indeed Nottingham with its bridge over the Trent was as strategically important to the parliamentary party as Newark was to the royalists.

The preservation of Nottingham was, however, going to be no easy matter and 'nothing but an invincible courage and a passionate zeal for the interest of God and his country could have engag'd Mr. Hutchinson in it', knowing as he did that the townspeople were 'more than halfe disaffected', that the place was too far from the centre to expect to receive much in the way of relief or assistance, and that he himself would be 'the forlorne hope of those who were engag'd with him'. If the worst came to the worst, outsiders, 'the gentlemen who were on horseback', would at least have an opportunity of saving their lives by rejoining the main army, but he would have no line of retreat and 'must stand victorious, or fall tying himselfe to an indefensible Towne'. All this had clearly been the subject of much anxious discussion between husband and wife, but both knew there could be only one possible course of action for a man so committed in his conscience to the cause.[49]

At the end of June Colonel Hutchinson was appointed Governor of Nottingham Castle, a heavy responsibility for a young man – he was still in his twenties and with no military experience. The castle was potentially a very strong place, built on a rock and commanding the principal streets of the town, but according to Lucy 'the buildings were very ruinous and unhabitable, neither affording roome to lodge souldiers or provisions'. Nor was it adequately fortified when the new governor took over, having 'only a little brestworke before the outmost gate'. Ramshackle buildings and shortage of provisions – no more than 10 barrels of powder, 11 quarters of bread corn and 15 hogsheads of beer – were not his only problems. At the beginning of July Sir John Meldrum, with all the force quartered in Nottingham, was called away to attempt the relief of Gainsborough, another Trent town currently being besieged by the Earl of Newcastle, leaving Nottingham to be guarded 'by few more than the very townsmen'.[50]

On 7 August Newcastle, having successfully retaken Gainsborough, sent to demand the surrender of the town and castle of Nottingham – a demand promptly rejected by both Hutchinson brothers. John scorned 'ever to yield on any terms to a Papisticall Armie led by an Atheisticall General', while George exclaimed that 'if my lord would have that poore Castle, he must wade to it in blood'.[51]

Fortunately for Nottingham, my lord and his army were at this point diverted to the siege of Hull, but the situation remained critical. Marauding cavalry from Newark plundered the local countryside at will, 'even to the walls of Nottingham', and Colonel Hutchinson continued to have serious doubts about the reliability of some of the leading townsmen. He had therefore forbidden any of the castle garrison to leave their quarters and planned to block up the alleys and lanes round the castle itself 'for the better securing of them'. But, on the night of 18 September, 'just the night before these lanes should have been block'd up, Alderman Toplady, a greate Malignant, having the watch, the enemie was by treacherie lett into the Towne'. It was not until reveille, when the soldiers who had been on guard came off duty and were fired on by the enemy's musketeers as they started to emerge from the castle gates, that the alarm was raised.

The Governor now made the horrifying discovery that not only was the enemy within the gates, but two-thirds of his garrison were missing. Those with wives and more comfortable accommodation in the town had been in the habit of sleeping out against orders, and consequently more than half of them had been 'betrey'd, surpriz'd, and seiz'd on in their bedds'. Some were later able to get away and return to their posts, but on that first morning there were no more than eighty men in the castle and no officers, apart from George Hutchinson, 'nor so much as a Surgeon among them'. Faced with this emergency, the Governor sent urgent appeals for help to the garrisons at Leicester and Derby, and then 'play'd his Ordinance into the Towne, which seldome fail'd of execution upon the enemie', although the enemy musketeers on the steeple of St Nicholas' Church were able to rake the outer ward of the castle with their fire.

Meanwhile, the cavaliers, a raiding party of six hundred or so from Newark led by Sir Richard Byron, 'fell to ransack and plunder all the honest men's houses', helped, naturally, by those disaffected citizens who had called them in. They also set to work throwing down the demilunes and defensive ramparts which had been raised about the town and erecting a fort at Trent Bridge, from which they were able to send prisoners and plunder back to Newark by boat. This went on for five days 'and all that time' remembered the Governor's wife, 'the Governor and his souldiers, none of them were off from the guard, but if they slept, which they never did in the night, it was by them that watch't'. Inevitably there were civilian casualties – a weak old man in the castle, shot on the first day, who bled to death for want of a surgeon, and an old woman in the town whose head was taken off by a cannon ball. Lucy also recorded the 'remarkable providence there was concerning a Cannon shott that came through a house which was deserted of all its inhabitants but only a girle that rockt a little child in a cradle. The girle was struck dead and kill'd with the wind of the bullett, which past by and went through the wall and a bed's-head in the next house, and did some execution there, while the child in the cradle remain'd unhurt.'[52]

At last, on the afternoon of Saturday 23 September, help arrived in the shape of a detachment of 400 horse and foot from Leicester, and the cavaliers, having achieved their main objective of closing the bridge, 'had nothing more to doe but to gett safe off, which they endeavour'd with more hast and disorder than became good and stout souldiers'. Seeing the enemy in retreat, John Hutchinson sent brother George with all the musketeers that could be spared to speed them on their way. But as soon as he came into the town with his men 'they, greedie of knowing what was become of their wives and houses, dropt so fast from behind him to make the enquirie that they had left him only in the head of sixteene men'. It was at this point that George came face to face with his cousin Richard Byron, 'follow'd by a whole Troope of horse and a foote company'. Undismayed, George yelled to his men to charge and not to let Byron escape, 'though they cut his leggs off'. However, in the general scrimmage, Sir Richard did get away, though he left his hat behind and his horse was so badly hurt that it fell dead in the next street.[53]

Up at the castle the women were busy preparing a victory supper, as large as the time and present conditions could permit, and in the absence of a surgeon the governor's wife was attending to the wounded. 'She having some excellent balsoms and plaisters in her closett, with the assistance of a gentleman that had some skill, drest all their wounds (whereof some were dangerous, being all shotts) with such good successe that they were all well cured in convenient time.' Later, as she stood at her chamber door, she saw some of the royalist prisoners badly cut and bleeding being hustled down into the castle's underground prison, known as the Lion's Den, and 'desir'd the Marshall to bring them in to her, and bound up and drest their wounds alsoe'. While she was doing this, one of the more fanatically Puritan officers came in and rebuked her, telling her that 'his soule abhorr'd to see this favour to the enemies of God'. But Lucy, who never had any time for zealots, retorted that 'she had done nothing but what she thought was her duty in humanity to them, as creatures, not as enemies'.[54]

Early in October Colonel Hutchinson was presented with an opportunity to dislodge the cavaliers from their foothold at Trent Bridge, and later in the month the Nottingham garrison was further heartened by news of a parliamentary victory at Winceby on the edge of the Lincolnshire Wolds. But Hutchinson could not afford to relax his guard and 'having a very ingenuous person, Mr. Hooper, who was his Engeneer, and one that understood all kind of operation in all things allmost imaginable, they procur'd some saltpeter men and other necessary labourers, and sett up the making of match and pouder in the Castle . . . they alsoe cast mortar pieces in the Towne, and finisht many other inventions for the defence of the place'.[55] These included a platform for artillery, and 'a new worke before the Castle Gates to keep off approaches', for the colonel was becoming acutely conscious of a renewed threat from the north.

The now Marquis of Newcastle had been forced to break off the siege of Hull, but this meant that he and his army were free to return to the vicinity of the vital Trent crossings and perhaps at last to make the long-desired push southward to join hands with the king at Oxford. The late autumn of 1643 was thus a particularly anxious time for the defenders of

Nottingham Castle and Lucy believed it was only the mercy of God which restrained the enemy from occupying the town, which then 'lay soe open that they might have come in at their pleasure'. In fact, of course, it was the approach of the Scots which saved Nottingham, and the beginning of the new year saw Newcastle hurrying back to Yorkshire. But if his lordship had gone again – for the last time as it turned out – the cavaliers were still in Newark and as belligerent as ever.

On 15 January Colonel Hutchinson received intelligence that a considerable force was being mustered at Newark and that its objective was the Lincolnshire town of Sleaford. However, the colonel was not convinced and ordered a special watch to be kept that night. Sure enough, next morning 'two of his intelligencers came and brought him word very early that the designe was against Nottingham'. Almost at once the scouts arrived with news of the enemy's approach over the frozen winter landscape, and a company of foot and some horse were sent to man the defences 'and dispute the enemy's entrance into the Towne'. But the horse, seeing themselves outnumbered, fell back in sudden panic and the infantry, unsupported and getting no help from the townspeople, quickly followed. The royalists were therefore able to press on unopposed through the still uncompleted fortifications, seizing St Peter's Church and several other buildings, 'though the Cannon that play'd upon them from the Castle tooke off wholly the second file of Musketeers that enter'd the Gates, and kill'd them'.

Hutchinson had by this time managed to rally the horse 'and stirr'd them up to such generous shame that they dismounted and all tooke muskets to serve as foote'. They were then sent out to clear the enemy from the lanes and houses nearest to the castle and did so well that they quite retrieved their reputations. It was now about midday, and the Governor despatched the rest of the garrison – 400 horse and foot – with orders to beat the cavaliers out of the town.

Meanwhile, Charles Lucas, the royalist commander, had written a letter to the Governor, threatening to sack and burn the town if the castle was not immediately surrendered, but could find no one willing to deliver it. 'Whereupon they tooke the Mayor's wife, and with threats compell'd her to undertake it; but just as she went out of the house from them, she heard an outcrie among them that "the roundheads were sallying forth", whereupon she flung down their letter and ran away.' The cavaliers, too, now fled, some firing their pistols into the thatched houses and hay barns as they went, in an unsuccessful attempt to set them alight.

The royalists had suffered heavy losses. 'Betweene thirty and forty of them were kill'd in the streetes,' reported Lucy, 'fourscore were taken prisoners, and abundance of armes were gather'd up, which the men flung away in hast as they ran.' Nor was this all. 'Many of them died in their returne, and were found dead in the woods and in the townes they past through . . . For two miles they left a great track of blood which froze as it fell upon the snow, for it was such bitter weather the foote had waded allmost to the middle in snow as they came in, and were so nummed with the colde when they came into the Towne that they were faine to be rubbed to gett life in them.'

It seems that to begin with the raiders had been more interested in thawing themselves out than in plunder, 'which sav'd many men's goods', and had also been overconfident, not expecting that the garrison which, as the Governor's wife was bound to admit, had 'so unhandsomely' allowed them to enter the town, would then have turned round and 'durst at such greate odds to have sett upon driving them out'. Indeed, Lucy was moved to reflect that no one who had not actually been there would believe 'what a strange ebbe and flow of courage and cowardize there was in both parties that day. The Cavaliers marcht in with such terror to the Garrison, and such gallantry that they startled not when one of their leading files fell before them all at once, but marcht boldly over the dead bodies of their friends under the mouth of their enemies' cannon . . . Our horse, who ranne away frighted at the sight of their foes when they had brestworkes before them, and the advantage of freshnesse to beate back assaylants allready vanquisht with the sharpnesse of the cold and a killing march, within three or four howers, as men that thought nothing too greate for them, return'd fiercely upon the same men after their refreshment, when they were enter'd into defensible houses . . .'

'If it were a Romance', wrote Lucy, 'we should say after the successe that the Heroes did it out of excesse of gallantry.' But this was no romance, and 'to those who saw it and shar'd in it, it was a greate instruction that even the best and highest courages are but the beames of the Almighty, and when he with-holds his influence, the brave turne cowards, feare unnerves the most mighty, makes the most generous base, and greate men to doe those things they blush to thinke on . . . The events of this day humbled the pride of many of our stout men, and made them after more carefully seeke God, as well to inspire as prosper their vallour.'[56]

John and Lucy Hutchinson stayed on in Nottingham Castle until the end of the First or Great Civil War, although the Governor was to become embroiled in a long-drawn-out and acrimonious dispute with the committee of townsmen supposedly working with him but which made a number of determined attempts to unseat him. 'Allmost all the Parliament Garrisons were infested and disturb'd with like factious little people,' wrote the Governor's wife indignantly, ' . . . meane sort of people . . . Worsted stocking men.'[57] For all her high-minded Christian principles Lucy retained a keen eye for social distinctions.

In July 1647 the colonel finally relinquished his command, handing over the much reduced garrison to a junior officer and taking his wife and children back to Owthorpe. They found the house, which had stood empty throughout the war, had been stripped of everything the neighbouring royalists could carry away and was 'so ruinated that it could not be repair'd to make a convenient habitation without as much charge as would allmost build another'. This the colonel was not yet able to do 'by reason of the debt that his publick employment had runne him into', and the family was therefore obliged to camp out in conditions of considerable discomfort for the rest of that year.[58]

John Hutchinson's public career had now changed direction. He had been elected Member of Parliament for Nottinghamshire, and as soon as the county was cleared of all the enemy's garrisons he went up to London to attend the House of Commons 'and to serve his country as faithfully in the capacity of Senator as he had before in that of a souldier'.[59] In January 1649 he was named one of the panel of commissioners appointed to sit in judgement on the king and was one of the signatories to the royal death warrant, believing, according to his wife, that if they did not execute justice on one so clearly bent 'to the ruine of all that had oppos'd him . . . God would require at their hands all the blood and desolation which should ensue by their suffering him to escape'.[60] Mr Hutchinson also now became a member of the Council of State, but grew steadily more disenchanted with the new regime and increasingly suspicious of the political ambitions of Cromwell and his army. In 1651, therefore, 'while the grand quarrel slept', he retired to Owthorpe and private life, and Lucy contentedly resumed the duties and responsibilities of a country housewife.

Lucy Hutchinson was highly intelligent, well educated, well informed and independent minded, but she was still very much a woman of her times, sustained by a deep, unquestioning religious faith – although she did have doubts as to the existence of scriptural authority for infant baptism. She was, however, in full agreement with St Paul on the subject of wifely submission and wrote scathingly about men like King Charles and Thomas Fairfax who allowed themselves to be governed by their wives.

For Lucy, as for Ann Fanshawe and indeed for Henrietta Maria, her husband was the centre of her universe and when, after his death, she came to write his biography, both for her own consolation and the edification of his children, desiring 'if my treacherous memory have not lost the dearest treasure that ever I committed to its trust', to relate to them the story of 'his holy, vertuous, honorable life', she knew she would never be able to do justice to the many gifts and graces of one of the best of men.

CHAPTER FOUR

'A Courage Even Above Her Sex'

> Tell that insolent rebell, he shall have neither
> persons, goods nor house . . . if the Providence of God
> prevent it not, my goods and house shall burne in
> his sight: myself, children and souldiers will seale
> our religion and loyalty in the same flame.
>
> The Countess of Derby

The year 1643 is generally conceded to have belonged to the king, but Clarendon's assessment of the situation in the north-west proved to be unduly optimistic. By the end of the summer parliament was very much stronger there than it had been at the beginning of the year, controlling nearly the whole of Lancashire and most of Cheshire. Chester, the port for Ireland, remained in royalist hands, though it came briefly under attack by the parliamentary commander Sir William Brereton in July, and seventeen-year-old Alice Wandesford, standing in a turret in her mother's house looking out of a window towards St Mary's Church, had a narrow escape from death. 'A cannon bullet flew so nigh the place where I stood that the window suddenly shut with such a force the whole turret shook. It pleased God I escaped without more harm, save that the waft took my breath from me for that present, and caused a great fear and trembling, not knowing from whence it came.'[1]

The Wandesford family, Alice, her widowed mother and two brothers, were refugees from the rebellion in Ireland, where they had lost everything but two trunkfuls of 'wearing linen'. They were now preparing to seek refuge with their relations in Yorkshire – a journey across a war-torn land and fraught with difficulty 'by reason of the interchange of the king's armies and the Parliament's'. However, they managed to get a pass from Colonel Shuttleworth of Gawthorpe Hall and at about ten o'clock at night 'came weary into the town of Warrington'. Next day they went on to Wigan, 'a town zealous for their king and church', but which had recently been taken and ransacked by the parliamentarians. 'We found it sorely demolished, and all the windows broken; many sad complaints of the poor inhabitants,' wrote Alice.

At the village of Downham, near the Lancashire–Yorkshire border, the travellers were stopped 'with harsh language and abuse by a Parliament corporal and his gang. They would not believe our pass, but took us down, swearing and threatening we should be stripped; so my dear mother and all of us were forced to come into a pitiful house for shelter, and lie there all night, with heavy hearts, lest we should have been used barbarously, as they continued in threatening against my father's widow and children.' Their nervousness was understandable, for Alice's father, Sir Christopher Wandesford, had been a cousin of the terrible Earl of Strafford and his second-in-command in Ireland. But fortunately his widow and children were not to suffer any further unpleasantness. The disputed pass was taken back to Colonel Shuttleworth, who expressed 'grand displeasure' at their ill-treatment and gave orders that Lady Wandesford and her family were to be conveyed safely 'as far as his quarters lay, wishing her a good journey'.[2]

In November and December the first contingents of royalist troops from Ireland began to arrive. These were soldiers of the army once commanded by Strafford and now released as the result of an armistice with the Irish rebels, the so-called Confederates, negotiated by the Marquis of Ormonde. The newcomers were predominantly English and Protestant, but unhappily the very name of Ireland struck such superstitious dread into English hearts that the 'Irish' auxiliaries were always deeply unpopular with both sides in the conflict. They were, however, warmly welcomed by John Byron, the Governor of Chester, and with their help he was able to halt William Brereton's inroads into North Wales, and take back Hawarden and Beeston Castles. But his assault on the town of Nantwich in January 1644 was heavily defeated by Brereton and Thomas Fairfax, the royalists losing 'many brave soldiers and commanders, besides many cartloads brought to Chester that were wounded and maimed'.

Among the horror stories being circulated about the 'Irish' was a report that they had with them a Female Regiment, that 'these were weaponed too; and when these degenerate into cruelty, there are none more bloody'. So the news that the prisoners taken at Nantwich included 120 Irish women, 'of whom many had long knives with which they were said to have done mischief', caused great excitement in London, where the equivalent of the tabloid press made the most of it. 'These cruell Irish queans', it seemed, were armed with great knives half a yard long, all ready 'to cut the throats of such as they should take prisoners, or finde wounded'. Worse still, the knives were said to have a hook at the end, 'made not only to stab but tear the flesh from the very bones'. Such harpies, raged *The True Informer*, should be 'put to the sword, or tied back to back and cast into the sea'.[3]

In fact, there appears to be absolutely no evidence to suggest that the Female Regiment consisted of anything other than members of that indomitable sisterhood which, from time immemorial, had followed in the tail of an army to forage, cook and care for their men, and for whom a knife was both a useful tool (they were enthusiastic looters when occasion offered) and a means of self-defence – also useful, bearing in mind the fate of the unlucky Irishwoman set upon by the people of Lyme. At any rate, General Fairfax, an officer and a gentleman and a sensible man, ignored the prevailing hysteria and made arrangements to have the prisoners exchanged in the usual way.

Having forced the royalists back on to the defensive in Cheshire, Fairfax now turned his attention to mopping up the few remaining pockets of resistence in Lancashire. Here, however, he was to come up against a far more intractable female force than anything encountered at Nantwich; and the siege of Lathom House, the most determined and aggressive defence of a family home in the whole of the English Civil War, became renowned for the heroism of the Lady of Lathom who was, ironically enough, a Frenchwoman.

Short of royalty, ladies did not come much grander than Charlotte Stanley, Countess of Derby. Born Charlotte de la Trémoille, daughter of the Duc de Thouars and granddaughter on her mother's side of the Dutch national hero William the Silent, she was impressively well connected. Louisa Juliana, wife of the Elector Palatine Frederick IV, was her aunt, the Duc de Bouillon, leader of the French Protestants, and Prince Maurice of Orange Nassau her uncles. The Duc de Thouars died when Charlotte was still quite young, and she and her brothers, who were brought up in the reformed religion according to their father's dying wish, seem to have spent most of their time at the family château in Poitou. The widowed duchess was away a good deal, either at the French court or with her relations in Holland, and Charlotte was about six years old when she wrote to her mother: 'Madame, – Since you have been gone, I have become very good, God be thanked. You will also find that I know a great deal. I know seventeen psalms; and more than that, I can talk Latin . . . Madame, I pray you to love me. Monsieur de St. Christophe tells me you are well, for which I have thanked God. I pray heartily to God for you. I am, Madame, your very humble and very obedient and good daughter.'[4]

In 1625 the Duchesse de Thouars came over to England in the train of the young Henrietta Maria and during her visit arranged a marriage for her daughter with the Earl of Derby's heir, the nineteen-year-old James Stanley, Lord Strange. The wedding took place at the Hague in July 1626 and shortly afterwards the couple returned to Lancashire to settle at Lathom House.

The Stanleys were one of the oldest noble families in England and among the most powerful territorially, owning vast estates in Lancashire, Cheshire and North Wales, as well as the lordship of the Isle of Man – that curious amalgam of Celtic and Norse culture seized from the Scots by Edward III. The family's close connection with the English royal house dated back to the 1480s, when Margaret Beaufort, the Lancastrian heiress and mother of the future King Henry VII, had married as her third husband Thomas, Lord Stanley, who tipped the balance in Henry's favour at the battle of Bosworth and was rewarded with the earldom of Derby. Seventy years later, Henry VIII's great-niece, Margaret Clifford, married the 4th Earl and their son, Ferdinando, Lord Strange, had been a prominent figure on the Elizabethan scene, as courtier, man of letters, and friend and patron of poets and actors.

The sixteenth-century Earls of Derby lived *en prince* at Lathom, employing upwards of two hundred household servants and dispensing hospitality on a regal scale, but Charlotte's father-in-law, the 6th earl, had retired to his house in Chester, preferring to hand over the reins to his son. He welcomed Charlotte kindly when the newly-weds went to visit him, speaking to her in French and telling her that she was to have full authority as mistress of Lathom. In spite of this, not everyone would have envied the new Lady Strange, for while James Stanley was a tall, athletic, good-looking young man in a dark, florid style, he had the reputation of being vain, arrogant, selfish and hot-tempered. But Charlotte apparently had no complaints. She found the grandeur of Lathom House very much to her liking and thanked her mother for having established her so comfortably. In a letter written about the time of her first wedding anniversary she says that her husband showed her great affection, adding that God had given them the grace to live in much happiness and tranquillity of mind.[5]

In January 1628 Lady Strange gave birth to her first child, a son christened Charles with all due pomp and ceremony by the Bishop of Chester in the chapel at Lathom. 'I had him dressed in white after the French fashion,' wrote the baby's mother, 'for here they dress children in colours, which I do not like.' There were other English ways which did not meet with her approval. 'I wish you could see the manner in which they swaddle infants in this country, for it is lamentable,' she told her French sister-in-law. 'Three days after mine was born, he was found in the middle of the night sucking his thumb. Imagine the rest!'[6]

Although fiercely loyal to the king, Lord Strange held no political office and for the next fifteen years he and Charlotte lived almost entirely in the north, with only occasional visits to London. The outbreak of the Civil War, which coincided very nearly with his succession to his father's title, brought an abrupt end to this uneventful career and he was later to be accused of having caused the first casualties of the war by his attempt to seize the arms depot at Manchester – a bustling community of Puritan weavers and clothiers – in July 1642. But this is disputable, for fighting was breaking out all over England that summer in isolated pustules of fear, rancour and petulance.

The new Earl of Derby, who tended to regard the rebellion in Lancashire as a personal insult directed at the house of Stanley, would no doubt have enjoyed teaching the impudent psalm-singing Mancunians a sharp lesson, but that pleasure was denied him. His assault on the town in September ended in failure, leaving it unsubdued and assertive, and an important base for future parliamentary operations. Loyalties in Lancashire were divided, but the bully-boy tactics of Lord Derby and his private army, which roamed the countryside in undisciplined marauding bands, did serious damage to the royalist cause. In the spring of 1643 they sacked and burnt the town of Lancaster and stormed into Preston, plundering the homes of all those suspected of disaffection. After this the parliamentary forces began to recover the initiative, repulsing an attack on Bolton and taking Wigan, which was only six miles from Lathom itself. Then, on 20 April, a few hundred musketeers under Colonel Shuttleworth surprised and utterly routed Derby's men as they crossed the Sabden Brook close to where it joins the River Calder between Whalley and Padiham.

This proved a decisive victory and put an end to the earl's military command. Early in June rumours of trouble in the Isle of Man (where his efforts to bring the ancient Manx system of land tenure into line with mainland practice had already caused acute irritation) gave him an excuse to abandon Lancashire for a visit to his island kingdom. During his absence Parliament seized the port of Liverpool, captured Warrington and reoccupied Preston, so that Lathom became one of only two royalist strongholds left in the county and no sooner had the Earl of Derby sailed for the Isle of Man than the countess received a peremptory summons from Colonel Holland, Governor of Manchester, ordering her either 'to subscribe to the propositions of parliament, or yield up Lathom House'.

'But', says the author of the *Briefe Journall of the Siege against Lathom*, 'her ladyship denyed both – shee would neither tamely give up her house, nor purchase her peace with the losse of her honour.' However, 'being then in noe condition to provoke a potent and malitious enemy, and seeing noe possibility of speedy assistance', her ladyship was obliged to make concessions, giving up the Lathom estate to parliament's disposal and promising to keep only as many men in arms as were necessary to defend herself and her household from 'the outrages of their common soldiers'.

For the rest of the year the family at Lathom was left more or less undisturbed, the parliamentary army in the north having more urgent business elsewhere. But Charlotte Derby and her two young daughters, the Ladies Mary and Catherine, were now confined to the gardens and walks close to the house, the countess suffering 'dayly affronts and indignities of unworthy persons, besides the unjust and undeserved censures of some that wore the name and face of friends; all which', according to the *Briefe Journall*, 'shee patiently endured, well knoweing it noe wisdome to quarrell with an evill she could not redresse'.[7]

The countess, it seemed, was still taking care not to offer the enemy any unnecessary provocation while she continued to collect men and supplies in readiness for the attack she knew must come. This, says the sympathetic *Journall*, 'was a hard worke, considering shee had been debarred of her estate for a whole yeare. Yett in these straites she used not the least vyolence to force releefe from any of her neighbours, though some of them were as bad tenants as subjects.' A less sympathetic account, by an officer in the enemy camp, accused 'the Countesse of Darbie of receiving very many Caviliers' into Lathom who terrorized parliament's friends in the district, 'fetching some of them from their houses in the night, keeping them prisoners to get money from them for their Ransoms, till at last the Colonells for the Parliament began to consider of it as an oppression and injustice to the People'.[8]

During the weekend of 24/25 February 1644 the countess received a warning from a 'secret friend' that a parliamentary force was on the march 'against a house that theire fathers and themselves, whilst their eyes were open, had ever honoured, reputing Lathom, in more innocent tymes, both for magnificence and hospitality, the only court of the northerne parts of this kingdom'. But times had changed and, as if to drive the point home, the preacher at Wigan that Sunday took as his text Jeremiah 50, 14: 'Put yourselves in array against Babylon all ye that bend the bow, shoot at her, spare no arrows; for she hath sinned against the Lord.' He further informed the congregation that he was keeping the next verse – 'Shout against her round about; her foundations are fallen, her walls are thrown down; for it is the vengeance of the Lord' – for his victory sermon.

On Tuesday the 27th Thomas Fairfax and his advance guard took up their quarters about two miles from Lathom, and on the following day a letter was delivered from the general requiring the countess to yield up Lathom House 'upon such honourable conditions as he should propose'. Charlotte's reply was predictable. 'She much wondered that Sir Thomas Fairfax would require her to give up her Lord's house without any offence on her part done to the Parliament', and asked for a week's grace in which to consider a matter of such importance, that so nearly concerned her conscience, her sovereign, her husband and her whole posterity.

Sir Thomas, who knew a delaying tactic when he saw one, instead invited her ladyship to come in her coach to New Park, a nearby house on the Lathom estate, where he and his officers would meet her for 'a full discourse and transaction of the business'. This drew a majestic put-down from her ladyship. 'Notwithstanding her present condition, she remembered both her Lord's honour and her own birth, conceaving it more knightly that Sir Thomas Fairfax should waite upon her, than shee upon him.'

Thursday and Friday were taken up with the exchange of letters and messages but at last, on Saturday 2 March, two emissaries, Colonel Rigby and Captain Ashton, were admitted to Lathom bearing Fairfax's terms. These were the immediate surrender of the house with all its arms and ammunition, the garrison having leave to depart for Chester or elsewhere with all their possessions. The countess could go with her household servants to live at Knowsley, another of the family homes and once a hunting lodge, with twenty musketeers for her protection. Alternatively, she might join her husband on the Isle of Man, but for the time being, until parliament could be consulted, her ladyship was to receive the earl's revenues from the Hundred of Derby for her maintenance and parliament would be asked to continue this arrangement.

These conditions were promptly rejected as being 'in part dishonorable, in part uncerteyne'. How was her ladyship to treat 'with them who had not power to performe theire own offers'? But for her part, 'shee would not move the good gentlemen to petition for her. Shee wold esteem it a greater favour to permitt her to continue in her present humble condition.'

On the following Monday Captain Ashton returned to hear Lady Derby's counter-proposals. She wanted a month's 'quyett continuance in Lathom' to prepare for her departure and then free transport to the Isle of Man for herself and her children, her friends and all her household. In the mean time the garrison should stay where it was, although she promised that the arms in the house would not be used against the parliament. She also asked for an undertaking that none of her tenants and neighbours who had supported her should suffer 'in their persons or estates' after she had left.

These propositions were interpreted as being 'too full of policy and danger to be allowed', and only intended to gain time. It was, in fact, becoming pretty obvious that any further efforts at negotiation would be a waste of time – especially as it now appeared that the only parliament her ladyship recognized was the assembly summoned to Oxford by the king. But Fairfax was not quite ready to give up, sending his engineer Colonel Morgan, 'a little man, short and peremptory', to make one more offer. The countess might have her month to pack and then liberty 'to transport her armes and goods to the Isle of Man' – all, that is, except the cannon. But she must disband her garrison by 10 o'clock the following day and agree to accept a guard of forty parliamentary soldiers.

Seeing that she could 'scrue them to no more delays', Charlotte Derby now issued an open defiance. She rejected their terms and was glad they had rejected hers, protesting 'she had rather hazard her life than offer the same again; that though a woman and a stranger, divorced from her friends and robbed of her estate, she was ready to receive their utmost vyolence'. She had not forgotten her duty to the Church of England, her prince and her lord her husband, and meant to defend her home to her last breath, trusting in God for protection and deliverance.[9]

The parliamentarians' first move was 'the taking of the Stand in the Parke which the Cavaliers was then possessed of'. They then began, unwisely as it turned out, to dig a line of trenches within musket range of the house; but little else was done that week. Ancient Lathom, with its yards thick walls and wide moat, its nine towers and medieval gatehouse, would have been a tough proposition even if it had not contained the Countess of Derby and her garrison of three hundred determined, well-drilled defenders – while its situation, protected on three sides by rising ground, made it very difficult to raise a battery against it 'so as to make a breach in the wall practicable to enter the house by way of storm'.[10] The besiegers, however, were hoping rather to starve the garrison out, believing mistakenly that it had provisions for only a couple of weeks, and even now had not given up all hope of persuading the countess to come to terms.

On Sunday 10 March a deputation of local gentry 'of the best rancke' was sent with a petition, beseeching her ladyship to consider her own danger and the damage likely to be done to the whole county, which she could prevent 'if she pleased to slacken something of her severe resolution'. Her ladyship responded by remarking that her neighbours would be better employed in petitioning 'the gentlemen who robb'd and spoyl'd their country, than her, who desyred only a quyett stay in her owne house', leaving them with little to say but 'God bless the king and the Earle of Derby'.

On Monday the 11th Captain Ashton returned once again with positively the last offer from Thomas Fairfax. All former conditions were to be waived, and the countess, the garrison and all the household were free to go where they pleased with all their arms, ordnance and personal possessions, on the understanding that the arms were never to be used against the parliament. But everyone must leave the house at once, except for a rearguard of a hundred persons who must go within ten days.

Lady Derby's reply was predictable. 'She scorned to be a ten dayes prisoner to her owne house, judging it more noble, whilst shee could, to preserve her liberty by armes, than to buy a peace with slavery'; "and what assurance", said shee, "have I ever of liberty, or the performance of any condition, when my strength is gone? . . . 'Tis dangerous treating when the sword is given to the enemies hand." And therefore her Ladiship added, "that not a man shold [de]part her house, that she wold keepe it, whilst God enabled her, against all the Kings enemyes, and in breefe, that she wold receave no more messages without an expresse of her Lords pleasure, whoe shee now heard was returned from the Isle of Man".'[11]

The earl had indeed returned some months ago and had spent part of the winter with the king at Oxford. He was now back on the Wirral peninsula and, not knowing either 'how his house was provided with victuals and ammunition, or strengthened for resistance', had sent a letter to Fairfax requesting free passage out for his wife and daughters, being loath to expose them to the 'uncertain hazard' of a siege. But although her ladyship declared herself willing to submit to her lord's commands, she had no intention of doing anything so poor-spirited as to desert her post unless and until she was assured that this really was his pleasure, and she contrived to despatch a messenger to him at Chester with a full report on the situation at Lathom.[12]

Whether or not they had been impressed by the strength of the garrison or influenced by the immense local prestige of the Stanleys, which in spite of everything remained a potent factor in South Lancashire, the besiegers were showing a marked reluctance to fire the first shot in the battle for Lathom House. The defenders suffered from no such inhibitions and on Tuesday 12 March a hundred foot led by Captain Farmer, a professional soldier who had been put in overall command of the garrison, and a dozen horse – 'our whole cavalry' – sallied forth to attack the enemy's trenches, killing about thirty and taking six prisoners. Five days later the commanders under her ladyship decided to test the night watches, and in the early hours of 18 March Captain Chisenhall, 'a man of known courage and resolution', with two other officers and a party of thirty musketeers 'issued out of the backe gate to surprize the enemy in their new trenches'. This sortie, too, was successful, the enemy being chased into a nearby wood where the captain left them, killing only two or three.[13]

The parliamentary troops, numbering between two and three thousand altogether, were drawn from the various shire hundreds by turns. Each company was on duty every third day and night, their pay and provisions being levied from the towns where they were raised and the men quartered in such houses as were able to receive them. 'It was', remarked one commentator gloomily, 'a very costly siege to the County.' Thomas Fairfax, whose presence was now required in Yorkshire, had left the proceedings by the end of March and command of the leaguer, or siege, devolved upon Colonel Alexander Rigby, MP for Wigan and a fanatical supporter of the parliamentary cause. But notwithstanding his title and his zeal, Rigby was no military man and the bombardment of Lathom, which began on or about 20 March, was wasteful and ill-directed. 'There was needlessly spent against it in shot and Powder an Infinite quantity. Some was alwaies shooting at nothing they could see but the walls.'[14]

Little impression was made on the massive walls, but some of the towers were damaged and two defenders killed.

The besiegers had now succeeded in manoeuvring a large mortar into position, planting it on a mound of earth about half a musket shot from the house. This was an awesome weapon, capable of firing both explosive granadoes and stone balls weighing 80 pounds from a high trajectory, and was likely to be especially effective against Lathom which lay in a marshy hollow. The first two missiles were launched on 4 April but fortunately overshot their mark, although the household was standing anxiously on guard with wet hides ready to 'quench the burneing', fire being an ever-present danger among the wood and thatch inside the stone walls.

There followed an unexpected respite, while the enemy 'cast a shew of religion over their execrable work' in a four-day prayer meeting. It was decided to interrupt this pious exercise and on 11 April Captains Farmer and Radcliffe led about half the garrison out of a postern gate and 'beate the enemy from all theire worke and batteries, which were now cast up round the house, nail'd all theire cannon, killed about 50 men, took 60 armes, one collours, and 3 drumes; in which action Captain Rattcliffe deserves this remembrance, that with 3 souldiers, the rest of his squadron being scattered . . . he cleared 2 sconces and slew 7 men with his owne hand.' Captain Chisenhall was waiting with reinforcements in case of need, but the assault party 'bravely marched round the works, and came in at the great gates' where Captain Ogle with a body of musketeers guarded the passage. 'In all this service', records the *Briefe Journall*, 'we had but one man mortally wounded and we tooke onely one prisoner, an officer, for intelligence.' Although it occasioned 'a greater slaughter than either her Ladyship or the Captaynes desired', the garrison had stopped taking prisoners, being unable to keep them and not trusting the enemy to observe the agreed conditions for exchange.

Their efforts to put the enemy guns out of action had evidently not been all that successful, for the bombardment soon began again. A chance bullet even entered the window of her ladyship's own chamber, though it was 'too weake to fright her from the lodging'. But it was the mortar which had 'too wide a mouth to be stopt' which was doing the real damage. On 15 April one granadoe fell short of the house in a walk near the chapel tower, but fragments of shell two inches thick flew over the walls and were found in the furthest parts of the building. On the following day another shell scored a direct hit on an inner courtyard, making a crater half a yard deep and bringing down the weaker glass and clay structures round it, leaving only 'the carcase of the walls' standing. Fortunately no one was hurt, 'saveing that 2 women in a neere chamber had theire hands scorcht, to putt them in mind hereafter they were in [the] siege at Lathom'.[15]

Fear of the terrible 'mortar peece' was beginning to have a worrying effect on morale, but everyone cheered up when one of the engineers tending the monster was 'happily slaine by a marksman from one of our towers'. The Lathom marksmen were deadly. Former keepers and fowlers from the estate, they were posted on the battlements waiting patiently to pick off any parliamentary soldier in the trenches unwise enough to put his head above the parapet – and they very rarely missed.[16]

Easter fell on 21 April and in order to 'shew the people some pastime' during the holidays Rigby ordered the artillery to concentrate on Lathom's great Eagle Tower, 'against which they playd their culverin and demi-canon 23 tymes . . . 2 of the bulletts entred her Ladyship's chamber, which last made her Ladyship seeke a new lodgeing'. But she went under protest, making sure that everyone knew she meant to keep her house as long as there was still a building to cover her head.[17]

The siege had now lasted for two months. It was becoming an increasingly heavy financial burden on the local population and had also cost the lives of 'many pore honest men'. Continual alarms meant that the besiegers were getting very little rest, the soldiers having to mount guard every other night and sometimes two nights in succession; while Colonel Rigby, who came over every day from his base at Ormskirk, complained piteously that he was quite spent with anxiety and fatigue.[18] On 25 April, therefore, he made a determined effort to browbeat the countess into submission, sending her 'a furious summons' to yield up the house with all the persons, arms and goods within it, to receive the mercy of parliament and return her answer by two o'clock the next day. This, he indicated, would be her last chance to surrender.

Charlotte Derby was unmoved. Now a stout matronly figure in her middle forties, she received Rigby's messenger surrounded by her captains and household officers, and told him that he deserved to be hanged up at her gates for his pains. '"But", says she, "thou are but a foolish instrument of traytors pride: carry this answer back to Rigby" (with a noble scorne teareing the paper in his sight). "Tell that insolent rebell, hee shall neither have persons, goods, nor house: when our strength and provision is spent, we shall find a fire more mercyfull than

Rigby, and if the providence of God prevent it not, my goods and house shall burne in his sight: myselfe, children, and souldiers, rather than fall into his hands, will seale our religion and loyalty in the same flame."' The garrison broke into cheers and excitable shouts of 'We'll dye for his majesty and your Honour' and the messenger hurried away amid cries of 'God save the king!'

As soon as he had gone, her ladyship and her captains held a council of war to decide their next move. Something special seemed to be called for in reply to Rigby's ultimatum and now was 'the nicke and joynte of tyme'. Everyone agreed that it was the 'morter peece' which represented the greatest threat to their survival. Even 'the litle ladyes had stomack to digest canon, but the stoutest souldiers had noe hearts for granadoes; and might not they att once free themselves from the continuall expectation of death?' At last it was resolved 'to sally out the next morning and venture for all'.

So, just before daybreak on 26 April, Captain Chisenhall and the main party slipped silently out of the eastern gate, surprising the enemy and driving them from their trenches round the nearest gun emplacement, before making for the defensive earthworks protecting the great mortar piece itself. After some fierce fighting, they succeeded in forcing their way through musket and cannon fire and scaling the rampier, 'where many of the enemy fledd, the rest were slayne'. The main works having been seized, they were held by a squadron of musketeers against some parliamentary troops who attempted a counter-attack. Meanwhile, fresh soldiers from the garrison, supported by the Lathom servants, worked frantically to get ropes round the mortar, hoist it onto a sledge and drag it by their combined strength back into the house, 'Captain Ogle defending the passage against another companye of the enemye which played upon their retreate'.[19]

The action had lasted an hour and was without doubt the garrison's 'greatest and most fortunate exploit'. Their triumph tasted still sweeter when it became known that Colonel Rigby had been planning an all-out attack with fireballs and granadoes that very afternoon, and had invited his friends to come and share the thrill of seeing the house either surrendered or destroyed. Instead they could only commiserate with him 'who was sick of shame and dishonour, to be routed by a lady and a handful of men'.[20]

Although the besiegers had begun to try and cut off their water supply and had brought in an extra force of workmen to dig a channel to drain the moat, nothing any longer had the power seriously to trouble the garrison – not with their 'grand terror', which for the past three weeks had 'frighted 'em from theire meate and sleepe', lying harmlessly like a dead lion in their midst. Everyone came to give it a kick, 'shouteing and rejoyceing as merrily as they used to doe with theire ale and bagpypes'. Even her ladyship, who was not often 'overcarryed with any light expressions of joy', made no secret of her pleasure, ordering the chaplains to conduct a special service of thanksgiving.[21]

The leaguer remained in place but the heart had gone out of Colonel Rigby's troops with the capture of their most successful weapon, and many of their other guns were now being moved away out of reach of 'the madmen in the garrison'. Efforts to drain the moat were also getting nowhere and work was abandoned after heavy rain caused a fall of earth which killed three men. Inside the house the sight of the enemy's obvious discomfiture was keeping spirits high and the garrison amused itself with harassing tactics, 'either by the excursions of a few in the night, or by frequent alarums, which the captaines gave theire souldiers leave to invent and execute for theire recreation'.[22]

The Earl of Derby, who had been trying unsuccessfully all this time to raise a sufficient force to rescue his wife and daughters, had contrived to smuggle an occasional message in to them and by mid-May he would have had some encouraging news to pass on, for Prince Rupert had left Shrewsbury and was marching north. Rupert's objective was the relief of the hard-pressed Marquis of Newcastle at York, but he had been persuaded to come by way of Lancashire and Lord Derby was urging him to add the relief of Lathom to his already heavy workload.

On 23 May the countess received yet another summons from Colonels Holland and Rigby to submit herself, her children and servants to the mercy of parliament. But 'the mercyes of the wicked are cruell' remarked her ladyship with a smile. Not, of course, that she meant a wicked parliament, for which honourable assembly she had a very proper respect, only wicked factors and agents such as Rigby, 'who for the advantage of theire owne interests labour to turne kingdomes into blood and ruyne'. It was then hinted that she might now be granted her own original conditions for giving up the house, but Charlotte merely repeated that she would do nothing without authority from her husband. Until such time as she knew his pleasure, 'they should never have her, nor any of her friends alive'.

That same night a spy sent out from the garrison returned with the joyful news that Prince Rupert, whose name alone was said to be worth half a conquest, was in Cheshire and on his march for her ladyship's relief. Three more days passed 'in a hopefull ignorance' and then, on Monday the 27th, Colonel Rigby 'drew upp his companyes, and what fresh supplyes he could raise' and moved off in the direction of Bolton.[23] The siege of Lathom was over at last.

Two days previously Rupert had taken Stockport and, reinforced by the local royalists mustered by Lord Derby, he too made for Bolton, a Puritan stronghold known as the Geneva of the North, reaching it about two o'clock in the afternoon of 28 May. Rigby and his men, who had arrived only a few hours earlier, put up a valiant defence but they were heavily outnumbered and besides, 'what could naked men do against horse in an unfortified place?' After a short but desperate struggle in pouring rain, Rupert's dreaded cavalry had broken in and were rampaging through the town. Alexander Rigby escaped in the general confusion by pretending, of all things, to be a royalist officer. Others were not so fortunate. Rupert had apparently given orders forbidding quarter to any in arms, but precious little mercy was being shown to anyone on the streets of Bolton that dreadful day. 'Nothing was heard but kill dead, kill dead was the word in the Town' as the Lancashire Cavaliers took full advantage of this opportunity to pay off old scores against the hated Roundheads, 'their horsemen pursuing the poor amazed people, killing, stripping and spoiling all they could meet with'.

An eyewitness account of 'the bloody and barbarous Massacre at Bolton in the Moors' describes some of the atrocities perpetrated on individual townsmen and women. William Boulton was dragged from his house and butchered in front of his wife, 'who being greate with childe and ready to be delivered, fell on him to have saved him, but they pulled her off without compassion, and bade him call on his God to save him, whilest they cut him to pieces'. There was Katherine Saddon, 'an aged woman 72 years old, run with a sword to the very heart, because she had no money to give'; and Elizabeth Horrocks, 'a woman of good qualitie', dragged up and down by a rope and threatened with hanging 'unlesse she would tell them of her plate and money'. Although some of the stories and casualty figures may well be exaggerated, the massacre at Bolton which left 'a sweet godly place a nest of owles and a den of dragons' remains one of the ugliest episodes of the Civil War, and it was neither forgotten nor forgiven.[24]

Rupert sent Lady Derby the colours captured at Bolton 'which 3 dayes before were proudly flourisht before her house', but he did not go to Lathom himself until he had taken Liverpool, another useful port for Ireland. When he did arrive, to be warmly welcomed by his indomitable kinswoman, he did not linger – his presence was too urgently required in Yorkshire. But before he left, towards the end of June, he had supervised the strengthening of Lathom's defences, promoted Edward Rawsthorne, one of the garrison captains, to colonel and appointed him governor of the house. He had also strongly advised Lord Derby to send his wife and children away to the safety of the Isle of Man.

Although the siege of Lathom captured the public imagination, it was not, in fact, very significant from the purely military point of view. The house did not occupy a site of any great strategic importance, and while its garrison could always have nuisance value, the place was never likely to be strong enough to form a base for the reconquest of the north-west for the king. Nevertheless, Lady Derby's courage and obstinacy had raised royalist morale in the district and succeeded in immobilizing a large proportion of the parliament's forces in Lancashire, for whom the siege had been a humiliating failure. 'About twelve weeks the Leaguer lay there with little or no effect but the losse of mens lives and spending of much treasure and vituals.'[25]

For the Lady of Lathom herself it had been a personal triumph, earning her a special place on the honour roll of Civil War heroines. The author of the *Briefe Journall*, believed to have been Samuel Rutter, one of the domestic chaplains, naturally had nothing but praise for his patroness 'whose first care was the service of God' and who had regularly been present at public prayers four times a day, accompanied by 'the 2 litle ladyes her children . . . for piety and sweetness truelye the children of so princely a mother'. Charlotte throughout had 'commanded in cheefe', keeping a keen housewifely eye on every detail. She watched over the distribution of powder – the only item in seriously short supply and which had to be dispensed frugally – was often present to see the men's rations served out and, of course, saw to the care of the wounded, although, according to the *Journall*, casualties had been amazingly light: only six killed in the whole of the siege and two of them as a result of their own carelessness.[26] Not surprisingly her ladyship was widely held to have shown herself a better soldier than her husband or, as some said, to have stolen the earl's breeches. But she gave no sign of wishing to prolong her martial career. As soon as the siege was over she 'willingly resigned to her husband the authority which she had never exercised but in his name' and departed serenely for the Isle of Man, arriving there on 30 July.

She never saw Lathom again. The garrison was finally starved out and forced to surrender in December of the following year, after which the house was ransacked and demolished by the parliamentarians – the Ormskirk parish records contain receipts for the sale of planks, beams and lead from the old building. Another house was eventually built on or near the site of the original Lathom, but the family never lived in it, making their principal home at Knowsley on the outskirts of Liverpool.

Before Lady Derby reached the Isle of Man the royalist cause she had so doggedly defended had suffered a severe setback when, on 2 July 1644, the combined forces of Prince Rupert and the Marquis of Newcastle were heavily defeated at Marston Moor by the combined forces of the Scots, Sir Thomas Fairfax and the troops of the Eastern Association under the Earl of Manchester, with Oliver Cromwell as his Lieutenant-General of the Horse. Marston Moor, one of the greatest battles ever fought on British soil in terms of numbers, was also seminal in that it marked the effective loss of the north of England for the king and destroyed Rupert's reputation for invincibility as a cavalry general. Rupert, that tough, hard-bitten professional, rallied the remnants of his army and retreated to Chester to regroup and raise fresh recruits, but Newcastle had had enough. Unable to cope with the humiliation of defeat – 'I will not endure the laughter of the court' – he abandoned his command and took himself off into exile abroad.

The city of York surrendered on 16 July and now, as in Lancashire, only a few isolated royalist strongholds remained north of the Trent. One of these was Sheffield Castle, once the property of the Talbots, Earls of Shrewsbury, and the occasional residence of the 6th earl's involuntary house-guest Mary, Queen of Scots. The castle had passed by marriage into the hands of the Howard family, but no lord had lived there since the days of the Talbots and in the spring of 1643 Newcastle had put a garrison into it and left Sir William Savile of Thornhill in charge. Sir William had died at York in January 1644 but his widow was still at Sheffield when it was summoned to surrender by the victorious parliamentarians at the beginning of August.

Anne Savile, described as 'a gallant lady famous even for her warlike actions beyond her sex', is said to have been resolved to perish rather than surrender the castle, in spite of being so heavily pregnant as to be very near her time and the midwife refused 'the liberty of going to her'. However, on this occasion the gallant lady was overruled by the garrison. Once the enemy guns had made a breach in the walls which were, in any case, 'everywhere full of cracks with age and ready to fall', it was felt that honour had been satisfied and on 11 August a parley was called. In the terms of surrender it was agreed that Lady Savile with her children, servants and 'her own proper goods', might pass with coaches, horses and waggons to Thornhill or elsewhere 'with a sufficient guard, befitting her quality; and without injury to any of their persons . . . She, they, or any of them to go or stay at their own pleasure, until she or they be in a condition to remove themselves.' It does not seem to be recorded how soon Lady Savile was in a condition to remove herself, for she went into labour and was brought to bed the night after the castle surrendered. Nor does there seem to be any record of what became of the child born in such dramatic circumstances, but the mother survived and later remarried to Sir Thomas Chicheley of Wimpole.[27]

Another Yorkshirewoman caught up in the aftermath of the great battle was Alice Wandesford, now living with her mother at Hipswell near Richmond in the North Riding, where they were suffering from the depredations of the 'Scotch rebels' who were quartered all over the county, especially in and around Richmond, and were eating up all the available provisions. Lady Wandesford was being made to pay £25 a month in money to the soldiers, besides 'the quartering of a troop of Scots on free quarter' which was treble the value of her estate, so that she was forced to borrow to keep her family. Worse, from Alice's point of view, were the unwanted attentions of one Captain Innis, 'so wild a bloody-looked man' that she trembled at the sight of him. In spite of every discouragement he continued his pursuit, coming boldly into her mother's chamber and demanding to be put up in the house. He promised to stay in his own quarters, 'but we so ordered the matter that we got him out, by all fair means could be'. The captain, whose intentions appear to have been honourable, at any rate to begin with, then approached Alice's aunt, saying 'he would give all he was worth if she could procure me to be his wife, and offered three or four thousand pounds'. In the end, poor Alice had to run away into the town and hide herself 'in great fear and fright' with a good old woman, one of her mother's tenants. After which 'this villain captain did study to be revenged of my dear mother, and threatened cruelly what he would do to her because she hid me'. He demanded double the money she was required to pay him, and when she refused drove all her cattle away to Richmond, so that Lady Wandesford was forced to go there herself to appeal to the Scots general, Alexander Leslie, and tell him how she had been wronged and abused.

Alice was later to have a narrow escape 'from this beast, from being destroyed and deflowered by him' when she was warned by one of the soldiers, whose wounded hand she had dressed, not to walk out alone, because his captain 'did curse and swear that he would watch for me, and that very night he had designed with a great many of his comrades to catch me . . . and force me on horseback away with them, and God knows what end he would make of me'. After this, of course, she dared not go out at all, but was forced 'to keep like a prisoner while they was here'.[28]

Captain Innis and his troop did eventually march away and in 1651 Alice married William Thornton of East Newton, but her life was to be a hard one. Only three of her nine children survived and her husband died a bankrupt, leaving her to struggle with poverty and debt. All the same, she lived on into the next century, dying in 1706 in her eightieth year.

News of the disaster at Marston Moor reached the king on 12 July as he was making his way westward, but its impact was considerably softened by the royalist successes in Devon and Cornwall that summer. At the beginning of September the Earl of Essex, trapped with his army at Lostwithiel, decided it was every man for himself and slipped away out of Fowey in a fishing boat. Like the Marquis of Newcastle, his lordship could not face the consequences of admitting defeat and the scorn of his enemies, 'it being a greater terror to me to be a slave to their contempt than a thousand deaths'. His cavalry had managed to escape through the royalist lines but the infantry, abandoned, demoralized and soaking wet (as usual it was pouring with rain), were forced to sue for terms, handing over all their guns and ammunition – thirty-six cannon, ten thousand muskets and several waggonloads of powder and match – before being allowed to depart 'presst all of a heap like sheep, though not so innocent; so durty and so dejected as was rare to see'. After this the king started on a leisurely return journey in the direction of Oxford, not at all dissatisfied with the summer's campaign, although for very many of his subjects the war with its attendant miseries must by now have been looking set to go on indefinitely.

Typical of those families suffering most severely from the effects of the conflict were the Verneys of Claydon in Buckinghamshire and their neighbours and kinsfolk the Dentons of Hillesden. Sir Edmund Verney had borne the king's standard at Edgehill and had been killed there, while his son Ralph sat in the Long Parliament and was generally thought a staunch parliament man. But Ralph was also a staunch Church of England man and conscientiously objected to signing the Presbyterian Solemn League and Covenant when this was required of the members of the Commons as a condition of the Scottish alliance. As a result he found it prudent to go abroad in the winter of 1643, leaving his five unmarried sisters marooned at Claydon, unspoken for, unprotected and virtually penniless, the money for their portions having been tied up in the Aulnage (customs duties on woollen cloth), and now vanished into an impenetrable undergrowth of legal complications and delays.

The sisters, 'whose names read like the chorus of an old song', Sue and Pen and Peg and Molly and Betty the youngest, who was only ten and said to be 'unruly', inevitably grew querulous and touchy over trifles. 'I did speak to Peg,' wrote their aunt Elizabeth Isham, 'as her mayd might serve both her and Pen, but she will not let it be so by no meanes. I told her now their father and mother was dead, they should be a help one to the other, but all would not doe.' Mrs Isham thought a possible solution to this knotty problem would be if Peg agreed to take charge of Betty, 'all but the washing of her'. Then the nurse, Nan Fudd, would have more time to help Pen and Ralph 'need not be at any more charges for a mayd for Pen'.[29]

The household at Claydon was later joined by yet another sister, Cary, the only one to have been married before the outbreak of war and their father's death. But Cary's husband, a young captain of dragoons in the king's service, was killed in a skirmish near Aylesbury in the spring of 1645, leaving 'a sad disconsolate widow great with child' and still only eighteen years old. To make matters worse, 'when her husband died he left her not a penny in the house . . . She looks for her time within less than a month and I feare will want many necessaries,' wrote one of her uncles. To everyone's disappointment, Cary's baby was a girl and sickly, and her in-laws were so unsympathetic, even making difficulties over the payment of her jointure, that she was driven to take refuge at Claydon.[30]

The Verney girls did have the company and support of their Denton uncles, aunts and cousins at Hillesden. But Hillesden occupied a particularly exposed position on the borders of royalist and parliamentary territory. Sir Alexander Denton had fortified the house as best he could and early in 1644 Colonel Smith came to take command, digging trenches and building extra stabling for cavalry. The country all round was continually swept by foraging parties from both armies and it was not long before a dispute over compensation for some commandeered cattle drew the attention of the parliamentary authorities at Aylesbury to the unwelcome existence of a royalist outpost at Hillesden. An attack in some force was therefore mounted on the house and although Colonel Smith and his men put up a brave resistance they were quickly overwhelmed and forced to surrender. Alexander Denton and his brother were taken prisoner to Newport Pagnell and the house was ransacked and burnt to the ground. Pen Verney, who had been present during the attack, wrote to Ralph: 'When it pleased God to lay that great affliction on my uncle, I was more consarned for him, but I did stand so great a los in my own particular that it has been a half undoing to me. We were not shamefully used by the souldiers, but they took everything and I was not left scarce the clothes of my back.'[31]

'The ruine of sweet Hillesden' was a dreadful blow and Mrs Isham thought the Denton children would be 'like to beg', but the gloom was somewhat lightened by two love stories which blossomed unexpectedly among the ashes. First, and most suprisingly, was the romance of Sir Alexander's sister Susan and Captain Jeremiah Abercromby, one of the Roundhead officers who had apparently led the plunderers of her home. Hardly any details are known, but the courtship of this unlikely couple must have begun in the immediate aftermath of the destruction of the house, perhaps in the few hours before Susan and her nieces walked across the fields to seek shelter at Claydon, for it is first mentioned in a letter of 6 March only three days later.

In June Elizabeth Isham was writing: 'My sister Susan's marage is to be accomplished very suddenly if her captine be not killed . . . I think fue of her friends like it, but if she hath not him she will never have any, it is gone so far.' Sadly the captain – he was half Scots, half Irish with land in Ireland – was indeed killed the following year and was buried among the Dentons in the churchyard at Hillesden.[32]

William Smith, who had led the defence of Hillesden, had been taken prisoner with the two Dentons and they all three ended up in the Tower, where somehow – although the how is not explained – he contrived to get married to Sir Alexander's daughter Margaret. 'I think it will be a happy match if these ill times doth not hinder it,' Mrs Isham told Ralph Verney. 'But he is still a Prisener, so you may thinke it a bolde venture. But if these times hold, I think there will be none men lefte for women.' Later in the year Colonel Smith, who was clearly a resourceful character, managed to escape and in September Margaret, Elizabeth Isham and Susan Verney were arrested on suspicion of having aided and abetted him. 'When I was in prison, thaye would not lett me have so much as a Pene and Incke,' complained that indefatigable correspondent Mrs Isham, 'but all of us was innocent Prisnors, and so came out without examining, for none could have a worde against us.' Susan Verney also wrote to Ralph in October to tell him she had been kept in custody for eight days but never examined, for 'there was nothing could be brought against mee . . . Itt was thought that I had a hand in helping of my new cosin out of prison, butt indeed I had nott – I hope that I shall never under take to doe any such thing whereby I may bring my selfe into trouble.'[33]

Susan was then living in London with her uncle and aunt John and Dorothy Leeke but Tom Verney, another brother, was seriously worried about the sad condition of the girls at Claydon 'subject to the affrights of rude souldiers rushing in att all houres both by day and night, and not a man there that dares show himself in their defence. My sisters (God help them) are so sensible of their incivilitye allready that I have heard them say that they could not eat hardly in a week one meale's meat contentedly.'[34]

As the year drew to a close there was a determined air of optimism in the royalist camp in spite of Marston Moor and in spite of the fact that parliament now controlled approximately two-thirds of the country. Lord Digby told the Marquis of Ormonde that his majesty's affairs were 'in the best posture they have been at any time since these unhappy wars', while even the cautious Edward Hyde thought the king's condition was 'now much better than in the beginning of the summer he had reason to expect'. There had been another confused and inconclusive engagement at Newbury in October from which the royalists had withdrawn under cover of darkness, but they were later able to regroup and come back to rescue their artillery before marching off with drums beating, colours flying and trumpets sounding defiantly. The end of November saw the king once more back at Oxford, inspecting the new fortifications in gracious mode, complimenting the citizens on their hard work and assuring them that the war would soon be over.

In London, by contrast, the mood was one of gloom and recrimination. The whole southern army was in a bad way after a long season's campaigning in consistently cold wet weather, and the soldiers, ill-clad, underfed, their pay in arrears and with sickness growing in their ranks, were displaying an ominous disenchantment with the whole business of the war. At the same time, dissension among the generals was reaching crisis point. Essex and Waller had long been at loggerheads and now Cromwell, the rising star, was openly accusing the Earl of Manchester of 'backwardness to all action'.

It was Manchester who, in the aftermath of Newbury, had summed up the moderate parliamentarians' predicament when he pointed out that 'the King need not care how oft he fights, but it concerns us to be wary, for in fighting we venture all to nothing. If we beat him ninety and nine times yet he is king still and so will his posterity be after him; but if the King beat us once we shall all be hanged and our posterity made slaves.' But Cromwell had no patience with this kind of talk, or the half-hearted amateurish attitude of men like Manchester. It was clear to him and the other members of what was becoming known as the Independent Party that the army must be radically restructured and brought under unified command as soon as possible, and the incompetent generals cleared out of the way.

It was with this end in view that in December the so-called Self-Denying Ordinance was brought before parliament, making it unlawful for any member of either House to hold any military office or command. The Earls of Essex and Manchester were thus neatly disposed of but there was, of course, nothing to prevent the Commons from making exceptions from one of its own decrees for one of its own members. Sir Thomas Fairfax was presently appointed commander-in-chief of the New Model Army and, to no one's surprise, Oliver Cromwell, MP for Cambridge, became General of the Horse.

During the winter there had been another attempt by the more moderate parliamentarians to start discussing terms for a possible peace treaty, and at the end of January 1645 commissioners for both sides met at Uxbridge. News that the king was even considering a treaty brought an anxious letter from the queen. 'For the honour of God trust not yourself in the hands of those people. . . . I understand that the propositions for peace must begin by disbanding your army. If you consent to this you are lost . . .'.[35] Henrietta need not have worried. No one involved in the talks at Uxbridge had any real expectation of success and the negotiations soon ground to a halt.

The king had so far always been careful to keep his two sons close to him, especially the Prince of Wales: 'he had no resolution more fixed in him, than that the Prince should never be absent from him'. But now he was beginning to say that it was too dangerous for both of them to be together in the same place, and that anyway it was time to 'unboy' his heir by putting him into 'some action and acquaintance with business out of his own sight'. It was therefore decided to send the fourteen-year-old Charles down to Bristol, the West Country being the only district where he could now safely be sent, and where he was to have his own court and council.

The prince left Oxford at the beginning of March and one of those gentlemen who travelled with him was his Secretary for War, Sir Richard Fanshawe. It was a traumatic parting for the Fanshawes. Not only was it the first time they had been separated since their marriage, but Ann was then lying-in of her first child and the normally self-controlled Sir Richard was 'afflicted even to tears' at having to leave his young wife alone in a garrison town with a sick baby – a boy who died two days later – and herself 'extream weake and very poor'.

It was May before Ann was strong enough to leave her room and go to church, but after the service she was approached by 'a very honest gentleman', who brought her a letter from her husband and fifty pieces of gold. The money was welcome but it was the letter, summoning her to come and join him in Bristol, which did most to revive her and she went immediately to walk, or at least sit as she was still very weak, in the garden of St John's College and to tell her father the good news. It was there that she had a narrow escape, typical of the sort of casual danger always lurking in the wartime situation. 'We heard drums beat in the high way under the garden wall,' remembered Ann long afterwards. 'My father asked me if I would goe up upon the mount and see the souldiers march, for it was Sir Charles Lee's company of foot, an acquaintance of ours. I sayd yes, and went up, leaning my back to a tree that grew on the mount. The Commander, seeing us there, in compliment, gave us a volley of shott, and one of their muskets being loden, shot a brace of bullets not 2 inches above my head as I leaned to the tree.'

A few days later she set out on her journey, confident that the worst of her misfortunes were now past and blissfully unaware that she was in fact about to embark on an odyssey which would last for nearly a quarter of a century. 'Little thought I to leap into that sea that would tosse me untill it had racked me.' She was greeted joyfully by her husband, who took her in his arms and then presented her with the rest of his little store of gold, saying: 'I know that thou that keeps my heart so well will keep my fortune, which from this time I will ever put into thy hands as God shall bless me with increase.' But although Sir Richard was happy to trust her with his money, the classified details of his work were a different matter, as Ann was about to learn.

Countess Rivers, one of the senior ladies at Bristol, seeing an opportunity to profit by the youthful Lady Fanshawe's inexperience, let her know that nowadays it was considered perfectly acceptable, if not positively commendable, for the women of their circle to take an informed interest in political affairs; that she happened to know some letters had just arrived from the queen in France, 'and that she would be extream glad to hear what the Qween commanded the King in order to his affairs, saying if I would ask my husband privatly, he would tell me what he found in the packett, and I might tell her.'

Much impressed, and innocently believing that her husband would love her all the more if she showed an interest in 'the buseness of publick affaires', Ann waited until he next returned from a council meeting carrying his usual sheaf of papers and, after welcoming him home, followed him into his study. 'He turning hastyly sayd, "What wouldst thou have, my life?" I told him I heard the Prince had received a packet from the Qween, and I guessed it that in his hand, and I desired to know what was in it. He smiling replyed, "My love, I will immediately come to thee. Pray thee goe, for I am very busy." When he came out of his closet I revived my sute. He kissed me and talked of other things.'

Rebuffed, however gently, Ann sulked. 'At supper I would eat nothing.' At bedtime she asked again, 'and said I could not belive he loved me if he refused to tell me all he knew, but he answered nothing, but stopped my mouth with kisses, so we went to bed'. Ann cried and Richard went to sleep. In the morning she refused to speak to him. 'He rose, came on the other side of the bed and kissed me, and drew the curtaine softly and went to court.' When he came home to dinner she accused him of not caring to see her so troubled. 'To which he, taking me in his armes, answered, "My dearest soule, nothing upon earth can afflict me like that; and when you asked me of my busines, it was wholy out of my power to satisfy thee. For my life and fortune shall be thine, and every thought of my heart . . . but my honour is my own, which I cannot preserve if I communicate the Prince's affaires, and pray thee with this answer rest satisfied."' So very calm and reasonable was he that Ann realized how very foolish she had been, and 'from that day untill the day of his death I never thought fit to ask him any business, but that he communicated freely to me'.

By July the plague had become so bad in Bristol that the prince was moved with his retinue to Barnstaple. The Fanshawes followed two days later, Ann being careful to explain that all the time she was attached to his court she never travelled with the prince, 'nor ever saw him but at church, for it was not in those days the fashon for honest women, except they have business, to visit a man's court'.

She thought Barnstaple 'one of the finest towns I know in England', remembering it chiefly for the hundred-year-old parrot at the merchant's house where they lodged, and 'a fruit called a massard, like a cherry, but different in tast, and makes the best pyes, with their sort of cream, I ever eat'.[36]

But while Ann Fanshawe was enjoying cherry pie and cream in Devonshire, at the other end of the country another wife was enduring the discomforts and dangers of yet another siege. Elizabeth Twysden had married Hugh Cholmley in December 1622 at the church of St Mary Magdalen in Milk Street in the City of London. She was the eldest daughter of Sir William Twysden of East Peckham in Kent and his formidable and aristocratic wife Lady Anne Twysden. Hugh Cholmley was heir to a large estate at Whitby in the North Riding of Yorkshire but this, owing to his father's improvidence, was now heavily encumbered with debt.

The young Cholmleys lived with Elizabeth's parents, either in London or Kent, until the spring of 1626, when Hugh was summoned back to Yorkshire to try and sort out his father's chaotic finances and rescue what he could of his own inheritance from the creditors. Elizabeth joined him the following year with their two young sons and they all camped out in the gatehouse of the family mansion at Whitby, built of stone taken from the Abbey and itself then falling into ruin. Sir Hugh (he had been knighted in 1626) recalled in his Memoirs that 'though a time of trouble, I have heard my dear wife often say, she never lived with more content any part of her life than this winter; for ourselves, young people, loved much and joyed in one another.'[37]

The Cholmleys were to know the sorrow common to so many parents when their first-born son and eldest daughter both died in childhood, but two more sons and two daughters survived and, by means of selling land and frugal husbandry, Sir Hugh gradually succeeded in paying off his creditors and bringing the estate back into good order. All the same, it was the spring of 1636 before he was able to finish restoring the house at Whitby and take his wife and children to live there in proper state. 'My father being dead,' he wrote, a touch complacently, 'the country [county] looked upon me as the chief of my family; and having mastered my debts, I did not only appear at all public meetings in a very gentlemanly equipage, but lived in as handsome and plentiful fashion at home as any gentleman in all the country of my rank.'[38] To do him justice, he was careful to give credit to the homemaking talents of his wife. 'She contributed much to beautifying of the house at Whitby, being a good contriver within doors, and having a most singular faculty to make and order furniture for houses, and dress it after the best mode, which many cannot do though they have stuff.'[39] Sir Hugh and Lady Cholmley employed between thirty and forty people on their ordinary staff, with a chaplain who said prayers three times a day and a porter 'who merely attended the gates'. There was always more than enough to feed any unexpected guests, who could be sure of a hearty welcome at their hospitable dinner table, and twice a week the local poor were served with bread and 'good pottage made of beef'.

Sadly this period of peace and prosperity was to be all too short. A man in Hugh Cholmley's position could not avoid taking sides in the conflict between king and parliament, nor did he attempt to do so, refusing to pay the notorious Ship Money tax and joining with Sir John Hotham and others in petitioning the king to call a parliament in 1640, although like many other moderate men he was deeply unhappy about the intransigence being displayed by both parties.

In November 1641 he was returned to the Commons as member for Scarborough and in August 1642 was asked by the Earl of Essex to go back to Yorkshire and 'draw his regiment' – that is, raise the militia of which he was colonel – for the securing of Scarborough. Sir Hugh hesitated, but 'conceiving these preparations for war would end in a treaty, and that myself desired nothing but that the King might enjoy his just rights as well as the subjects theirs, and that I should in this matter be a more indifferent arbitrator than many I saw take arms, and more considerable with my sword in my hand . . . than by sitting in the House of Commons where I had but a bare vote, I accepted this employment.'[40]

However, when he reached Scarborough he found that most of his neighbours had already taken up arms for the king and, as the months passed, he became increasingly disenchanted with his parliamentary friends, who not only failed to send him any money, so that he was 'for his subsistence and security forced into many actions he never intended or foresaw at his first undertaking the business', but were also, in his opinion, noticeably failing to honour those principles for which they said they had gone to war: 'viz. the preservation of religion, protection of the King's person, and liberties of the subject'.[41]

Consequently, when the queen arrived at York in 1643 and Sir Hugh 'was earnestly solicited by some of her friends and allies to quitt the Parliament', he was ready to be convinced, making a secret excursion through enemy lines for an interview with Henrietta. He explained that 'before hee fullie declaired his resolution, hee must make two modest requests to her; 1. that she would be pleased to give him her royall assurance not to divert the King from performing those promises hee had made to the Kingdome; 2ndly, that shee would endeavour the speedie settling the peace of the Kingdome.' Having, unsurprisingly, been given 'a verie satisfactory answeare' by her majesty – he was, after all, a valuable acquisition for the northern royalists – Sir Hugh undertook 'to quitt the Parliament, and to serve the King to the uttmost of his power'.[42]

He had intended to fetch his wife and children from London before making his 'resolution' public, but the news leaked out and Elizabeth Cholmley was robbed of her coach horses and roughly treated by some of her husband's former colleagues, furious over his defection. She, too, disapproved of what he had done, but managed to procure a pass and with her two small daughters, 'the elder then not above eight years of age', travelled to Whitby by sea, 'having so quick and prosperous a passage, as she said she would never go up and down again to London but by ship'.

The Cholmleys had now been separated for almost a year and Elizabeth, 'not understanding . . . the true state of the difference between the King and Parliament, was very earnest and firm for their party'. But when the situation had been made clear to her, 'she then was as much against them and as earnest for the King, and continued so to her death'. As a loyal wife she knew where her duty lay.

After a few days at Whitby they moved to Scarborough, a busy little fishing port with some trade with northern Europe. Sir Hugh now held Lord Newcastle's commission as Governor of the town and castle, as well as a commission 'to order all marine affairs within all the ports from Tees to Bridlington', although he received no pay or allowance and had to maintain his position at his own expense. In the autumn of 1643 he made a short excursion to assist at the unsuccessful attack on Hull, taking with him his own regiment of horse, also raised at his own expense; but in Scarborough life, trade and fishing continued largely undisturbed by war, and for their first year the Governor and his family were able to live comfortably in a style suitable to their rank. Then came Marston Moor and the collapse of the north, and suddenly everything looked very different.

It was to Scarborough that the Marquis of Newcastle fled after the battle, spending two days with the Cholmleys while Sir Hugh found a ship to take him overseas. Newcastle told his hosts that 'he gave all for lost on the King's side' and tried to persuade them to leave with him, but Hugh Cholmley possessed more staying power than his former general and 'meant not to surrender till I heard from the King or was forced to it'.[43] It seemed only too probable that he would be forced to it, for Scarborough was unfortified and the ancient castle, built out on a promontory in the North Sea, though strong by situation, 'had not within itt either habitation for soldiers or places for magazine, and as the provision for victualls were but small, soe for warr less, there beeing but 23 barrells of powder and 3 bundles of match'.[44] Sir Hugh seems to have been anticipating an immediate onslaught, but fortunately the enemy had other priorities and he was to have several months' respite in which to 'put the town and castle into a much better posture of defence'.

He himself always dated the siege from Marston Moor, in the summer of 1644, but the attack on Scarborough did not in fact begin until the following February, when Lady Cholmley asked him to send their two girls to safety in Holland. Sir Hugh parted from his daughters reluctantly, but sent them off in the charge of the vicar of Whitby and his wife, with a French gentlewoman, a chambermaid and a manservant to wait on them. Lady Cholmley herself could not be persuaded to leave her husband and remained at his side throughout the siege. 'During which time', he wrote, 'my dear wife endured much hardship, and yet with little shew of trouble; and though by nature, according to her sex, timorous, yet in greatest danger would not be daunted, but shewed a courage even above her sex.'[45]

The town of Scarborough was, as Sir Hugh had always foreseen, untenable with the forces at his command. However, he did manage to hold on to it 'till some places for Magazines within the Castle were finished and provisions in the towne carried thither'. He then retreated behind its walls, together with the garrison of some 500 men, prepared to resist for as long as possible. Elizabeth Cholmley, of course, went too, and was soon fully occupied nursing the sick and wounded, taking 'an extraordinary care of them, making such helps and provisions as the place could afford'. In fact, she worked her maids so hard that one of them stole away in the night, hoping to get back into the town, 'but the enemy's guards, taking her for a spy, caused her to return, which was acceptable to her lady, there being not persons in health to attend the sick'. Scurvy was then rife in the castle and even Lady Cholmley got a touch of it.[46]

After about eight weeks, the castle – which was already in a poor state of repair – was so heavily bombarded that the great tower, or keep, was split in two, destroying the living quarters of the Governor and most of his officers, and forcing them to move out into some 'poore cabbins' built against the walls of the castle yard. Here they were constantly exposed to gunfire from enemy ships in the bay, and Lady Cholmley caught cold and 'took a defluxion of rheum upon one of her eyes, which troubled her ever after'.[47]

The fall of the tower had seemed to signal an end to any further resistance and the enemy commander, that grim old warrior Sir John Meldrum, sent Hugh Cholmley a summons to surrender, threatening that if it were not obeyed 'he would that night be master of all the works and the castle; and, in case one drop of his men's blood was shed, not give quarter to man or woman, but put all to the sword'. As soon as she heard about this, Elizabeth went to her husband 'and prayed me I would not, for any consideration of her, do aught that might be prejudicial to my own honour, or the King's affairs'.[48]

In the event, it was John Meldrum who was killed, receiving 'a shott in att the bellie and out of the backe' in a scuffle round the gatehouse a few days later, and the siege dragged on for another twelve weeks. By that time conditions inside the castle were becoming desperate, half the garrison being either slain (apparently most of the casualties were caused by falling stones dislodged by the enemy cannon), or dead from scurvy, with nearly all the rest too sick to move. Only about twenty-five of the common soldiers were fit for duty and the gentlemen and officers 'almost tired out of their skinns'. Ten men had died one night and lain unburied for two days 'for want of helpe to carrie them to the grave'. There was some corn, but no one with the strength to grind it, and a serious shortage of water – the well in the castle was insufficient and access to another below the cliffs was now barred by the enemy ships. At last, with the powder down to half a barrel, no medicine for the sick and wounded, and hardly anyone in a fit state to look over the walls, let alone stand sentinel, it was agreed that honour had been satisfied, and on 25 July the garrison surrendered to Sir Matthew Boynton, who had taken over from John Meldrum.[49]

Hugh Cholmley had been given the choice of joining the king or going overseas, but the king was now in Wales and, feeling too worn out after his recent exertions to undertake such a long journey through largely hostile country, Sir Hugh opted to go abroad, sailing from Bridlington to

Holland. There he found his daughters safe and sound and sent them back to their mother, who had stayed behind to save what she could of the family property. The estates were, of course, sequestrated, but it had been agreed at the surrender of the castle that the garrison then in the house at Whitby should be removed and that Lady Cholmley should 'have the liberty to live there'. Unfortunately, however, the parliamentary captain in residence liked his quarters so much that he refused to leave, so Lady Cholmley, homeless and with no more than ten pounds in her purse, took lodgings at Malton and waited developments. Her patience was rewarded that winter, when plague broke out at Whitby and one of the intransigent captain's servants died. He unwisely fled, and before he could return, Elizabeth, who was now in her mid-forties, set out alone to travel more than twenty miles across the snow-covered moors of North Yorkshire 'in a dangerous season'. But she reached the house and took possession, living there in considerable discomfort with only one maid for company and a manservant who did the cooking. Everything had been systematically looted by the parliamentary soldiers and she had to make do with what she could borrow, complaining only that her bed was so hard 'she could not be warm nor able to lie in it'.

Later she would remember this as 'the saddest and worst time of her life', with her family scattered and the future looking dark. But her spirit, as always, remained undaunted. The winter over and the house free of infection, she was able to collect her daughters from Malton and, with the help of her brother-in-law Henry Cholmley, secured her 'fifth' from the authorities, managing on this until her elder son William arrived from the Continent to lay claim to the manor of Whitby and some other lands which his father had previously made over to him. Between them, William and his uncle Henry succeeded in extracting enough of his property from the clutches of the parliamentary committee at York to provide a reasonably adequate income and in the spring of 1647 Elizabeth, William and the two girls went over to France to join Sir Hugh, now settled at Rouen. Soon afterwards the younger son, another Hugh, who had been at school in London, also joined them and the family, who had not been all together for five years, were joyfully reunited.

The Cholmleys remained in exile until February 1649, when the execution of the king put an end to any immediate hopes of a royalist revival and, money again becoming short, Elizabeth returned to England to arrange the composition for her husband's estate. Helped by family and friends, 'best discovered in adversity' remarked Sir Hugh, she paid the first instalment of his fine, after which he felt it was safe to return himself.[50] They spent most of the next three years living in London or with Elizabeth's relations at East Peckham, but in 1652 they went back to keep house at Whitby for the first time in seven years and Elizabeth set to work once again to make a home. Not, of course, on the same scale as before. 'Partly', wrote Sir Hugh, 'in respect my purse could not so well furnish her as before, partly in respect that it was not discretion to bestow much cost in furniture, considering the unsettledness of the times; so what was done now, was for necessity and present use, more than ornament; and truly the blankets and much of the bedding were made by her own housewifery, without much expense of money.' There was, however, 'a suit of green cloth hangings, with flowers of needlework, wrought by herself' which he greatly prized and hoped might be preserved for their posterity.[51]

In the summer of 1654 Hugh and Elizabeth came south for the wedding of their daughter Ann, and Elizabeth stayed on in London, wanting to be near her daughter and to support her through her first pregnancy. Hugh's various business interests took him back to Whitby and he was in Yorkshire in April 1655 when Elizabeth was taken suddenly ill with a fever, dying a week later in her cousin's house in Covent Garden. She was buried in the church at East Peckham, and although Hugh was not in time for the funeral, he travelled to Kent as soon as he could. He does not appear to have lived at Whitby again, 'being indeed not able to endure the sight of those rooms and places in which I had used to enjoy her company', and spent the rest of his life among her family and friends.[52]

Hugh Cholmley died in November 1657 and chose to lie beside his dear Elizabeth, who had never forsaken him in 'all the many troubles and tossings she had in her life' and to whose memory he had erected a black marble stone with this inscription: 'She was very beautiful, of great ingenuity, and a discerning judgement; in great dangers had a courage above her sex; of a most noble and sweet nature, compassionate to all in distress; a virtuous, chaste, loving wife, indulgent parent, and true friend; and, which was above all, a most pious and religious person.'[53]

CHAPTER FIVE

'*Love Loyalty*'

The earnest desire I had to serve the King made mee omitt
noe opportunity wherin I could bee usefull, and the zeal
I had for His Majesty made mee not see what inconveniencys
I exposed my selfe to.

Anne, Lady Halket

Early in May 1645 the king set out from Oxford to begin his summer campaign and in a letter to the queen dated the 12th explained that 'being now in my march, I cannot hope to hear so often from thee, or thou from me so often as before'. The army was on its way first to the relief of Chester, which had now been under siege for more than a year, and then to make a bid to recover the north, and Charles, although worried about Henrietta who had recently been ill again, was in optimistic mood, 'so that if I may be assured of thy health, I shall cheerfully proceed in this summer's work'.[1]

The work had not, however, proceeded very far when news arrived that Thomas Fairfax with the New Model Army was coming up from the south and, on Prince Rupert's advice, the king turned east to draw the enemy away from Oxford. On 31 May the royalists stormed and seized Leicester, a prosperous town of brewers and stocking-frame knitters, and that night Charles wrote to tell his wife 'of the good success which it hath pleased God to give me this day'. Rupert wanted to continue north, but was over-ruled and the royalists, weighed down by the plunder taken at Leicester, were taking their ease at Daventry – 'the soldiers in no order and their horses all at grass' – when Fairfax reached the village of Kislingbury some ten miles to the east. Next day, 13 June, he was joined by Cromwell with a contingent of Eastern Association Horse – the famous Ironsides who had wreaked so much havoc at Marston Moor – bringing his strength up to about 15,000 men. The royalists were now withdrawing to Market Harborough, where it was hoped that cavalry reinforcements would soon be arriving from the West Country, but Rupert was not happy about the situation and again urged going further north. Again he was overruled by those gung-ho members of the king's entourage who wanted to stand and fight rather than 'be sought and pursued', believing that here might be their chance to win a glorious victory over the 'new Noddle', as they had christened the New Model Army.

Naseby, the battle 'of all, for all', took place on 14 June and ended in disaster for the royal army. Estimates of its numbers vary widely, from 7,500 to 12,000, but superior generalship and discipline on the parliamentary side probably counted for more than numbers alone. The first cavalry charge, led by the Princes Rupert and Maurice, crashed through the left wing of the parliamentary horse but, just as at Edgehill, it was then allowed to bolt away out of control to squander precious time and energy plundering the enemy baggage train. 'Though the king's troops prevailed in the charge, and routed those they charged, they never rallied themselves again in order, nor could be brought to make a second charge again the same day.'[2]

The rock-steady Ironsides, meanwhile, were advancing against Marmaduke Langdale's Northern Horse, which gradually fell back across rough ground pitted with rabbit warrens towards the shelter of Prince Rupert's regiment of foot in the king's reserves, leaving the infantry in the centre dangerously exposed. This seems to have been the moment when Charles himself attempted to take a hand and ride forward with his reserve of horse 'which was his own guards'. But a zealous aide seized his bridle and dragged him to one side, exclaiming: 'Will you go upon your death in an instant?' An unlucky misunderstanding of this sudden commotion panicked the Lifeguard, which turned 'and rode upon the spur, as if they were every man to shift for himself', running almost a quarter of a mile without stopping.[3] By the time Rupert had succeeded in regrouping and getting his men back to the battle, it was too late to save the situation or the infantry who, unsupported and unprotected by their own cavalry and under attack from the enemy horse, were now surrendering *en masse*.

By early afternoon Rupert and the king, with their 'broken troops', were in full flight, leaving Fairfax and Cromwell in possession of the field, between four and five thousand prisoners, the entire royal artillery train with its powder and ammunition, about eight thousand other weapons and a whole forest of colours. No attempt had been made to guard the clutter of sumpter waggons, coaches and carts which trailed in the wake of the army, and there were some very nasty scenes along the road to Leicester as the victors took advantage of their turn to plunder. 'The enemy', says Clarendon indignantly, 'left no manner of barbarous cruelty unexercised that day, and in the pursuit killed above one hundred women, whereof some were officers' wives of quality.' In fact, the officers' wives and anyone else with money, jewellery, or even 'rich apparel' in their possession would in most cases have been able to buy their lives. Less fortunate were the humble 'leaguer bitches' and camp sluts who were slaughtered without mercy or had their noses slit, the customary judicial disfigurement of a prostitute. The old bogey of Irishwomen with 'cruel countenances' and long knives was later raised in extenuation, but it seems more likely that the victims were Welsh women belonging to the royalist foot soldiers drawn from the recruiting grounds of North Wales.[4]

The value of the booty taken from the royal baggage train has been estimated at a hundred thousand pounds in gold, silver and jewels, but for the king by far the most serious loss was the capture of his private papers, consisting mainly of his correspondence with the queen going back over the past three years and giving details of their increasingly desperate efforts to raise money and armies from abroad – from Denmark, from France, from the Duke of Lorraine, from the Vatican and, worst of all, from Ireland. These letters, sent down to London and promptly published by the parliamentary propaganda machine under the title *The King's Cabinet Opened*, provided conclusive evidence that Charles and Henrietta had been actively plotting to bring foreigners and papists into the country and did irreparable damage to their cause.

Naseby and its aftermath was only one of a string of disasters in that disastrous year. While the king retreated into South Wales to enjoy the comforting hospitality of the Marquis of Worcester at Raglan Castle, Fairfax was cutting a swathe through the West Country, where the oppressive behaviour of incompetent and dissolute royalist commanders and the unrestrained extortions of their troops had begun to alienate even that once dependably loyal territory. On 14 July the New Model Army defeated Lord Goring at Langport near Ilminster. Bridgwater fell on 23 July, Sherborne Castle on 14 August, and on 10 September Rupert was forced to surrender Bristol, a calamity which caused 'a new earthquake in all the little quarters the King had left'.

Things were no better in the north-west. Back in May Helen Neale, wife of the Governor of Hawarden Castle, then under siege by William Brereton and threatened by an enemy mine and mortar piece, had written to her absent husband: 'Our condition is at this tyme very desperate.' All the same, she intended 'to hould out as long as there is meate for man for none of these eminent daingers shall ever frighten mee from my loyalty but in life and death I will be the King's faithfull subject and thy constant loveing wife and humble servant.'⁵

The pressure on Hawarden and nearby Chester had been temporarily relieved in the summer by the king's march northward and in September he was again on his way north, lured by the hope of being able to join up with the Marquis of Montrose, who had been conducting a spectacularly successful guerilla war against the Scottish Covenanters. But once again hope proved illusory. Montrose and his Highlanders and a handful of Irish were crushed at Philiphaugh on 13 September, and ten days later Charles and the remnants of his cavalry were themselves heavily defeated at Rowton Heath outside the walls of Chester. After that there was nothing for it but another retreat and while the king wandered across the Midlands looking for a safe haven, Fairfax and Cromwell were mopping up in the south.

Basing House in Hampshire, the great fortified mansion of the Marquis of Winchester – a 'place seated and built as if for Royaltie, having a proper motto Aymez Loyalte' – which stood astride the main road to the south-west, had been defying the parliament since the autumn of 1643 when William Waller had led the first assault against it. The marquis, a devout Catholic and a subject who took his family motto as seriously as his religion, plainly deserved no consideration, but Waller found himself in something of a quandary when it came to the lady of the house.

The Marchioness of Winchester, born Lady Honora de Burgh, daughter of the Earl of St Albans and Clanricarde and a granddaughter of Sir Francis Walsingham of Elizabethan fame, was also half-sister to parliament's Earl of Essex. It would be embarrassing if any harm befell her, and William Waller therefore made a special point of offering free passage to her ladyship and all the other women and children. He was severely snubbed for his pains. The marchioness 'thanked God that she was not in that condition to accept of fair quarter at Sir William Waller's hands, being resolved to run the same fortune as her Lord, knowing that there was a just and all-seeing Judge above, who she hoped would have an especial hand in this business, from whom Sir William Waller could pretend no commission. Whatever befel she was not unprepared to bear it.'⁶

The bombardment of Loyalty House, as it became known, began on 6 November and lasted for several days. It was followed up by an attempt to storm the walls with scaling ladders, during which the women joined the defenders, hurling bricks, tiles and stones from the roofs of the various buildings. Everyone in the house resisted valiantly. Colonel Rawdon, commander of the garrison, and his officers fought side by side with their men, while the marchioness and her ladies cast bullets with the lead hastily stripped from roofs and turrets.[7]

Shortage of ammunition, November rain and fog, and reports of the approach of a relieving force eventually forced Waller to call off the attack, but the following spring 'proud, stubborn and malignant Basing' was once more under siege, this time by Colonel Norton, 'a stout and diligent officer, who had a body of horse and foot equal to the service'. After three months' close investment the marquis was sending out urgent appeals for help and the marchioness, who had managed to travel to Oxford, was doing her best to procure relief for her husband, 'who was in respect of his religion sure to be ill-treated if he fell into the enemy's hands'. Everyone, says Clarendon, was anxious to gratify her, 'being a lady of great honour and alliance', while the Catholics, who were numerous in Oxford, 'looked upon themselves as concerned to contribute all they could'. But Sir Arthur Aston, the Governor of the city, took a less quixotic view of the matter, pointing out that Basing was almost forty miles away, that the enemy's garrisons in Abingdon, Reading and Newbury regularly patrolled the highways, and that even if it were possible to reach the house, it would certainly be impossible to return. Sir Arthur, in short, flatly refused to allow any of the men under his command 'to be hazarded in the attempt'. In the end, after a desperate last message from the marquis that he could not hold out for more than another ten days at most and 'new instances from his lady', Colonel Henry Gage, an experienced professional soldier recently arrived in Oxford, undertook to organize a relief column made up in part of gentlemen volunteers and augmented by Colonel Hawkins's regiment from Greenland House near Henley which had just been surrendered to the parliament.[8]

This small but determined force left Oxford at 10 o'clock on the night of Monday 9 September, carrying with them twelve barrels of powder and twelve hundredweight of match. Travelling by back roads and wearing the orange-tawny scarves and ribbons of parliament men, they reached their objective in less than thirty-six hours and, assisted by the Basing garrison, successfully fought their way through the besiegers' lines. Leaving a hundred of Hawkins's musketeers to reinforce the defenders, Gage then mounted a lightning raid on the nearby market town of Basingstoke, where he commandeered forty or fifty head of cattle, a hundred sheep and as much wheat, malt, salt, oats, bacon, cheese and butter as he could find horses and carts to transport. Reckoning that they had put at least a month's provisions into the house, the column now prepared to withdraw under cover of darkness 'without sound of drum or trumpet' and ready, if challenged, to pass themselves off as parliament soldiers marching to the River Kennet to lie in wait for the Oxford troops. But, with the help of local guides, they were able to ford the Kennet undetected and arrived safely back at Oxford on Saturday 14 September, having suffered only a handful of casualties.[9]

Thanks to Colonel Gage, Basing had been granted a reprieve and that November, when supplies were again running very low, Richard Norton finally lifted his twenty-four week blockade. Then, in August 1645, another enemy appeared at the gates and this time there would be no rescue operation. Colonel John, or Jan, Dalbier, described as 'the Cunning Engineer', was a Dutchman with a distinguished record of service to the parliamentary cause. Having assessed the situation with a trained eye, he sited his batteries and began methodically to pound Loyalty House into rubble. The great tower of the castle, as the old part of the building was known, collapsed on 22 September. Next day Dalbier turned his cannon on the so-called New House, which dated from Tudor times, 'and after many shots against the midst of the House, which loosened the bricks and made a long crack in the wall, he made another shot or two at the top of the House which brought down the high turret, the fall whereof so shook that part of the house, which before was weakened, that the outmost wall fell down all at once'. So great was the damage that the gunners could see 'bedding and other goods fall out of the House into the court'.[10]

On 8 October John Dalbier was joined by no less a personage than General Cromwell himself. Fresh from a triumphal progress through Wiltshire, Cromwell had just taken Winchester Castle and was now ready to turn his attention to Basing, that well-known nest of Romanists and the only surviving royalist stronghold between London and the West Country. Having peremptorily summoned the garrison to surrender and been as peremptorily refused, he wasted no more time. The additional heavy siege artillery he had brought with him was already deployed on the south-east side of the house and on 12 October the bombardment resumed. One shell landed in Lady Winchester's rooms and killed one of her waiting women and a chambermaid, she herself 'very narrowly escaping'. In fact, there seems to be some doubt as to whether the marchioness was still in the building at this time. According to one account she was taken prisoner and subsequently exchanged; two others say that she got out on the day of Cromwell's arrival, 'before the siege was close laid'.[11]

By nightfall on 13 October two serviceable breaches had been made in the outer walls and the final assault began at dawn on the 14th. It was a savage business. The New House was stormed first and, in the words of the correspondent of one parliamentary news sheet, the enemy 'desired no quarter, and I believe that they had but little offered them . . . They were most of them Papists, therefore our musquets and our swords did show but little compassion.' The New House having fallen, 'our men . . . were more eager and resolute to subdue the Old . . . There the besieged showed incredible boldness, for although they knew that it was impossible for them to subsist, yet they fought it out to the last, and disputed every entry and pass with the edge of the sword.'[12] It was all over in a couple of hours and the great house, which for two years had withstood storm and siege, lay at the mercy of its captors.

'We have had little loss', remarked Cromwell in his report to the Speaker of the Commons; 'many of the enemy our men put to the sword, and some officers of quality.' Several Catholic priests found sheltering in the house were killed on the spot, and 'one Robinson, sone to the Clowne at Blackfriars Playhouse' and himself a comedian at Drury Lane in civil life was shot down by the fanatic Major Harrison as he tried to escape or, in another account, as he tried to surrender. By the laws of siege warfare, any garrison which put the other side to the trouble of taking it by storm was not entitled to expect quarter. Another casualty was 'a gallant gentlewoman', the daughter of Dr Griffiths, a rector of St Mary Magdalen in Old Fish Street, who tried to protect her father from being roughed up and, with more courage than common sense, 'fell a-railing against our soldiers, calling them Roundheads and rebels to the King'. Thus provoked, one of the troopers turned on her and beat her brains out. Other women were wounded 'who hung upon the soldiers to keep them from killing their friends'. Altogether about a hundred were killed, many in cold blood according to the royalist *Mercurius Rusticus*, and the estimate of the numbers of prisoners taken varies from two to four hundred.

Luckily the soldiers soon became more interested in plunder than slaughter. 'Eight or nine gentlewomen of rank, running forth together, were entertained by the common soldiers somewhat coarsely; yet not uncivilly, considering the action in hand.' The ladies were left with some clothes on them. Less fortunate was the architect Inigo Jones, who had been brought in to advise on the fortifications. The old man, who in happier times had been the king's surveyor and 'contriver of scenes for the Queen's dancing barne', had to be carried out wrapped in a blanket to cover his nakedness.[13]

The pillage went on all day. The Marquis of Winchester had been immensely wealthy and the treasure waiting to be seized at Basing was 'of greater value than any single garrison could be imagined, in money, plate, jewels, household stuff and riches'. People from the neighbouring farms and villages, as well as dealers from London, came flocking in search of bargains and soon the seventeenth-century equivalent of a gigantic car boot sale was in progress – the country people loading carts with 'household stuff' and provisions, while the London men snapped up plate and hangings and works of art at knockdown prices from soldiers eager to turn their loot into cash.

That evening an incendiary device which had been launched at some point during the siege and had been smouldering unnoticed in the general uproar suddenly burst into flames, and before long the whole building was ablaze. The fire burned unchecked for nearly twenty hours and by the morning of Thursday 16 October nothing but bare walls and chimneys remained of the two houses, Old and New, either of which had been 'fit to make an Emperor's court'. Tragically, some of the prisoners and a number of other unfortunates still hiding in the cellars were trapped inside and Hugh Peters, Cromwell's chaplain, says that 'we heard divers crying in the vaults for quarter, but our men could neither come to them nor they to us'.[14]

The marquis himself, who had been taken up to London, was brought to the bar of the House of Commons and committed to the Tower for the high offence of 'taking up arms against the Parliament and kingdom contrary to his duty'. The following January, 'being for the present somewhat infirm' and in want of many comforts in prison, he petitioned for his wife to be allowed to join him with some servants and other necessaries. This was granted and a weekly allowance of ten pounds, later increased to fifteen, was paid for the support of the marchioness and her children, with the stipulation that they should be raised in the Protestant religion. The Winchesters were presently given leave to go abroad and after the Restoration they retired to live at Englefield near Reading. No attempt was made to rebuild Loyalty House, of which only the foundations are now visible.

Early in November, some three weeks after the fall of Basing, the king returned to Oxford for what was to be the last time. The Prince of Wales was still in the west, but fears for his safety were growing as Cromwell and Fairfax between them continued to drive the crumbling Western Army further down the peninsula towards Cornwall. Early in the New Year Cromwell encountered the royalist cavalry at Bovey Tracey and cut them to pieces. On 19 January Fairfax stormed Dartmouth and laid siege to Exeter. When Torrington fell on 16 February the prince's anxious retinue hurried him away to Truro. Two days later he reached Pendennis Castle above Falmouth and on 2 March went on board the frigate *Phoenix*, which had been standing by in readiness for his escape, and set sail for the Scilly Isles.

After him went Ann and Richard Fanshawe, who were obliged to put 'all our present estate into two trunks' which they carried with them on board a ship commanded by Sir Nicholas Crispe, 'whose skill and honesty the master and seamen had no opinion of'. Sir Richard was forced to appease the seamen with money, but during the night 'they broke open one of our trunks and took out a bag of £60 and a quantity of gold lace, with our best clothes and linnin and all my combs, gloves and ribonds'. This was a cruel loss and Ann, six months pregnant and very seasick, was set ashore 'almost dead' on St Mary's. She went straight to bed but their quarters were primitive in the extreme, the whole house consisting of '2 low rooms and 2 little lofts with a ladder to goe up'. One of the rooms was used to store dried fish and Ann's accommodation was meaner than anything her own servants had ever had to put up with. Worse was to follow, for 'when I awaked in the morning, I was so cold I knew not what to doe, but the daylight discovered that our bed was neer swimming with the sea' a phenomenon which, as their landlord explained apologetically, only occurred at the spring tides.

The Scillonians' resources were, of course, quite inadequate to meet the demands of this sudden influx of grand strangers, and there was an acute shortage of food and fuel. 'We begg'd our dayly bread of God', wrote Ann Fanshawe feelingly, 'for we thought every meal our last.' Some provisions were sent over from France, 'but they were bad and little of them.' Finally, after three very uncomfortable weeks, the refugees sailed on to Jersey, where the Governor, Sir George Carteret, 'indeavoured with all his power to entertain His Highness and court with all plenty and kindness posible, both which the iland afforded'.

Certainly loyal Jersey was a great improvement on the Scillies. 'Ther is many gentleman's houses at which we were entertained. They have fine walkes along to their dores of double elmes and oakes, which is extream pleasant.' The people, too, were cheerful and good-natured. Their chief occupation appeared to be knitting and the Fanshawes were lodged in the house of a stocking merchant, the widowed Madame de Pommes, in the market place at St Helier. It was there, on 7 June, that Ann gave birth to her second child, a girl christened Anne. At the beginning of July the Prince of Wales left to join his mother in Paris and a month later the Fanshawes followed him to France, leaving their baby daughter behind with a nurse under the care of Lady Carteret.[15]

Back in England the Great Civil War was over. The last royal army had been defeated at Stow-on-the-Wold on 21 March and at the end of April the king slipped quietly out of Oxford on his way to give himself up to the Scots, then camped near Newark. The war in the west had also come to an end by this time. Exeter surrendered to Thomas Fairfax on 9 April and Princess Henrietta Anne 'the last of the royal offspring but the first that was in any town when it stooped to the obedience of the Parliament, came out with her governess'.

When Henrietta Maria fled from Exeter in the summer of 1644, she had left her newborn daughter in the care of Lady Dalkeith, wife of the Earl of Morton's heir. Anne Dalkeith, born Anne Villiers of the family whose fortunes were so intimately connected with the Stuarts, possessed her full share of Villiers good looks but, more importantly, was to prove herself to be strong-minded, brave, resourceful and devoted. The previous autumn the queen had written ordering her to take the princess away to a place of greater safety and she had tried to get a pass to go into Cornwall, but everyone's attention just then was concentrated on the Prince of Wales and Henrietta Anne had stayed where she was. Poor Lady Dalkeith was most unfairly blamed for this, but found a champion in Edward Hyde, who declared her to have been 'as punctual, as solicitous, and as impatient to obey the queen's directions, as she could be to save her soul'. But what could she have done? 'She could not act her part without assistance, and what assistance could she have? How could she have left Exeter, and whither have gone?'[16]

When the city surrendered Lady Dalkeith was granted a safe conduct to take her charge with her household servants, plate and money to any place she chose. Transport would be provided and the princess's future maintenance would be allowed by parliament. Meanwhile, her ladyship was given leave to send a messenger to the king for further instructions. As a result she was able to tell General Fairfax that his majesty wished her to remain with the princess at any one of his houses about London.

Lady Dalkeith had chosen Richmond Palace as being the most suitable but, for reasons undisclosed, ended up at Oatlands instead. Here she was soon faced with financial problems of an acute kind. Contrary to the assurances she had been given at Exeter, no money was forthcoming to meet the household's expenses and she found herself having to pay for the essentials out of her own pocket. Appeals to the generals of the army, to parliament and, finally, to the Committee of Justices for the County of Surrey at Kingston produced no result. But the Surrey magistrates got in touch with the Westminster committee which was now effectively running the country and on 24 May an order was issued that the Princess Henrietta's household was to be broken up and she herself brought to London to join her brother and sister, the ten-year-old Princess Elizabeth and little Henry, Duke of Gloucester, who had been in parliamentary custody ever since 1642, and were now based at St James's Palace under the guardianship of the Earl and Countess of Northumberland.

It obviously made better sense from parliament's point of view to keep all the royal children together, but Anne Dalkeith was not going to be parted from her nurseling without a struggle. She wrote again to both Houses, begging them to consider that the king himself had entrusted the child to her care, that she had 'preserved her highness – not without many cares and fears – from a weak to a very hopeful condition of health', and was best acquainted with her constitution. She was quite prepared to be subordinate to Lord and Lady Northumberland, 'and from time to time receive and follow their directions'. All she asked was to be allowed to stay with the princess 'without being any kind of burden to the parliament, or inconvenience to my Lord and Lady of Northumberland'. But if this was not possible, she went on, 'I have only these requests, that I may be reimbursed the money I have laid out during my attendance . . . and that I may have a pass to send one to his majesty to know his pleasure, without which, in honour and honesty, I cannot deliver up his child.'[17]

Evidently afraid that in the end she would be forced to deliver up the princess, Lady Dalkeith now came to the bold decision that she would somehow find a way to smuggle the child over to the queen in France. Taking only two trusted servants into her confidence, she disguised herself in a shabby gown and cloak, with a bundle of rags stuffed into one shoulder to give a hunchback appearance. Posing as a Frenchwoman and accompanied by a French valet de chambre as her 'husband', the valiant governess set out on 25 July to walk to Dover, carrying the little princess, who was passed off as a boy called Pierre. A few hours after their departure, a letter was carried back to Oatlands addressed to the gentlewomen of the Princess Henrietta's household, requesting them, as a mark of faithfulness and kindness to their mistress, to conceal her absence for as long as they could. The gentlewomen waited faithfully for three days before raising the alarm, but it seems that the authorities in London were frankly relieved to be spared the expense and responsibility of another royal child. At any rate there was no attempt at pursuit and the travellers' only anxiety was caused by the two-year-old Henrietta Anne, who insisted on informing all and sundry that her name was not Pierre but princess and that the rough clothes she was wearing were not her own. On reaching the port they sailed to Calais by the ordinary cross-Channel packet and were rapturously received by Henrietta Maria at St Germain. 'O, the transports of joy! O, the excessive consolation to the heart of the queen! She embraced, she hugged, she kissed again and again the royal infant.'[18]

The French court was charmed by the 'pretty romance' of little Henrietta's escape and Lady Dalkeith became quite a heroine. For the older Henrietta this unexpected reunion with her youngest child was the first piece of good fortune to have come her way since her arrival in France, and was especially welcome at a time when the news from England was uniformly grim. The king had been escorted up to Newcastle by the Scots, but his hopes of being able to make a separate peace with them were looking more and more unrealistic and he was now to all intents and purposes a prisoner in their hands. Oxford had surrendered in June and everywhere the defeated and dispossessed cavaliers were counting the cost of their loyalty to a ruined cause.

Some of these unfortunates chose exile and the precarious hand-to-mouth existence of the political refugee; some turned to an equally precarious life of crime at home, but most swallowed their pride and prepared to do what was necessary to come to terms with their new masters. This involved 'compounding', or buying a pardon, for past 'delinquency' – the price of forgiveness normally being the equivalent of two years' income from their estates. The business of conducting negotiations on behalf of delinquents already abroad or in prison frequently fell to their womenfolk, so that wives who had suffered the discomforts, disruption and dangers of the war years, and who in many cases had lost their homes, now found themselves called upon to appear before hostile committees and act as 'pleaders, attorneys, petitioners and the like'. Although at first glance these might appear to be unladylike activities, there could be no denying that the female sex was peculiarly well suited to the role of suppliant and William Denton, writing to Ralph Verney, made no bones about it. 'Women were never so useful as now . . . their sexe intitles them to many privileges, and we find the comfort of them more now then ever.'[19]

Richard Fanshawe evidently shared this point of view, for the Fanshawes had no sooner arrived in France than he despatched his 21-year-old wife back to England on a fund-raising expedition. It was, she recorded, 'the first manage of business hee ever put into my hand, in which I thank God I had good success'. Success in such matters always depended heavily on having friends and contacts in the right places, and Ann had been fortunate in being able to make use of the good offices of Colonel Copley, 'a great Parlement man, whose wife had formerly been obliged to our family', in procuring a pass for Sir Richard to come over and compound for £300 a year. But it was only a pretence, she added, for her father had to produce the money 'and deliver it us free'.[20]

The Verneys' problems were considerably more complicated. Sir Ralph, his wife Mary and their two older children had been living in France for nearly three years now. Much to his distress, Ralph Verney had been voted out of the House of Commons and named a delinquent, and had a sequestration order made on his estate, all, it seemed, for no worse a crime than absence – as he pointed out indignantly he had never been inside the king's quarters or done anything to assist him in his life. There was a nice legal point involved: the mere absence of a Member of Parliament from his duties had been declared to be delinquency by an order of the Commons, but this had never been confirmed by the Lords – and could such an important question be decided by anything short of an Ordinance of both Houses? Sir Ralph's friends were of the opinion that he had a case but that if he was to get the sequestration lifted without having to compound, it would have to be 'by speciall favour'.[21] They therefore urged him to send his wife over to tackle the committees, with the added recommendation that 'certainly it would not do amiss if shee can bring hir spirit to a soliciting temper and can tell how to use the juyce of an onion sometimes to soften hard hearts'.[22]

The Verneys were a devoted couple – she was his 'Mischiefe' or 'Budd', he her 'dearest Rogue' – and he was reluctant to let her undertake such an onerous task, especially as she was in the early stages of pregnancy. But after some delay because of the weather, which was 'wonderfull stormie', she sailed from Dieppe in November 1646 and was able to write on the 26th that she had 'this very instant safely arrived here in Southwark, but so extreamly weary that I can scarce hold my penn'. She found London very expensive and had to pay twelve shillings a week for lodgings – two rooms for herself and her maid up two flights of stairs, with fire, candles, washing, breakfast and 'diet' all extra. Coaches, too, were horribly dear but there was no stirring forth without one, or a chair, for 'the towne was neavor so full as tis now'.[23]

In her next letter Mary explained that nothing could be done until she was able to get a certificate from the local Buckinghamshire committee giving the reason for the sequestration, 'and then they say we must petition the committees in both Houses after we have made all the frendes that possebly we can'; although, she went on bitterly, 'the greatest freyndshipp one can expect from most here is nott to be one's enymie'. The Verneys had been counting on the support of one particularly influential acquaintance, Eleanor, formerly Countess of Sussex and now married to the parliamentarian Earl of Warwick; but when Mary went to visit her, hinting as broadly as she dared 'that itt was frends which did all', the result was disappointing, for though Lady Warwick was very civil and made kind enquiries after the family, she 'did not offer to engadge her selfe for her husband nor any other curtesy'.[24]

Mary fell ill over Christmas and it was January before she was able to report that the fever had left her, 'only itt hath brought me soe low that I am not able to goe twise the length of the chamber, and I am soe extreamly opressed with mellenchollick that I am almost ready to burst'. More than anything she longed to be back with Ralph and the children, but it was now looking very much as if she would not be able to get home in time for her confinement and the prospect of having to go through the birth on her own in London terrified her. 'To lye inn without thee, is a greater affliction then I feare I shall be able to beare', she told Ralph, 'but I shall dayly pray for patience.'[25]

She was to need all the patience she could muster in her battles with the new officialdom. The Buckinghamshire committee was being especially obstructive. 'Those villaines in the country might have given me a certifycate, if they had pleased, without putting me to this trouble,' she wrote in February; and, 'the committee in the country are very malitious and extreamly Insolent'.[26] She was still doing her best to cultivate Lady Warwick, who had now promised to speak to her husband – not that Mary expected anything to come of it: 'I neavor since I came receaved any curtesie from eyther of them.' Then, at last, at the beginning of April, the all-important certificate came through from Aylesbury. 'It is for noething but absence . . . They tell me they beleeve it must be referred to the House [of Commons] before I can come off cleare . . . It will cost us a great deale of money by the tediousness and delayes that I know we shall find there.'[27]

As she began to make preparations for her lying-in, Mary found herself coming up against another aspect of life in this strange new England of committees and church elders. Ralph had wanted her to try and find a minister who would come to the house and perform the christening ceremony in the old way, for godparents had become a thing of the past and nowadays the father was expected to bring the child to church and 'answer for it' himself. 'Truly one lives like a heathen in this place,' Mary complained, and to those accustomed to the Anglican rite the new Presbyterian-type service with its total absence of ceremonial and heavy emphasis on preaching seemed alien and almost laughable. Then again, anyone wishing to receive communion had first to be examined before the elders who, it was said, were liable to ask the most blush-making questions. In the end Ralph thought it better not to worry too much about the christening. It would not do to risk offending the authorities, and so long as the words 'I baptise thee in the name of the Father and of the Son and of the Holy Ghost' were used with the water, that was all that really mattered. But he urged his wife to take the sacrament as soon as she could, if not in church then privately at home, 'for you know not how soone you may lye in'.[28]

The baby arrived safely on 3 June and was a 'lusty boy', but the mother took a long time to recover her strength and it was nearly six weeks before she was able to get about again. Meanwhile, progress in the matter of the sequestration had come to a standstill, owing not so much to Mary's weakness – 'since I was brought to bed, I have neavor been able to sitt upp an hower at a time' – than to the current disturbed state of the political situation, for the summer of 1647 saw the beginning of the power struggle between parliament and the army. 'Every body flyes out of town,' Mary wrote on 17 June, 'some say we shall have a nue warr and some say noe . . . that which afrights me most is the delayes that these combustions is like to putt upon our busenes.' On 24 June she was telling Ralph, 'I hope you will not any longer account itt a misfortune that you were turned out of the House . . . You cannott posseble Imagion the change without you saw itt.' And, in mid-July: 'there is noe hopes of ending our busenes untell the great buseness betweene the armye and the parlyament be ended'.[29]

Mary had been meaning to go down to see to things at Claydon for some time, but it was August before she was strong enough to make the journey. Years of neglect and the damage caused by relays of soldiers billeted there had left the house in a shocking state. All the linen was quite worn out, the feather beds eaten by rats, and the fire irons, spits and other such things so rusted away that they would never be of any use again. The upholstery of the 'Musk-coloured stools' had been spoiled and the dining-room chairs were in rags. It was all very depressing, especially as the country round about was still crawling with the military – 'I protest I know nott which way we shall live if the countrey may allwayes quarter soldiers' – but Mary did have the joy of a reunion with her second son Jack, who had been considered too young to go to France with the rest of the family. Jack was now nearly seven and apart from crooked legs, caused by rickets, and an 'imperfection' in his speech, he seemed a bright, healthy little boy. 'A very ready witted child,' reported his mother, and very good company. 'He is allwayes with me from the first hower that I came, and tells me that he would very fayne goe into France to his father.' Mary felt it was high time his father took him in hand, 'for he learnes noething here' and had of course been utterly spoilt by Nan Fudd and his aunts.[30]

Mary made no secret of her poor opinion of those forlorn creatures her sisters-in-law – 'I did neavor in my life see or hear of soe much indiscretion as is amongst them' – and was thankful that four of them at least were now safely married. The sad little widowed Cary had come off best with a wealthy and good-natured man of property, and was now a lady of consequence with a large household to manage. Sue's husband, Richard Alport, was a widower, a drunkard and heavily in debt, so that she had to spend the first two years of her married life with him in the Fleet Prison. All the same, she seemed happy. 'If you did butt see him', Mary wrote to Ralph, 'you would wonder how she could be soe fond of him, butt indeed I think he is very kind to her.' 'Poore Pegg' was less fortunate, having 'soe ill a husband that I cannott give you a caracter badd enoughe of him.' The couple quarrelled constantly – their language was 'not to be matched in Billingsgate' according to William Denton – and they later separated. Pen Verney married a brute who knocked her about, but after his death she, too, did better the second time round and lived on to enjoy a comfortable old age. In 1647, therefore, only Mall and Betty had still to be settled and their future was the subject of much anxious discussion in the family. In the end Mall went to live with Cary, and the youngest, Betty, always a problem child, so cross and wilful that nobody wanted her, was sent to school. This appears to have done her the world of good, for when Dr Denton went to see her he could hardly believe the improvement in her countenance, humour and disposition which had been wrought in so short a time.[31]

After a month at Claydon spent in making inventories with the housekeeper, going through the accounts with the steward, Will Roades, and trying to find a safe place to stow the remaining valuables – she strongly suspected her sisters-in-law had been helping themselves to items of linen and furniture – Mary left for a visit to Ralph's aunt, Margaret Eure, in Leicestershire. She was back in London in October, having much enjoyed her brief holiday and feeling refreshed and ready to go into battle again. She had left Jack and the baby at Claydon. Little Ralph (christened after his father, although Ralph senior thought it an unlucky name) had appeared to be thriving well when she last saw him, but now came the news that he had died suddenly of convulsions; almost simultaneously a letter arrived from France to say that her daughter, nine-year-old Pegg, was also dead from fever and dysentery. The death of a child was an all-too-common occurrence and a grief which few families escaped, but this double bereavement was very hard to bear and both parents were distraught. Dr William Denton, who had looked after Mary during her confinement and was doing his best to comfort her now, told Ralph that she had collapsed completely for two days and nights and 'sometimes did not know her friends'.[32]

Mary was now more than ever determined to bring her business to a successful conclusion and things were at last beginning to move. On 10 November a petition was presented to the Commons in the name of 'the Lady Verney, wife to Sir Ralph Verney' praying that the matter of his sequestration be referred to a joint committee of Lords and Commons and, against most people's expectations, for there were some important papers to be considered that day and the House was unusually full, the Verney petition was read and granted. There was still plenty of anxious lobbying to be done – ''tis necessary we should have as many Lords at the hearing of our busenes as we can gett' – and Mary entertained a number of carefully chosen 'Parliament men' to dinner during December. 'This charge I am forced to be att, butt I hope I shall reape the benefitt.' The case finally came before the joint committee in the first week of the New

Year and on 6 January 1648 she was able to tell Ralph that 'thy buseness was yesterday donn according to thy hartes desire'. It seems that Lady Warwick had after all 'in some measure played her parte' by persuading her husband to attend the hearing. But, wrote Mary, 'I putt her soundly to itt for I have bin 4 or 5 times with her this week'.[33]

The case might have been won and the sequestration order lifted, but Mary was not yet free to go home. She had to make arrangements for settling with Ralph's most pressing creditors – he had inherited a legacy of debt from his father and this had grown with interest charges over the past four years. She had to write letters of thanks to everyone who had helped her in the business which had cost her 'many a troublesom and many a sadd howr', and she had some shopping to do. She was determined that Ralph should have a new suit of clothes, 'because I know you will weare any rusty old thing rather than bestow a new one upon yourselfe'. But she could begin to plan her journey. 'My dearest Rogue itt joyes my hart to think how soone I shall be with you.'[34]

Mary and Ralph were reunited in April but Mary had never been strong and now, sadly, her health began to fail. She was thirty-four when she died of 'a consumption' in the spring of 1650 leaving Ralph inconsolable. He was to outlive her by nearly half a century but, unusually, never remarried. No one could ever take the place of that 'Best of Wifes' who had solicited his business 'with all the care that posibly might be' and who, by her 'most exemplary goodness and patience', had both helped him and taught him to bear the burden of his many troubles.[35]

Another woman forced by circumstances to appear before committees and plead her cause was Isabella Twysden, wife of Sir Roger Twysden of East Peckham and also, incidentally, sister-in-law of Elizabeth Cholmley née Twysden. Sir Roger, an antiquary and scholar with a wide knowledge of ancient law and a member of that not inconsiderable body of opinion which wanted reform but not revolution, had got into trouble with parliament as early as April 1642 by helping to draw up a petition protesting against the more arbitrary proceedings at Westminster. This was considered seditious and against privilege and Sir Roger was arrested and held without charge until September, when he was released on bail but warned not to go back to Kent. In May 1643 he attempted to leave the country but was stopped, re-arrested and committed to the Counter, a particularly unpleasant prison. Meanwhile, a sequestration order had been made on his estate.

Isabella now had to start on the wearisome business of claiming her 'fifth' from the local committee, which told her that unless her husband acknowledged his delinquency and the justice of the sequestration she would get nothing. This he refused to do, maintaining that he had merely sought to uphold the liberty of the subject in strict accordance with the law. Roger Twysden himself always believed that he was the victim of the private malice of his neighbours and enemies Sir John Sidley and Sir Anthony Weldon who were said to rule all Kent, and certainly the consistently antagonistic attitude of the Kent committee (Anthony Weldon was its chairman) seems to bear this out. Sir Roger therefore appealed to the Committee of Lords and Commons for Sequestrations which sat at Westminster. He also managed to organize his transfer from the Counter to more salubrious accommodation at Lambeth Palace, where he was assigned 'a Lodging had formerly beene one of the Archbishop's Chaplayns which had three roomes and a studdy' and where, in February 1644, his wife was able to join him. After several adjournments his petition was eventually considered on 21 August and, although the joint committee seemed impressed by the arguments put forward on his behalf, the implacable hostility of the witnesses from Kent carried the day, it being felt inexpedient 'for one man's sake to disoblige a whole county'. The Westminster committee did, however, make an order that Dame Isabella should be granted her 'fifth', adding a recommendation that she should also be allowed to occupy Roydon Hall, the family home at East Peckham. But when she applied again to Kent she was refused, this time on the pretext of requiring details of the rent roll of the estate from her, though, as she pointed out, the Kent committee was better placed than she to provide it.

Back at Westminster, she appealed again to the Lords and Commons who told her that they had done as much as they could for her and advised her to re-apply to Kent. So, on 2 November, she appeared once more before the hateful Anthony Weldon, only to be told that she would get nothing until she had supplied full particulars of the value of her husband's property. This was no easy task, bearing in mind that all Sir Roger's papers had been seized and the estate had now been in the hands of the sequestrators for a year and a half. But the indomitable Isabella was not to be put off, visiting all the tenants and laboriously compiling the required return. At long last, on 31 December, she was grudgingly allowed a fifth of the rents and profits for the support of herself and her children, although the order was not back-dated as was customary but framed to begin on a date deliberately chosen to deprive her of her share of the Michaelmas rents.

The Twysdens' troubles were still far from over. Sir Roger was becoming increasingly uneasy about his woods at East Peckham, which he feared were being felled indiscriminately by the sequestrators in spite of repeated restraining orders from Westminster. In January 1645 Isabella herself petitioned the Westminster committee that the woods adjoining the mansion house of Roydon Hall 'beeing as she conceived in her fifte part . . . might bee stopt from felling', and in February she was once more on her way down to Kent armed with yet another order. Riding pillion over bad roads in all weathers and often on an undistinguished mount – Mary Verney had complained of her discomfort on the back of 'a cruell trotting horse' – these constant journeys would have been a strain on a strong young woman but Isabella, who had married at the unusually advanced age of thirty and who had borne five children in the seven years between 1635 and 1642, was now approaching forty. What was more, in February 1645 she was again heavily pregnant. 'I came to Peckham great with child, and ride all the waye a hors back, and I thank God had no hurt.' Her child, a boy christened Charles, was born on 6 March, but it was May before she was well enough to go back to London.

It was to be another two years before Sir Roger was able to return home to Roydon Hall and two years after that before he was allowed to compound at the rate of a tenth, that is two years' revenue of his estate. 'His sufferings from the first to this last,' wrote his wife, 'has ben a great hardship, being for nothing but in tending a petition to themselves [parliament].' Isabella died in 1657 at the age of fifty-two sincerely mourned by her husband, who remembered her as the saver of his estate. 'Never man had a better wife, never children a better mother.'[36]

In the strange 'world turned upside down' of the late 1640s even the greatest ladies were sometimes obliged to adopt 'a soliciting temper'. Even the redoubtable Countess of Derby, the Lady of Lathom herself, came to London in 1647 to try and persuade the House of Lords to remove her husband's name from parliament's blacklist of those royalists considered to have put themselves beyond pardon. She was philosophical about her own situation. 'I am advised to go to Lancashire', she told her sister-in-law the Duchesse de la Trémoille, 'and live there on the little which has been allowed to my children, for I receive nothing; and I hope that I may be able to make it go further if I am on the spot. One must live economically, and make the best of what one has.'[37]

Nor could husbands, even those of the highest rank, afford to be too proud and financial necessity obliged the Marquis of Newcastle to send his second wife, whom he had married in the first year of his exile, back to England 'to seek for relief'. Margaret Newcastle, born Margaret Lucas, had been one of Henrietta Maria's maids of honour and had shared the queen's adventurous journey from Falmouth to Brittany in 1644. Regarded by some as England's first woman writer, her prolific output of turgid verse, bad plays, essays, biography and science fiction, combined with a deliberate eccentricity of dress and behaviour, was to earn her the half-admiring nickname Mad Madge, but she did not impress the authorities when she applied to be granted her 'fifth'. 'I found their hearts as hard as my fortunes, and their natures as cruel as my miseries.' She was anxious it should be clearly understood that she never stood 'as a beggar' at parliament's door, 'for I never was at the Parliament House as a petitioner, neither did I haunt the committees, but one in my life'. That one was the much-dreaded Committee for Compounding, which sat at Goldsmiths Hall in the City of London. 'But', says Lady Newcastle bitterly, 'I received neither gold nor silver from them.' On the contrary, when she appeared, escorted by her brother Lord Lucas, she was told 'that by reason I was married since my lord was made a delinquent, I could have nothing, nor should have anything, he being the greatest traitor to the State'. Disdaining to plead her cause before such an ill-bred assembly, Margaret whispered to her brother to conduct her out of 'that ungentlemanly place' and left without uttering a word.[38]

Events had been moving fast during 1647, as 'the great buseness between the armye and the parlyament' referred to by Mary Verney gathered momentum. Having failed in their efforts to induce the king to accept Presbyterianism as the state religion, the Scots had finally agreed to hand him over to a delegation of parliamentary commissioners in return for £400,000 in payment for their services during the war – with a rare flick of sarcastic humour, Charles reproached them for selling him so cheap. At the end of January he was taken south to Holdenby, the great Northamptonshire mansion built by Christopher Hatton in the unfulfilled expectation of a visit from Queen Elizabeth, and there remained in a kind of not uncomfortable limbo while parliament and the army tried, in Clarendon's words, to 'determine what should farther be done'.

The king had now become a pawn in the battle between the authoritarian Presbyterians, who dominated parliament, and the so-called Independents, who favoured greater freedom and decentralization of church government and who formed a majority in the army. Nervous of the army's size and strength and the popularity of its victorious generals, parliament now attempted to begin a programme of cut-price demobilization but quickly discovered that the formidable instrument it had created was not so easily disposed of. Soldiers who were owed up to nine months' back pay were not going to go quietly and on the morning of 4 June a business-like troop of horse arrived unheralded at Holdenby to take the king into their possession. In what amounted to a *coup d'état* Cromwell and the New Model Army had effectively seized power, although they were no nearer to reaching any decision about the future.

Meanwhile the king was installed at Hampton Court where, having given his parole that he would not try to escape, he was allowed the freedom to hunt in Richmond Park, to worship as he pleased, to write letters and receive visitors. Best of all, he was able to see his children. Elizabeth and Henry had now been joined by the thirteen-year-old James, who had been left behind in Oxford. All three were staying at nearby Syon House and came over frequently to Hampton Court to play in the gardens.

Charles was also able to have several discussions with his old friend Sir Richard Fanshawe, giving him messages and instructions to be passed on to the Prince of Wales and letters to be delivered to the queen. Lady Fanshawe, too, although only recently risen from her third childbed, came three times to pay her duty, 'both as I was the daughter of his servant and wife to his servant. The last time I ever saw him', she remembered, 'when I took my leave, I could not refraine weeping. When he had saluted me, I prayd to God to preserve His Majesty with long life and happy years. He stroked me on my cheek and sayd, "Child, if God pleaseth, it shall be so, but both you and I must submitt to God's will, and you know in what hands I am in." The king then embraced Sir Richard, saying, "Thou hast ever been an honest man, and I hope God will bless thee and make thee a happy servant to my son, whom I have charged in my letter to continue his love and trust to you", adding, "And I doe promiss you both that if ever I am restored to my dignity, I will bountifully reward you both for your servise and sufferings."' 'Thus', wrote Ann sadly, 'did we part from that glorious sun that within a few months after sett, to the grief of all Christians that were not forsaken by God.'[39]

Another visitor to Hampton Court was the enterprising Jane Whorwood, 'the most loyal person to King Charles I in his miseries as any woman in England'. Jane, who would then have been in her early thirties, is described as being red-haired, 'a tall, well-fashioned and well languaged gentlewoman' with a pock-marked face. She was the daughter of William Ryder of Kingston in Surrey, former surveyor of the stables to James I and wife of Brome Whorwood, eldest son of an Oxfordshire squire. Whether or not she was separated from her husband or a widow at this time is unclear, but she appears to have been a free agent and it was presumably because of her known loyalty and family connections with the royal household that she had been chosen by Alderman Thomas Adams, leader of the City of London royalists, to deliver the first instalment of the thousand pounds in gold which had been collected for the king.

Aware that Charles, his parole notwithstanding, was now contemplating escape, Jane consulted William Lilly, the fashionable astrologer, to discover where he could go to be 'most safe'. Lilly would not let her in at first, as there had recently been a case of plague in his household. But: '"I fear not the plague, but the pox", quoth she; so up we went.' After casting his 'figure' or horoscope, Lilly gave it as his opinion that twenty miles from London, preferably somewhere in Essex, would be the king's best choice of destination. 'She like my judgement very well', he wrote, 'and being herself of a sharp judgement, remembered a place in Essex about that distance, where was an excellent house, and all conveniences for his reception.'[40] Unfortunately, before this useful information could be acted upon, Charles had already, on 11 November, absconded from Hampton Court and, in what must surely have been one of the most irresolute and badly managed escape attempts on record, ended up at Carisbrooke Castle on the Isle of Wight, believing, quite wrongly as it happened, that the Governor, Colonel Hammond, would be favourable to his cause.

The Isle of Wight had been in parliamentary hands since the first year of the war, when the Earl of Portland, then Captain of the Island, was removed by order of the House of Commons. The Countess of Portland, left behind at Carisbrooke, had vowed, 'with the magnanimity of a Roman matron', to defend the castle to the utmost extremity and, advancing to the platform with a match in her hand, had offered to fire the first cannon herself. But her bluff was called by the Mayor of Newport at the head of the local militia, reinforced by several hundred naval auxiliaries. The castle, with a garrison of twenty men and provisioned for no more than three days, was in no position to resist any kind of attack and surrender terms were quickly negotiated.[41]

The king was received politely when he arrived on the island, but was soon to make the depressing discovery that he had merely exchanged one prison for another and by the spring of 1648 was again making plans to escape. Once more Jane Whorwood was eager to be of use. Hearing that Charles had tried unsuccessfully to squeeze through the bars on his bedroom window, she visited William Lilly again, and with his help acquired a supply of aqua fortis – nitric acid – to weaken the bars and Lilly also got 'a most ingenious locksmith' named Farmer, who lived in Bow Lane, to make a saw which would cut iron bars asunder. Most of the aqua fortis was unfortunately spilt in transit but in any case, before an assault could be made on the bars, the king was transferred to new quarters on the north side of the castle. An elaborate scheme was now being hatched to get him over to the Continent – he was to cross to Portsmouth and then ride cross-country to the Medway, where Jane would be waiting on board a ship she had chartered using some of Alderman Adams's gold and which would 'waft him to Holland'.[42]

But this and various other equally optimistic plans came to nothing: far too many people were in the know, too many people had to be bribed and the enemy's intelligence was too good. Jane did, however, contrive to come over to the island later in the summer and she and Charles exchanged affectionate little notes, which have inevitably given rise to the suggestion that they had an affair. This seems highly unlikely, given the king's character and his circumstances, but her sympathetic presence may well have given him comfort and it is perhaps significant that he seems never to have mentioned her in his letters to the queen.[43]

Curiously enough, just at the time when Jane Whorwood was making such efforts for the king, another royal escape was being arranged with the assistance of another ardently loyal young woman, even more closely connected with the Stuarts. Anne Murray's father had once been Charles's tutor, her mother was governess to Princess Elizabeth and she herself may briefly have been one of Henrietta Maria's maids. Like Lucy Hutchinson and Ann Fanshawe she had been carefully trained in the accomplishments necessary for a career as a wife and mother, but Anne Murray was destined to be unlucky in affairs of the heart. When she was twenty-one she fell in love with the son of Lord Howard of Escrick, but since it was necessary for the young man to marry money their romance was ruthlessly nipped in the bud by their respective families.

After her mother's death in the summer of 1647, Anne went to live with her brother and his wife where she made the acquaintance of the Irish adventurer and royalist agent Colonel Joseph Bampfield, who 'came to see mee sometimes in the company of ladys who had beene my mother's neighbours in St. Martin's Lane, and sometimes alone'. Anne was greatly taken with Bampfield, or C.B. as she calls him in her Memoirs. 'His discourse was serious, handsome, and tending to imprese the advantages of piety, loyalty, and vertue; and these subjects were so agreeable to my own inclination that I could nott butt give them a good reception.' The colonel was evidently an experienced charmer who knew exactly how to make himself agreeable to a serious-minded and virtuous young lady. He was also married, but explained to Anne that, being engaged in the king's service, he was obliged to be in London and it was more convenient for his wife to live with her friends in the country.

The royal business which engaged Bampfield in the spring of 1648 was arranging the Duke of York's escape from St James's Palace. The king was extremely anxious that his second son should be got out of the country. 'I looke upon James's escape as Charles's preservation,' he had written in one of his letters to Bampfield which the colonel showed to Anne when he let her into the secret. The idea was to disguise young James as a girl and Anne's help was needed in getting suitable clothes made for him. Bampfield had managed, through one of his contacts in the palace, to get in to see James in private and Anne 'desired him to take a ribban with him and bring me the bignese of the Duke's waist and his length to have cloaths made fitt for him . . . When I gave the measure to my tailor,' she went on, 'to inquire how much mohair would serve to make a petticoate and wastcoate to a young gentlewoman of that bignesse and stature, he considered it a long time and said hee had made many gownes and suites, but he had never made any to such a person in his life.' Anne thought he was more right about that than he knew, 'butt his meaning was, hee had never seene any woman of so low a stature have so big a waist'. However, he went ahead and produced the required garment of mixed light and dark coloured mohair with a scarlet underskirt.

The date of the escape was now fixed for 20 April. James had already established a routine of playing hide-and-seek with his brother and sister after supper, 'and sometimes hee would hide himselfe so well that in halfe an hower's time they could not find him. His Highnese had so used them to this', wrote Anne, 'that when he wentt really away they thought he was butt att the usuall sport.' The plan worked well. When the day came James was able to persuade one of the gardeners to lend him a key to the gate which led into the park and immediately after supper, under cover of his 'usuall sport', he slipped off down the privy stairs to the garden gate where Bampfield was waiting.

Anne, meanwhile, had been installed in a house hired by the colonel on the river by London Bridge, with instructions not to wait after ten o'clock. If he and James had not arrived by then – they were coming by boat from Westminster stairs – it would mean they had been discovered and she must shift for herself. Ten o'clock struck with no sign of the fugitives and Bampfield's man who was acting as look-out became increasingly agitated. But although nervous herself, Anne refused to desert her post. 'I had come with a resolution to serve His Highnese and I was fully determined nott to leave that place till I was out of hopes of doing what I came there for.' Then, at last, she heard 'a great noise of many as I thought comming up staires, which I expected to bee soldiers to take mee'. But all was well, and James burst in shouting 'Quickley, quickley, drese mee.' His girl's clothes were a great success and Anne thought he looked very pretty in them. She had a snack ready in case his highness should be hungry and a Woodstreet cake, 'which I knew he loved', for him to take on the journey. There was no time to linger and within a few minutes they were off again, the colonel leading the 'young gentlewoman' in his unaccustomed petticoats to the four-oared barge which was to take them down-river to Gravesend and a ship to Holland.

As soon as they were out of sight Anne and her faithful maid Miriam who had waited with her, hurried away back to her brother's house. They saw nothing on the way to make them think a hue and cry had been raised and it was not until the following day that any news of the escape was 'noised abroad'. Order were sent to the Cinque Ports to stop all sailings until passengers had been examined and ships searched, but Anne heard there had been so much confusion and delay among the clerks at the House of Commons that James was safely at sea before these instructions reached the port officials.

After delivering the Duke of York safely to his sister Mary at the Hague, 'C.B.' returned to lie low in London. As soon as he arrived he sent a message to Anne Murray 'as beeing the only person who att that time he could trust' and for the next few months she ran errands and collected information for him, paying frequent private visits to his lodgings. She was aware that this highly unconventional behaviour might be misconstrued, but excused it to herself as the earnest desire she had to serve the king. On one occasion she found the colonel lying on his bed and when she asked if anything was the matter he replied that he was 'well enough', but had just heard that his wife was dead. He did not appear unduly griefstricken and seemed to want to keep the news quiet, 'lest the fortune hee had by his wife and shee enjoyed while she lived should be sequestred'. Not long afterwards he began to suggest to Anne that now he was a free man they might reasonably consider getting married since, if the king were to be restored, they could count on a joint income of about eight hundred a year. After some hesitation she accepted his proposal, but they agreed to postpone the wedding until they knew whether the king's affairs would prosper.[44]

But in the second half of 1648 the king's tragedy was moving inexorably towards its final act. Both at Hampton Court and on the Isle of Wight Charles had been conducting clandestine negotiations with the Scots, and had finally agreed to sanction the establishment of Presbyterianism for a trial period, to suppress the Independents and appoint 'a considerable and competent number of Scotsmen' to his Privy Council. In return the Scots 'engaged' to restore him to his throne, by force if necessary. A Scots invasion was intended to coincide with a series of royalist uprisings in England, but the so-called Second Civil War turned into a brief and bloody fiasco, culminating in a particularly gruesome siege at Colchester and Cromwell's annihilation of the Duke of Hamilton at Preston in August.

Parliament was still trying rather desperately to reach an agreement with the king which would have preserved the monarchy, albeit in a severely emasculated form, and curbed the power of the generals; but Cromwell and the army were now coming to the conclusion that there was only one way to deal with Charles Stuart, 'that Man of Blood' and the grandest delinquent of them all. At the end of November they brought him over to the mainland and lodged him at Hurst Castle, a gloomy little fortress built by Henry VIII on a spit of sand and shingle overlooking the Solent. Five days later a detachment of regular troops took over from the City militia at the approaches to the Houses of Parliament while Colonel Thomas Pride, said to have started his career as a brewer's drayman, supervised the forcible exclusion of all those members of the Commons regarded as opponents of the army. On New Year's Day the survivors of Pride's Purge, a body known to history as the Rump, passed an Ordinance for the trial of 'Charles Stuart, the now King of England' on a charge of treason.

Charles had been transferred to Windsor Castle just before Christmas and on 19 January he came back to his capital, which he had last seen almost exactly seven years ago. His trial opened in Westminster Hall on the following day, but many people remained deeply unhappy over the way events were moving and the army commander, Thomas Fairfax himself, was conspicuously absent when the roll call of Commissioners, or judges, was read. 'He has more wit than to be here', cried a masked lady, later identified as the general's strong-minded wife, from one of the public galleries. Her voice was quickly drowned as the clerk hurried on with his reading but on 27 January, as the President of the Court, an undistinguished lawyer named Bradshaw, embarked on his closing address, declaring that the prisoner at the bar had been brought before the court to answer a charge of high treason and other high crimes made against him in the name of the people of England, the same masked lady interrupted again, calling out: 'No, not a half, not a quarter of them! Oliver Cromwell is a traitor!' This time there was something of a commotion. Some of the soldiers present were seen to level their muskets in the direction of the gallery; there were shouts of 'Down with the whores!' and Lady Fairfax was hustled away by her companions.[45]

Across the Channel Henrietta Maria waited in a state of agonized suspense. France was just then distracted by a series of insurrections known as the Wars of the Fronde, and in the winter of 1649 Paris was surrounded by the rebel forces. The queen regent and her young son, the ten-year-old Louis XIV, had retreated to St Germain, but the Queen of England insisted on remaining at the Louvre, believing that news from London would reach her more quickly there. Her situation was one of considerable discomfort. Owing to the present state of civil unrest her pension from the French government had not been paid for several months and now, with the royal family away and the city in a state of siege, the Parisian shopkeepers were refusing to extend her credit any further. The weather had turned very cold, and with no money for fuel she and little Henrietta Anne shivered in their fireless apartments.

All this though was as nothing compared to her mental anguish. On 6 January Henrietta had written, via the French ambassador, to both Houses of Parliament and to the Lord General Fairfax begging to be allowed the consolation of going to her dearest lord the king. 'I have specified nothing to the Parliaments and the general', she told the ambassador, 'but to give me the liberty to go to see the king my lord. You must know, then, that you are to ask passports for me to go there, to stay as long as they will permit me.'[46] But her letters were never answered. They were not even opened and the sad responsibility of saying goodbye and recording the king's last messages fell to the thirteen-year-old Princess Elizabeth.

After sentence had been passed – 'that the said Charles Stuart, as a Tyrant, Traitor, Murderer and Public Enemy shall be put to death by the severing his head from his body' – they took him back to St James's for the last two days of his life. He had asked to see his children and on the afternoon of Monday 29 January Elizabeth and Harry came up from Syon House. He kissed them both and gave them his blessing and then turned to Elizabeth, who was already in tears. 'He told me he was glad I was come, and although he had not time to say much, yet somewhat he had to say to me.'

Elizabeth's recollection of her father's words, set down immediately after the event, still echoes painfully across the years. 'He wished me not to grieve and torment myself for him, for that would be a glorious death that he should die, it being for the laws and liberties of this land, and for maintaining the true Protestant religion . . . He told me, he had forgiven all his enemies, and hoped God would forgive them also, and commanded us, and all the rest of my brothers and sisters to forgive them. He bid me tell my mother that his thoughts had never strayed from her, and that his love should be the same to the last. Withal he commanded me and my brother to be obedient to her, and bid me send his blessing to the rest of my brothers and sisters, with commendation to all his friends.'[47]

'Sweetheart, you'll forget this,' said Charles to his weeping daughter. '"No" (said she), "I shall never forget it while I live." The king then took the little Duke of Gloucester on his knee and said, "Sweetheart, now they will cut off thy father's head." (Upon which words the child looked very steadfastly on him.) "Mark, child, what I say. They will cut off my head, and perhaps make thee a King. But mark what I say, you must not be a King, so long as your brothers Charles and James do live; for they will cut off your brothers' heads (when they can catch them) and cut off thy head too at the last; and therefore I charge you, do not be made a king by them." At which the child, sighing, said "I will be torn in pieces first."'

These words, according to the account printed in the *Eikon Basilike*, 'falling so unexpectedly from one so young' – Gloucester was still only eight – 'made the King rejoice exceedingly'.[48]

Charles gave the children some of his few remaining pieces of jewellery and, perhaps in an attempt to comfort them, told them once more not to grieve for him, 'for he should die a martyr'. He kissed them both again before turning away to go into his bedroom. But a fresh despairing outburst of grief from Elizabeth brought him back for one last embrace. 'Most sorrowful was this parting,' wrote an eyewitness to the scene, 'the young princess shedding tears and crying lamentably, so as moved others to pity that formerly were hardhearted'.[49]

Next morning the soldiers came for Charles Stuart just before ten o'clock and as he left the palace for Whitehall accompanied by Bishop Juxon, who stayed with him to the end, the faithful, red-headed figure of Jane Whorwood stepped forward to greet him, thus inevitably reviving the rumours that they had been lovers at Carisbrooke.[50] So it was that in those last dreadful days the only two people to risk making any open demonstration of support and sympathy were women.

News of the king's death took nearly a fortnight to reach his widow. According to her friend Madame de Motteville, Henrietta heard a rumour that Charles had actually been rescued on the steps of the scaffold by a mob of outraged Londoners and had half believed it, knowing 'how dearly the king was beloved by many who were ready still to sacrifice life and fortune in his service'. But at last the truth had to be told and her confessor, Père Cyprien de Gamache, was warned to stay behind after saying grace at dinner, 'and not to leave her Majesty, but stop and comfort her, upon the sad tidings which were likely to be brought her'. The task of actually breaking the news was undertaken by Henry Jermyn, and Père Gamache says the queen was so deeply shocked that she stood motionless as a statue, without words and without tears. 'The words and the reasons that we employed to rouse her, found her deaf and insensible.' It was not until evening, when the Duchesse de Vendôme, Henrietta's sister-in-law and close friend, came in weeping to kiss her hand that her frozen silence finally melted in a gush of tears.[51]

A few days later, when Madame de Motteville came to pay a visit of condolence, the widow took the opportunity to send an urgent message to the French queen regent. 'She commanded me to tell my queen', remembered Françoise de Motteville, 'that King Charles, her lord, whose death had made her the most afflicted woman on the wide earth, had been lost because none of those in whom he trusted had told him the truth; and that a people, when irritated, was like a ferocious beast, whose rage nothing can moderate . . . and that she prayed God that the queen regent might be more fortunate in France than she and King Charles had been in England. But above all, she counselled her to hear the truth, and to labour to discover it; for she believed that the greatest evil that could befall sovereigns was to rest in ignorance of the truth, which ignorance reverses thrones and destroys empires.'[52] It was sound and, as it turned out, prophetic advice. The only pity was that Charles and Henrietta had never followed it themselves.

CHAPTER SIX

In a Free Republic

The King being a little surprized to see a woman (no good
concealer of a secret) said cheerfully to her, 'Good woman,
can you be faithful to a distressed cavalier?' She answered,
'Yes, sir, I will die rather than discover you.'

from *Thomas Blount's Boscobel*

On the morning of the day they killed the king, the House of Commons,
what was left of it, hastily passed a measure forbidding any person
whatsoever to presume 'to declare Charles Stuart, commonly called the
Prince of Wales, or any other person to be king or chief magistrate of
England and Ireland'. There would not, after all, be much point in
cutting off the head of one king if the crown was merely passed on to the
next in line.

Charles Stuart, commonly called the Prince of Wales, was nineteen
years old when his father died and his future looked unpromising. Only
from Scotland, in fact, came a faint gleam of hope. The Scots had taken
serious umbrage over the arbitrary manner in which the English had
tried, condemned and executed the king without reference to his
Scottish subjects, and on 5 February they proclaimed his son king at the
Mercat Cross in Edinburgh in a deliberate snub to the new rulers in
London. So, when Cromwell's suppression of the last vestiges of royalist
resistance in Ireland put an end to any chance of establishing a
bridgehead there, the new king had little choice but to turn to the Scots,
even though this involved the repudiation of Montrose, who was
currently attempting to raise the Highlands for him. The gallant
marquis was betrayed into the hands of his bitter enemy, Campbell of
Argyll, and was hanged, drawn and quartered a few weeks before Charles
landed at the mouth of the Spey on 23 June 1650. But the ill-fated
Scottish venture, undertaken against the advice of most of his English
friends, was to have unhappy consequences for many others besides the
Great Montrose, one of the first to feel its effects being the king's own
sister.

After that distressing farewell scene at St James's, Elizabeth and Harry had been taken back to Syon House, but a change in their guardianship was about to come under consideration. The Earl of Northumberland, one of the small handful of peers who had opposed their father's execution, was no longer regarded as quite sound by the ruling junta, while he himself was eager to be released from his duty. Like other minders of royalty before him, he was finding it an increasingly thankless and expensive task, and in April 1649 had written to the Council of State complaining that he had for several months 'been put to maintain the Duke of Gloucester and his sister out of my own purse; and, for want of those allowances which I should have received by appointment of the Parliament, have run myself so far out of money, that I am altogether destitute of means to provide longer for them, or indeed for my own poor family'.[1]

On receipt of this *cri de coeur*, the matter of the children's custody was laid before the Commons. Elizabeth had already asked to be allowed to go to Holland to her elder sister, the Princess of Orange, but her petition, presented in the hectic weeks leading up to her father's trial, had been ignored. Now, faced with the prospect of a new and perhaps less sympathetic guardian, she renewed her request. It was debated in the Commons but this humane and, as someone pointed out, economical solution to the problem of her future, was rejected, a small majority voting that the Princess Elizabeth 'should not have liberty to go beyond the seas'. After some delay, Northumberland succeeded in persuading his sister, the Countess of Leicester, to take over from him, and Elizabeth and her little brother had come to Penshurst, 'abode of the noble Sidneys', in the middle of June.

As England was now a republic, the monarchy along with the House of Lords having been officially abolished, Lady Leicester received instructions to see that her charges were accorded no more respect than the children of any noble family. No one was to bend the knee or remain uncovered in their presence, and their meals were no longer to be served with special ceremony. The various royalist propaganda sheets were naturally full of lurid reports regarding the projected degradation of 'Bessy and Harry Stuart'; how Elizabeth was to be married to one of Cromwell's sons 'to see if they can beget a new royal progeny to heir the crown when they have killed all the rest'; while Harry would be apprenticed to some menial trade – Cromwell, it was said, had suggested setting him up as a cobbler or a brewer. In fact, although young

Gloucester came to be addressed as Master Harry by his attendants, his sister was always given her title. As for Lady Leicester, that kind and strong-minded soul continued to treat both children with as much deference as she thought proper, and the ailing Elizabeth at least with particular tenderness. The princess had never been strong, and the emotional trauma of her father's death seems to have drained the last of her reserves, for it was noticed how from that time 'she fell into great sorrow, whereby all the other ailments from which she suffered were increased'.

The quiet months at Penshurst came to an end in August 1650. News that Charles II had arrived in Scotland at the invitation of the Covenanters caused a flurry of alarm in Whitehall, where executive power now rested in the hands of the Council of State. This body had no intention of allowing either king or presbytery to be foisted on it by the Scots, but as Cromwell, recently returned from Ireland, prepared to take the army north, rumours of royalist plots in the West Country began to circulate, causing nervous members of the Council to consider the wisdom of taking further precautions. A letter signed by the President, John Bradshaw, was therefore despatched to the Governor of the Isle of Wight, informing him that 'the parliament hath appointed that the two children of the late king, who are now at the Earl of Leicester's at Penshurst, shall be sent out of the limits of the Commonwealth'.[2] At the same time, orders went to Anthony Mildmay, the new Governor of Carisbrooke Castle, that he and his wife were to collect the children from the Countess of Leicester and escort them to the island.

The party landed at Cowes on 13 August, but Elizabeth's stay in the castle where her father had spent the last year of his life was destined to be brief. It is said that she and her brother were playing bowls on the green which had been provided for King Charles when they were caught in a summer rainstorm. The princess got very wet and next day complained of the chill which led to her death. In fact, it seems pretty certain that she was already in the terminal stages of tuberculosis when she came to Carisbrooke. She took to her bed within a few days of her arrival, and although the Mildmays summoned Dr Bagnall from Newport and sent urgent requests for assistance to old Theodore Mayerne in London, Elizabeth was beyond medical help. She died on the afternoon of Sunday 8 September at the age of fourteen years and eight months, one of the saddest of the innocent victims of the Great Civil War.

Meanwhile, in Scotland, Charles was suffering acute boredom and humiliation at the hands of the extremist wing of the Covenanting party led by Argyll, who had risen to power in the aftermath of the debacle at Preston. The unfortunate young man, subjected to interminable scolding harangues by the ministers of the Kirk and repeatedly made to repent not only of his own sins but those of his father and mother before him, kept his temper with remarkable self-control, concealing a deep and steadily increasing loathing for all things Scottish behind a mask of well-bred forbearance.

His easy unaffected charm of manner was already highly developed as Anne Murray, now living in Scotland as a guest of the Countess of Dunfermline, discovered when she was presented to him at a public assembly. Charles apologized for having been so long in speaking to her, because, he said, he had not known how to thank her enough for the service she had performed for his brother. '"But"', he went on, '"if ever I can command what I have a right to as my own, there shall be nothing in my power I will not do for you." And with that', wrote Anne, 'the King laid his hand upon both mine as they lay upon my breast.' Quite overcome, she curtsied very low, murmuring that she had done nothing but her duty and had recompense enough if his majesty accepted it and allowed her his favour. Charles then kissed her on the cheek, honouring her with the same farewell he gave the other ladies present of higher rank. After which, Anne remarked with a certain wry amusement, she was treated with considerably more attention by those who had seen the king take notice of her.

Not long after this encounter, on 3 September, Cromwell and the Ironsides comprehensively defeated the Scots army at Dunbar, and Anne Murray, travelling north to Fyvie Castle with Lady Dunfermline a few days later, saw a number of badly wounded soldiers on the road. When the party halted at Kinross, Anne who, like Lucy Hutchinson, kept a good stock of 'balsoms and plaisters', set up an impromptu dressing station and, with the help of her maid and a man she employed for 'such as was unfitt for me to drese', reckoned she had been able to attend to at least threescore casualties of the battle.

Among the many wounds she saw, two stood out in her memory. 'One was a man whose head was cutt so that the [brain] was very visibly seene and the watter came bubling up.' When her assistant saw this he cried out, 'Lord have mercy upon thee, for thou art butt a dead man.' Like any good nurse, Anne would have nothing to do with such unhelpful talk, and told the patient that he need not be discouraged, 'for if itt pleased God to blese what I should give him hee might doe well enough'; although she admitted, 'this I said more to harten him up then otherways, for I saw itt a very dangerous wound. And yett it pleased God hee recovered, as I heard afftterwards.' The other case was a youth of about sixteen who had been run through the body with a rapier. 'Itt went in under his right shoulder and came outt under his left breast, and yett he had litle inconvenience by itt.' But the wound was crawling with maggots – 'so infinitt a swarme of creatures that itt is incredible for any that were nott eye witnesses of itt'. The boy's clothes had to be burnt and Anne contributed towards buying him new ones. 'Of all these poore soldiers', she wrote, 'there was few of them had ever beene drest from the time they receaved there wounds till they came to Kinrose, and then itt may be imagined they were very noisome.' One man in particular who had been shot in the arm, stank so terribly that no one else could bear to stay in the room. But a gentleman coming in by chance and seeing Anne 'nott without reluctancy' struggling to cut away the man's sleeve, 'was so charitable as to take a knife and cutt it off and fling [it] in the fire'. It was this same anonymous gentleman who presently gave the king and council an account of what she had done for 'the poore soldiers' at Kinross, representing 'the sad condittion they had beene in withoutt that releefe'. As a result, some rudimentary provision was made for the care of the wounded and the king sent Mistress Murray his thanks for her charity and a gift of fifty gold pieces.[3]

Anne spent the next two years at Fyvie Castle, where she was visited by the enigmatic 'C.B.' In spite of persistent rumours that his wife was not dead after all, Anne found it hard to believe that her lover could be deceiving her and it was not until the spring of 1653, after she had returned to Edinburgh, that she learned for certain that Mrs Bampfield was very much alive and had come to London to prove it. Fortunately, by this time Anne had been introduced to Sir James Halket who was indisputably a widower. They were married in March 1656 and appear to have been happy together, although Anne always regretted that she had not been able to bring her husband a fortune 'as great as his affection'. Her money was tied up in one of those everlasting lawsuits and consequently she carried a permanent burden of debt.

The king's large promises notwithstanding, the only compensation she seems to have received for her services to the royal cause was a single sum of £500 paid out of the Exchequer in 1661, although to be fair to

James, he did grant her a pension of £100 a year when he came to the throne. Anne, Lady Halket lived on to the end of the century, supplementing her income by boarding the motherless children of various noble families – a pious elderly widow far removed from the reckless young woman who had been prepared to risk her good name in the king's service. All the same, it's tempting to wonder if she ever entertained her charges with tales of her adventures in the bad old days of the Great Rebellion.

On 1 January 1651 Charles finally reaped the reward of his months of patient endurance when he was crowned King of Scotland with Bruce's gold circlet at Scone Abbey. Their defeat at Dunbar had disconcerted the Covenanters and, for the time being at least, loosened their stranglehold, so that Charles, helped by his personal popularity and the prestige conferred by his coronation, was able to create a fragile alliance between them and the old cavaliers, the so-called Engagers who had followed the Duke of Hamilton in 1648, and assemble an army roughly 20,000 strong for an invasion of England. But the Scots in general remained lukewarm about the project, and it was the beginning of August before they were ready to cross the border at Carlisle.

The king's plan was to cut Cromwell's lines of communication (he and his army were still in Scotland, based on Edinburgh and occupying a large swathe of the south-east) and then make for London in a desperate bid to regain the throne. It was a plan which relied heavily on the assumption that the English royalists would rise in sufficient numbers to overwhelm the enemy, but in 1651 the English royalists were a spent force. Bankrupt, battle-weary and discredited, they were in no mood to rise – especially not for a king leading an army of Scots. The only royalist magnate who did answer the call was the Earl of Derby, who emerged from his lair on the Isle of Man and attempted to rally his followers. But they were badly mauled by the local militia at Wigan and the earl himself was wounded, only narrowly escaping capture. He found temporary refuge with a family of humble Catholic tenant farmers at Boscobel, a remote house lying deep in the oak woods on the Staffordshire–Shropshire borders, and did not catch up with the king until 2 September.

Failure to attract any meaningful support, plus the fact that Cromwell and the New Model Army were now storming down from the north-east, put an end to all hope of reaching London, and Charles therefore had no choice but to continue his march on through the West Midlands. By the time they reached the loyal city of Worcester on 22 August, the army was tired, footsore and discouraged, its numbers reduced by sickness and desertion to not much more than 16,000 men. A week later Cromwell, with some 30,000 seasoned troops, had arrived and was deploying to the south and east of the town. At five o'clock on the morning of 3 September he attacked and although Charles and a hard core of royalists fought with the courage of desperation, the outcome was never really in doubt. So at least the Scots general David Leslie thought, as he prudently kept his cavalry well out of harm's way. But it was not until dusk was falling, after several hours of bitter hand-to-hand fighting in streets reeking with blood and spilled entrails, with two thousand of his men killed and many thousands more beginning to throw down their arms and the scale of his defeat starkly obvious that Charles, still miraculously unhurt in spite of having 'hazarded his person much more than any officer of his army', was finally forced to think of the best way of saving himself. Worcester marked the end of a conflict which had lasted for nine years and cost an estimated 190,000 English lives.[4] For the king it was the ultimate humiliation, for Cromwell the crowning mercy. All that was needed now to make the victory complete was the capture of the second Charles Stuart and that, it seemed reasonable to assume, would only be a matter of time.

In the circumstances it did seem perfectly reasonable to assume that Charles would be taken, perhaps within a matter of days. Having made a scrambling last minute exit from the town by way of the St Martin's Gate, he had joined forces with a group of about sixty fugitives, officers and gentlemen led by the Duke of Buckingham, the Earls of Derby and Lauderdale, and the Lords Talbot and Wilmot. They were travelling north on the Wolverhampton road with no very clear destination, conscious only of the need to put as much distance as possible between themselves and the enemy. There was some talk of trying to get back to Scotland and Charles thought his best plan would be to get to London before the news of his defeat became generally known. But the most urgent necessity was to get him under cover and into some safe hiding place until the first hue and cry had died down. It was then that Lord Derby remembered the honest Penderel brothers at Boscobel. As luck would have it, another Catholic, Charles Giffard, whose family owned the Boscobel estate, was riding with the king's party and immediately offered his hospitality and the services of his servant Francis Yates as guide. Turning off the main highway, now thronged with the mass of retreating Scots, they reached Whiteladies, another even more remote manor about half a mile from Boscobel, at four in the morning and were received by George Penderel, a servant in the house. Brothers William and Richard were hastily summoned and taken to an inner parlour, where Charles was being revived with sherry and biscuits. 'This is the King,' said Derby simply. 'Thou must have a care of him and preserve him, as thou didst me.' After this, he and the others got ready to move on before their presence attracted unwelcome attention, leaving only Henry Wilmot who, it was agreed, would stay in the neighbourhood and keep in touch with the king.

It was now beginning to get light and Charles, with his long hair roughly cut and wearing Richard Penderel's best breeches and leather doublet, was hurried out of the back door to spend the day concealed in the surrounding woods. It had begun to rain and some long, damp, depressing hours lay ahead, although his anxious guardians had found a blanket for him to sit on and Francis Yates's wife, another Penderel, brought him 'a messe of milke, and some butter and eggs' in a black earthen cup. Charles 'being a little surprized to see a woman (no good concealer of a secret) said cheerfully to her, "Good woman, can you be faithfull to a distressed cavalier?" She answered, "Yes, sir, I will die rather than discover you." With which answer His Majesty was well satisfied.' Margaret Yates thus became the first of the gallant little band of women who played such an important part in the great escape.

Charles had now abandoned his idea of walking to London and decided instead to try for Wales, where he knew he would find friends. So that evening, after eating a meal of bacon and eggs provided by Richard's wife, making friends with Richard's small daughter Nan and being charming to old Mrs Penderel, the mother of the clan, he set out on foot with Richard as his guide for the house of a Mr Woolf at Madeley about nine miles to the west, from where it should be easy to cross the Severn. But Mr Woolf, who proved to be a very nervous old gentleman, warned him that there were two companies of militia in the town guarding the ferry and examining everybody who came that way. There was nothing for it but to return to Boscobel. The king spent another day in hiding, behind the stored corn and hay in Mr Woolf's barn, and 'as soon as ever it began to be a little darkish' he and Richard prepared to set out again. Before they left Mrs Woolf made her contribution by producing a decoction of walnut leaves to give his face and hands a suitably weathered-looking tan. The trudge back to Boscobel was slow and painful, for to add to his other troubles the king's feet were rubbed raw by his ill-fitting borrowed shoes, which were now not only soaking wet but full of gravel. But since no others were available, William Penderel's wife Joan was obliged to put hot embers in them to dry them. She also washed her guest's tortured feet, found him some clean stockings and made him up a posset of thin milk and small beer, apparently considered a special treat.

That day, Saturday 6 September, was passed in the celebrated Boscobel oak in company with Colonel Carlis, another fugitive from Worcester. Charles was by now so exhausted that he slept for some of the time with his head in Carlis's lap, but he remembered that 'while we were in this tree we see soldiers going up and down, in the thicket of the wood, searching for persons escaped'. The king had now been in the neighbourhood for three days and it was high time he moved on. Already a reward of a thousand pounds, more money than most of his subjects could hope to see in a lifetime's toil, was being offered for information leading to the arrest of 'Charles Stuart, son to the late Tyrant'. The Penderels' loyalty and discretion was beyond question, but as known recusants they would inevitably come under suspicion and both Whiteladies and Boscobel were liable to be searched at any moment – as indeed they were within forty-eight hours of the king's departure. But thanks to the efficiency of the local Catholic network, another safe house had now been found and on the Sunday night Charles was conveyed on the back of an old mill-horse belonging to Humphrey Penderel the ten miles to Moseley Hall on the eastern outskirts of Wolverhampton.[5]

Moseley belonged to the Whitgreaves, another recusant family, and boasted a particularly secure secret hiding place. Here the king was reunited with Lord Wilmot, and was able to rest and recuperate for two days in the care of Thomas Whitgreave, his mother and a Catholic priest, Father Huddlestone. Better still, after so much aimless hide-and-seek, a definite plan of action had now been devised and on Tuesday night Charles was passed into the hands of Colonel Lane of Bentley Hall, a few miles to the south-east.

The Lanes were not recusants, but staunch Anglicans and king's men. However, it was not the colonel who was best placed to serve the king in his present predicament but his sister Jane, who possessed a priceless asset – a pass issued by the local parliamentary commander for herself and a manservant to travel to Bristol, where she was to visit her best friend, a Mrs Norton who was expecting shortly to be confined. This offered a heaven-sent opportunity to get Charles out of the area, and at Bristol it would surely be possible to find a ship to carry him to France.

He was to escort Mrs Jane in the character of William Jackson, son of one of the Lanes' tenants, and was at last able to exchange Richard Penderel's breeches for a decent suit of country grey cloth, 'as neer as could be contrived like the holy-day suit of a farmer's son', and those dreadful shoes for a comfortable pair of boots.

The party, which consisted of Jane, riding pillion behind 'William Jackson', Henry Lassels, 'who was [a] kinsman and had been Cornet to the Colonel in the late warrs', and Mr and Mrs Petre, Jane's sister and brother-in-law, who would be going with them as far as Stratford, was ready to set out at daybreak on Wednesday 10 September. There was one slightly awkward moment when Charles, helping Jane to mount, offered her the wrong hand and old Mrs Lane, who had come out to see them off and, not being in the secret, laughed and asked the colonel what goodly horseman her daughter had got to ride before her.

About two hours into the journey the double gelding Jane and the king were riding cast a shoe and William Jackson had to take it to the smithy. Chatting away to the smith while holding the horse's foot, he remarked that that rogue Charles Stuart deserved to be hanged for bringing in the Scots, and was told that he spoke like an honest man. Approaching Stratford, an old woman gleaning in a field by the roadside called out a warning to the travellers, 'Master, don't you see a troop of horse before you!' and John Petre at once took fright, insisting on turning back. He had been beaten up by some parliamentary soldiers on a previous occasion and would not risk it again. Charles, knowing it might be dangerous to be seen to avoid the troopers, 'begged Mrs. Lane softly in her ear, that we might not turn back but go on . . . But all she could say in the world would not do, but her brother-in-law turned quite round and went into Stratford another way.' It was all for nothing, because they met the same troop again in the town and passed through them without any difficulty.[6]

That night was spent with friends of the Lanes at the village of Long Marston and Will Jackson 'being in the kitchen in pursuance of his disguise', the cook told him to wind up the jack – a clockwork mechanism used for turning joints on the spit. This he obediently attempted but failed to do. 'What countryman are you', snapped the cook, 'that you know not how to wind up a jack?' Will Jackson, now thoroughly into his part, answered meekly that he was only a poor tenant's son from Staffordshire. 'We seldom have roast meat, but when we have, we don't make use of a jack.'[7]

After this the journey passed without further incident, and Charles with his two companions reached Abbots Leigh, home of Jane's friends the Nortons, on the afternoon of Friday 12 September. The household was a large one and the king, who had spotted at least one old acquaintance, began to be nervous of being recognized; so Jane Lane, who possessed presence of mind as well as courage, had a word with the butler, explaining that poor Will Jackson had recently been sick of an ague and was still not quite recovered, 'whereof she procured him the better chamber and accommodation without any suspicion'. She had also procured him some privacy, but John Pope the butler, previously a royal servant, did recognize him and, after some hesitation, was let into the secret. This turned out to be just as well. "I am extremely happy I know you', he told Charles, 'for otherways you might run great danger in this house. For though my master and mistress are good people, yet there are at this time one or two in it that are very great rogues.'

Having offered his services, Pope was despatched to Bristol to try and find a ship sailing either to France or Spain, 'but could hear of none ready to depart beyond sea sooner than within a month'. This was no good, since Abbots Leigh was obviously not a place to linger in, and after some discussion with John Pope and Lord Wilmot, who had followed the royal party from Bentley, the king decided to make instead for one of the smaller south coast ports. He would use Trent near Sherborne, home of the impeccably royalist Wyndham family, as his base and sent Wilmot on ahead to prepare the way.

Then, on the Monday, Ellen Norton went into premature labour, miscarried of a dead child and was very ill. This presented a serious problem. William Jackson could hardly leave Abbots Leigh without his supposed mistress and Jane could hardly leave her friend at such a moment without a very good reason. It was Charles who found the solution. 'Consulting with Mr. Lassells, I thought the best way to counterfeit a letter from her father's house, old Mr. Lane's, to tell her that her father was extremely ill, and commanded her to come away immediately, for fear that she should not otherways find him alive; which letter Pope delivered so well, while they were all at supper, and Mrs. Lane playing her part so dexterously, that all believed old Mr. Lane to be indeed in great danger, and gave his daughter the excuse to go away with me the very next morning early.'[8]

The travellers reached Trent on the morning of Wednesday the 17th, to be greeted with joyful tears by Colonel Wyndham, his wife and mother.

The two ladies had been given no more than a couple of hours' notice of the dangerous honour in store for them but, according to Anne Wyndham, the news 'did not (through the weakness of their sex) bring upon them any womanish passion, but surprized with joy, they most cheerfully resolve (without the least shew of fear) to hazard all, for the safety of the King', and they at once began to contrive how his majesty might be brought into the house without arousing suspicion.

The 'family' or household at Trent consisted of 'above twenty persons', but it was decided that only Juliana Coningsby, who was old Lady Wyndham's niece, two trusted maids, Eleanor Withers and Joan Halsenoth, and Frank Wyndham's man Henry Peters, should be told of the king's presence. The rest of the servants must be found jobs to take them out of the way at the time of his arrival and he could be concealed in Lady Wyndham's room, where he would have access to the 'secret chamber' in case of search or imminent danger. As for Jane Lane, they would call her cousin and 'entertain her with the same Familiarity as if she had been their nearest Relation'.[9] But Jane stayed only one night at Trent. Her part in the adventure was now over, and besides she had to hurry home to her father's 'sickbed', in case the deception became known.

Colonel Wyndham now began the search for a ship and within two days had struck a bargain with William Ellesden, a merchant from Lyme, who produced one Stephen Limbry, the master of a small coasting vessel, assuring the colonel that he was 'a right honest man'. It was agreed that Limbry should bring his vessel along the coast to Charmouth on the night of Monday 22 September, pick up a couple of royalist gentlemen from the beach and carry them over to France. He would be paid sixty pounds on his return, 'upon sight of a Certificate under the Passengers hands of their landing there'.

A story now had to be concocted to cover the time that Wilmot and the king would have to wait at Charmouth. So next day Henry Peters paid a visit to the Queen's Arms where, over a convivial glass of wine, he told the hostess, Margaret Wade, how his master, a very gallant gentleman, had long been in love with a young lady and was beloved in return, but although her equal in birth and fortune, her friends would not agree to the match and therefore they had agreed to steal away privately to get married. They would be coming through Charmouth on the following Monday and would need somewhere to rest and refresh themselves. Much impressed by this tale of star-crossed lovers, as well as by a generous payment in advance, Mistress Wade promised that her house and servants would be at their command.

The party duly arrived at Charmouth about sunset on the Monday evening. Wyndham's cousin Juliana Coningsby was playing the part of the bride, riding pillion behind the king, still in the part of Will Jackson. Wilmot was the bridegroom, and they were escorted by Frank Wyndham and Henry Peters. While Juliana, Wilmot and Charles waited upstairs – Limbry was not expected before midnight, at the turn of the tide – Wyndham and Peters kept watch, ostensibly in case the runaways were being pursued. The hours passed, midnight came and went and there was no sign of the long-boat which was supposed to be coming ashore. The sky began to lighten and it was obvious that something had gone badly wrong. After some discussion, it was decided that Charles, with Juliana and Wyndham, should ride on in the direction of Dorchester, while the others tried to find out what had happened to Limbry. They would meet at Bridport, the next town on the road.

It did not take long to discover what had happened to Limbry. It seemed that his wife had been at Lyme fair on the previous day and had heard the government proclamations giving details of the dire penalties attached to aiding and abetting Charles Stuart or any of those engaged with him at Worcester. So, when her husband came in that evening, calling for his sea-chest and telling her that Mr Ellesden had provided him with a freight which would be worth much more to him than if his ship were fully laden with goods, that intelligent woman promptly put two and two together. Being strong-minded as well as quick witted – 'the grey mare was the better horse' as one account put it – she proceeded to lock the doors on the unfortunate Limbry, and 'by the help of her two daughters, kept him in by force . . . and threatened him that if he did but offer to stir out of doors, she would forthwith go to Lyme and give information against him'. The more he protested, the louder her scolding grew and, since her cries and lamentations seemed likely to bring the neighbours in on them, he was forced to give up the struggle, fearing 'if he should any longer contend, both himself and the Gentlemen he promised to transport would be cast away in this storm, without ever going to Sea'. His keepers let him out in the morning and he was to be seen trudging dolefully along the shore, his footsteps still dogged by the three women who were evidently determined not to let him out of their sight.

Bridport proved to be swarming with red-coats, part of the Cromwellian expeditionary force on its way to Jersey, the last bastion of royalism, but Charles, who remained convinced that boldness was the safest policy, insisted on going on into the town. 'So we rode directly into the best inn of the place and found the yard very full of soldiers. I alighted, and taking the horses thought it the best way to go blundering in amongst them, and lead them thro' the middle of the soldiers into the stable, which I did.' Wyndham managed to reserve a room, and while they snatched a quick meal, Juliana, who was looking out of the window, saw Henry Peters ride into the yard. 'He (being beckoned up) acquainted His Majesty that the Lord Wilmot humbly petitioned him to make Haste out of that Place, and to overtake him slowly passing on the road.' After another hurried council of war, it was agreed that the only thing to do now was to return to Trent, and since neither Wyndham or Peters knew that part of the country, they took the first left hand turn they came to, hoping it would lead them back towards Yeovil and Sherborne.

Had they but known it, Charles was in greater danger at that moment than at any other time in his wanderings, for Mrs Limbry had not been the only person in Charmouth with her wits about her. The ostler at the Queen's Arms had watched the comings and goings of the mysterious strangers with considerable interest. For one thing, their horses had not been unsaddled and they themselves had sat up all night, while their servants had been several times up and down to the beach. They said they came from Exeter, but one of the horses had certainly been shod in the north. Perhaps they were noblemen escaping from Worcester, perhaps the king himself was among them, disguised as a woman. The ostler, 'a very officious and prying knave', took his suspicions to the minister, one Benjamin Westley, a zealous Commonwealth man. The minister was at his devotions and not to be disturbed, but when he did eventually emerge and heard the ostler's tale, he bustled round to the Queen's Arms, where the following exchange took place between him and the landlady. '"Why how now, Margaret? you are a maid of honour now." "What mean you by that, Master Parson?" quoth she. Said he, "Why Charles Stuart lay last night at your house, and kissed you at his departure; so that now you can't but be a maid of honour." The woman began then to be very angry, and told him he was a scurvy-conditioned man to go about to bring her and her house into trouble. "But", said she, "if I thought it was the king, as you say it was, I would think the better of my lips all the days of my life; and so, Mr. Parson, get you out of my house, or else I'll get those shall kick you out."'

Having been thus comprehensively seen off by Mistress Wade, the Reverend Westley approached the local Justice of the Peace but that worthy, thinking it most unlikely that the king should be in those parts, 'notwithstanding all the parson's bawling', and unwilling to risk making a fool of himself by stirring up the neighbourhood for a false alarm, refused to take any action. After this, Westley seems to have lost heart, but the ostler was not giving up and took himself off to Lyme, to Captain Macy who commanded a company of foot stationed in the town. It was now about midday, but Macy's reaction was immediate, and calling for his horse and quickly rounding up some men to accompany him, he galloped off to Bridport, arriving little more than a quarter of an hour after the king had left. It did not take long to pick up the scent and the huntsmen were away again, thundering down the Dorchester road barely five minutes after the quarry had turned up Lee Lane leading to the village of Bradpole.

Charles and his companions spent the afternoon getting lost in a tangle of Dorset lanes. It was almost dark when they finally fetched up at Broadwindsor, a village in the hills behind Bridport, and here they had another stroke of luck, for it turned out that the George – the only inn in the place – was kept by a man called Rhys Jones, a staunch royalist and old acquaintance of Frank Wyndham's. On being told that Wyndham and Wilmot, who was passed off as his brother-in-law, had broken their parole by being more than five miles from home and did not want to attract attention, the landlord obligingly took them up to the attics and served their supper himself. But the adventures of that amazing day were not over yet. A detachment of soldiers on their way to the coast arrived in the village demanding billets and every available room at the inn was requisitioned, leaving Charles and the others trapped upstairs. About midnight sounds of commotion, mixed with a woman's screams, rose from below, as one of the 'leaguer wenches' went into labour on the kitchen floor. The noise woke the neighbours, and the all-too-strong probability that the military would be away in the morning, leaving mother and child to be supported by the parish, brought the constable and the overseers round in a hurry, 'and with great Clamour, [to] scold and wrangle with the Souldiers, about the nursing of the Child, and charge for the maintenance of the Mother'. This went on until daybreak when order was given to march, and although it meant that no one at the George got to sleep that night, 'this quarrelsom gossipping' had provided a welcome diversion, 'exercising

the minds of those troublesom Fellows, who otherwise were likely to
have proved too inquisitive after the Guests in the House'.

The next day, Wednesday 24 September, the royal party split up.
Wilmot, accompanied by Henry Peters, set off towards Salisbury to try
for a ship at one of the Hampshire or Sussex ports, while Charles, with
Juliana and Frank Wyndham, resumed his journey to Trent. There were
no more alarms, but the hunt had come unpleasantly close. Having
failed to find any trace of the king at Dorchester, Captain Macy rode
back to Bridport in no very good temper and proceeded to institute a
search of the houses of all known royalist gentlemen in the area. One of
these, at Pilsdon, only two or three miles from Broadwindsor, happened
to belong to Colonel Wyndham's uncle, Sir Hugh Wyndham. The
soldiers turned the place inside out and then, 'violently apprehending
the whole Family, they suspect a young Gentlewoman, of exceeding great
Beauty and rare endowments, as if she had been the King disguised;
neither did they discharge her of this suspition, before they had tried by
undoubted experiment, of what Sex she was'. Perhaps it was the
opportunity afforded for experiments of this kind which explains the
persistent notion that the king, described on the Wanted posters as
'a tall Black man above 2 yards high', was going about disguised as a
woman.

Back at Trent Charles settled down peacefully to await developments
and after a few days, 'all being now quiet', the colonel's wife decided to
pay a visit to Sherborne 'to hear what news was abroad of the King'.
Towards evening, just as she was about to start for home, 'a Troop of
Horse clapt privately into the town. This silent way of entring the
Quarters, in so triumphant a time, gave a strong alarm to this careful
Lady, whose thoughts were much troubled concerning her Royal Guest.'
She was unable to discover what had brought the troopers to the district
or where they were going, and although the king laughed at their fears,
the Wyndhams redoubled their precautions, until it became clear that
this was just another party on its way to the Channel Islands with no
interest in Trent. In fact, and in spite of the Charmouth episode, it seems
that the government still had no idea of the king's whereabouts. Nor
were they even sure if he was still alive – there were several quite
circumstantial reports that he had been killed at Worcester and buried
among the slain. One of these tales had reached Trent, whereupon the
'Sectaries' in the village celebrated by lighting bonfires and ringing the
church bells, much to the mortification of the Wyndhams.

Charles stayed holed up at the manor house for the best part of a fortnight and it was not until the morning of Monday 6 October that 'his Majesty took leave of old Lady Wyndham, the Colonels Lady and Family, not omitting the meanest of them that served him. But to the good old Lady he vouchsafed more than an ordinary respect, who accounted it her highest honour, that she had three Sons and one Grandchild slain in the defence of the Father, and that she her self in her old age had been instrumental in the protection of the Son, both Kings of England. Thus', wrote Anne Wyndham, 'his Sacred Majesty . . . bad farewel to Trent, the Ark in which God shut him up, when the Floods of Rebellion had covered the face of his Dominions.'[10]

His sacred majesty was bound for Heale House near Salisbury, and since the role of mounted servant riding with his lady had served as such convincing cover on previous occasions, Juliana Coningsby was once more behind him on the pillion. His guide this time was Colonel Robert Philips of Montacute House, who 'knowing all that country perfectly well brought them in such privat ways that they came nere very few houses', although Charles, who was hungry, insisted on stopping at Mere for a meal at the George Inn. He parted from Juliana somewhere in the vicinity of Salisbury. Although she had played her part as faithfully and bravely as Jane Lane, not a great deal appears to be known about Juliana Coningsby, except that she subsequently married a man called Amias Hext of Redlinch in Somerset and after the Restoration was granted a pension of £200 a year in recognition of her services. Now, though, her usefulness was over and she turned back to Trent escorted by Henry Peters.

The king's new hostess was Mrs Amphillis Hyde, the widow of one of Edward Hyde's cousins. This 'worthy discreet Loyall Lady' had not been told who she was to entertain, but when Charles arrived at her door, just as it was getting dark, she knew him immediately, although, according to his own narrative, 'she had never seen me but once in her life, and that was with the King, my father, in the army, when we marched by Salisbury, some years before, in the time of the war; but she being a discreet woman took no notice at that time of me, I passing only for a friend of Robin Philips, by whose advice I went thither.'

Discreet she may have been, but poor Mrs Hyde was 'so transported with zeal and loyalty' that at supper, although Robin Philips's friend was sitting at the lower end of the table, she had much ado to contain herself and not carve for him first. However, 'she could not refrain from drinking to him in a glasse of wine, and giving him two larks when others had but one'. Since 'William Jackson' was still wearing the plain grey cloth suit provided for him at Bentley, this preferential treatment not surprisingly gave rise to some curious glances from Mrs Hyde's sister and brother-in-law, who were also present. Later that evening, when Charles 'discovered' himself to her, she told him she had a very safe place to hide him in, but also said 'it was not safe for her to trust any body but herself and her sister; and therefore advised me to take my horse next morning, and make as if I quitted the house, and return again about night; for she would order it so that all her servants and everybody should be out of the house but herself and her sister. So Robin Philips and I took our horses, and went as far as Stonehenge; and there we staid looking upon the stones for some time.' Colonel Philips noted that 'the King's Arithmetick gave the lie to the fabulous tale that those stones cannot be told alike twice together'. They rode back to Heale at nightfall as arranged, and Philips then went away to see if any progress had been made in the so far unsuccessful quest for a ship.[11]

As well as Colonel Philips, the escape committee now included Laurence Hyde of Hinton Daubney, a clergyman Dr Henchman, and Colonel George Gounter of Racton near Chichester and his cousin Thomas. George Gounter had been away in London raising the money to pay his delinquency fine to the Committee for Compounding and arrived home on the evening of 7 October to be met by his wife with the news that a strange gentleman calling himself Mr Barlowe was waiting in the parlour, sent by Mr Hyde on some mysterious business 'which none but yourself can decide'. Gounter at once recognized the visitor as Lord Wilmot, 'which the noble lord perceiving took the colonel aside to the window: "I see you know me" (said he) "do not own me."' But later, when Gounter escorted him up to bed, they were able to have a private conversation, Wilmot announcing impressively: 'The King of England, my master, your master and the master of all good Englishmen, is near you and in great distress; can you help us to a boat?' The colonel replied that for all he lived so near the coast, he knew very little about ships and the sea. However, 'as he thought himself bound by all obligations, sacred and civil, to do his utmost to preserve his king, so he would faithfully promise, with all possible care . . . to acquit himself of his duty'.

Having said goodnight to Wilmot, he went to his own room where he found his wife waiting up for him. Katherine Gounter had been growing progressively more uneasy and now she confronted her husband, demanding to know what was going on. Just who was this Mr Barlowe,

Dorothy Spencer, Countess of Sunderland, born Dorothy Sidney; the Sacharissa so eloquently adored by the poet Edmund Waller, she was widowed at the first battle of Newbury. (By kind permission of Earl Spencer)

Ann Fanshawe, who has left her own vivid account of her adventurous married life.
(Valence House Museum, London)

Sir Richard Fanshawe, a career diplomat whose devotion to the Stuart cause took him and his wife half way round Europe in the war years and after. (Valence House Museum, London)

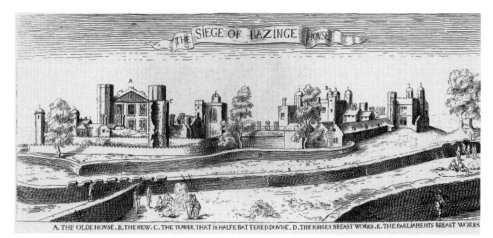

The siege of Basing House, Hampshire. (Ashmolean Museum, University of Oxford)

Charles I and Henrietta Maria, who said their last goodbyes at Abingdon in April 1644.
(The Duke of Northumberland: photograph Courtauld Institute of Art)

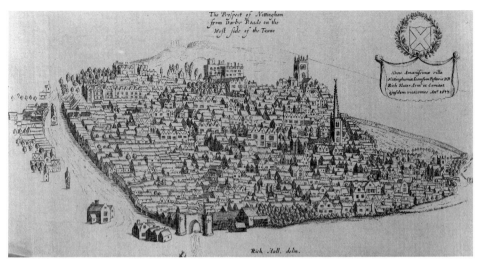

Nottingham, a vital strategic town held for parliament by John Hutchinson against the royalists of neighbouring Newark. (Nottingham County Council: Leisure Services)

A view of Nottingham from the River Trent by Jan Siberechts. (Lord Middleton: photograph The Paul Mellon Centre for Studies in British Art)

Charlotte Stanley, the redoubtable Countess of Derby, who commanded the garrison of Lathom House during an epic three-month siege in the spring of 1644. (V & A Picture Library)

Roaring Meg – a 'morter peece' similar to the one whose granadoes frightened the defenders of Lathom House from their meat and sleep. (Hereford City Museum)

Mary Verney, one of the numerous wives called upon to act as 'pleaders, attornies, petitioners and the like' for delinquent husbands in exile or in gaol. (Sir Ralph Verney, Bt: photograph Courtauld Institute of Art)

Jane Lane, the young Staffordshire woman who risked her life to help Charles II escape after the disaster of Worcester Fight. (By courtesy of the National Portrait Gallery, London)

Jane Lane riding pillion behind Charles, who is disguised as her servant 'Will Jackson'. (By courtesy of the National Portrait Gallery, London)

and what exactly was his business? Gounter tried to reassure her, telling her 'it was nothing concerning her, or that would anyways damnify her'. But she would not be put off. 'She was confident there was more in it than so, and enough she doubted to ruin him and all his family; "and in that", said she, "I am concerned", breaking out into a very great passion of weeping.' Defeated, the colonel took his candle and went back to Lord Wilmot to ask if he might tell his wife the whole. He could vouch for her loyalty and integrity, but without Wilmot's allowance she should know nothing. 'No, no; by all means acquaint her with it', said his lordship hastily, so Gounter, 'coming into his chamber unfolded the business, wiped the tears off his lady's eyes, who, smiling, said: "Go on and prosper; yet I fear you will hardly do it." "However," said the colonel, "I must endeavour, and will do my best, leaving the success to God Almighty." His lady deporting herself during the whole business, with so much discretion, courage, and fidelity, that (without vanity be it spoken) she seemed, her danger considered, to outgo her sex.'

Despite his doubts, and after a couple of false starts, Gounter succeeded in freighting a bark from Francis Mansel of Chichester, a merchant in the French trade, and Charles spent his last night on English soil at Hambledon, on the chalk downs above Portsmouth, in the house of George Gounter's sister Ursula. 'Alighting at the door, the colonel led them in, Lord Wilmot following, the king putting Colonel Robert Philips before him, saying, "Thou lookest the most like a gentleman now". Coming in, the colonel's sister met him; they all saluted her. She brought them into a little parlour where was a good fire. This was about candle-lighting. Wine, ale and biscuits were presently set before them with a very cheerful countenance, as though the king's presence had some secret influence upon her, who suspected nothing less than that a king was present.' However, when Ursula Symonds's husband appeared, having clearly spent the day 'playing the good fellow at an ale-house in the town', that honest man looked with deep suspicion at Charles's cropped hair, wanting to know whether he was not 'some round-headed rogue's son'.

The next morning, Tuesday 14 October, the king left for Brighthemston (Brighton) and a rendezvous with Francis Mansel and Nicholas Tattersall, master of the *Surprise*. This time all went well, and at two o'clock in the morning of 15 October Charles and Wilmot went on board the *Surprise*, then lying in Shoreham harbour waiting for the tide to lift her off the mud. High water was at seven and about an hour later, Gounter, who was still waiting nearby with the horses in case anything went wrong at the last minute, saw them hoist sail. It was midday before the little vessel was out of sight and the colonel finally felt free to go home to his long-suffering wife, whose concurrence had made such a difference to the success of the business. He had not been gone out of the town two hours, 'but soldiers came thither to search for a tall black man, 6 feet 2 inches high'.[12]

Charles had been on the run for six weeks and Thomas Blount, author of *Boscobel; or, the Complete History of His Sacred Majesty's Most Miraculous Preservation after the Battle of Worcester*, one of the first accounts to be printed after the Restoration, considered it was indeed a miracle 'that so many men, and (which is far more) so many women should faithfully conceal so important and unusual a secret'. The king, too, kept faith with all those devoted men and women who had so willingly risked their lives for him, carefully laying false trails when asked questions about his adventures. Following the news of his safe arrival in France, a number of reports, more distinguished for the creative imagination of their authors than for their accuracy, began to appear in the English press, but there was a description of how the King of Scots had travelled to Bristol riding before a lady on one horse. This was close enough to the facts to alarm the Lane family and make them decide to get Jane out of the country. She arrived in France in December and Charles rode out from Paris to welcome her, greeting her with an affectionate kiss and calling her his 'Life'. Jane was presently offered a home in the household of the Princess of Orange, and after the Restoration the House of Commons voted her £1,000 to buy herself a jewel and granted her a pension of £1,000 a year, which was paid with 'fair regularity'. She married Sir Clement Fisher, a family friend and neighbour of the Lanes at Bentley, and lived on until 1689, a tough old lady who reputedly refused to make a will, saying that her hands should be her executors as she intended to spend everything she had.

In the autumn of 1651 Charles faced nine years of exile, boredom, frustration and penury, but he had none the less been a good deal more fortunate than some of the other members of that little party of fugitives which had paused briefly at Whiteladies in the early hours of 4 September – the most prominent victim being the Earl of Derby, who, together with Charles Giffard, had surrendered to a Captain Oliver Edge a little beyond the town of Newport later that same day.

Lord Derby was taken to Chester Castle as a prisoner of war, but quickly discovered that he was to be treated as a war criminal and on

30 September was tried by court martial on charges of having invaded the realm with intent to levy war on the parliament and Commonwealth of England, and to set up Charles Stuart, a declared traitor and enemy of the people as king. The outcome of these proceedings was never in any doubt. Other considerations apart, James Stanley had made too many personal enemies since the outbreak of war, and memories of the burning of Lancaster and the sack of Puritan Bolton were still green – it was no coincidence that his execution was to take place in Bolton market-place.

In his last letter to his wife, written on 12 October, three days before his death, the earl warned her that a force under Colonel Duckenfield, the Governor of Chester, would soon be coming to demand the surrender of the Isle of Man. 'And however you might doe for the present', he wrote, 'in time it would be a grievous and troublesome business to resist, especially them that at this hour command three nations.' Duckenfield was a gentleman who might be trusted to deal fairly and therefore, despite his great affection for the island, the earl's advice to his lady was that she should submit to the will of God and make the best conditions she could for herself, 'and children, and servants, and people, and such as came over with me, to the end you may go to some place of rest where you may not be concerned in warr . . . I conjure you, my dearest heart,' he went on, 'by all those graces which God has given you, that you exercise your patience in this great and strange trial. If harm come to you, then I am dead indeed.'[13]

Whatever the countess might have been planning to do, and there is some reason to believe that she had been hoping to use the Isle of Man as a bargaining counter in an attempt to save her husband's life, she was frustrated by the prompt action of Manx patriot William Christian, also known as Illiam Dhone, or Blond William. Christian, a member of one of the most influential island families and already at loggerheads with the Stanleys over the land tenure question, had no intention of allowing the heroine of Lathom to put his people at risk by staging a repeat performance at Castle Rushen. He therefore mustered the community leaders, and as soon as the commonwealth forces landed at Ramsey a deputation of Manxmen formally surrendered to Colonel Duckenfield without reference to her ladyship.

The countess was back in London by the spring of 1652 and told her sister-in-law in a letter dated 25 March that 'there is nothing left for me but to mourn and weep, since all my joy is in the grave. I look with astonishment at myself that I am still alive after so many misfortunes; but

God has been pleased to sustain me wonderfully, and I know that without his help I could never have survived all my miseries.'[14] She continued to survive, fighting financial battles with the new regime – 'after incredible trouble, I have succeeded in getting my marriage contract allowed, which settled on me besides my dowry, certain estates bought with my own money' – finding suitable husbands for her daughters, worrying about the education of her two younger sons and pursuing a long-standing feud with her eldest son and his wife.

After the Restoration she lived mostly in London, taking a close interest in court matters and writing gossipy letters to her sister-in-law in France. She was present at the coronation of Charles II, 'and it was a very grand and imposing sight, the lords in the robes proper for the occasion, which are very becoming. It is the last thing of the kind I shall see; and I have greatly desired to witness it, having prayed with tears to be permitted to behold this crown on the head of His Majesty.'[15] Charlotte, Countess of Derby died at Knowsley in March 1664, a great lady of the old school whose life had been governed by the rigid concepts of honour and duty epitomized by the mottoes borne by her mother's and her husband's families: *Je maintiendrai* and *Sans changer*.

Another of the prisoners taken at Worcester was Sir Richard Fanshawe who, although a non-combatant, had followed the king from Scotland. The Fanshawes had been through some extraordinary adventures since that autumn day at Hampton Court in 1647 when they had said a sad farewell to Charles I. Carrying his letters to the queen they had then set out for France by way of Portsmouth where, 'walking by the sea side about a mile from our lodging, 2 ships of the Dutch then in war with England shot bulletts at us so near that we heard them wiss by us'. Ann had called to her husband to make haste and began to run. 'But he altered not his pace, saying if we must be kill'd, it were as good to be kill'd walking as running.' Having escaped this danger, they embarked the next day, and on their way collected the baby girl they had left in Jersey. They returned to England on family business the following year and Ann gave birth to another son in June. In November Sir Richard was summoned back to France and sent for his wife to follow him, bringing £300 of his money. She spent six weeks in Paris on this occasion, 'with delight in very good company'. The queen was gracious, Princess Henrietta's governess, now Countess of Morton, was very kind, and Lady Fanshawe had the satisfaction of seeing her own little daughter 'admitted to play with the princess dayly, and presented with many toys'.

At the beginning of 1649 Ann was once more on her travels. 'My husband thought it convenient to send me into England again there to try what sums I could raise both for his subsistence abroad and mine at home.' Richard Fanshawe had now been appointed Treasurer of the Navy by Charles II and in February left for Ireland, where Prince Rupert was commanding that part of the fleet which had recently declared for the king. Royalist prospects in Ireland just then looking fairly hopeful, Sir Richard again sent for his family to join him. 'We went by Bristoll very cheerfully towards my North Star, that only had the power to fix me', wrote Ann. She was also pleased because she had been able to sell land worth £300 a year 'to him that is now Judge Archer, in Essex, for which he gave me £4,000, which at that time I thought a vast sum. But be it more or less, I am sure it was all spent in 7 years' time in the King's servise; and to this hour I repent it not.'

The Fanshawes were reunited at Cork, where 'for six months we lived so much to our satisfaction, that we begun to think of making our abode there during the war, for the country was fertil and all provisions cheap, and the houses good, and we were placed in Red Abby, a house of Dean Boyle's in Cork'. Lord Ormonde had a good army, everybody was very civil and the country seemed quiet, until, on 15 August, Cromwell landed near Dublin and at the beginning of October Cork revolted against the royalist Confederates.

It was midnight when Ann heard the great guns go off. 'Hearing lamentable scricks [shrieks] of men and women and children, I asked at a window the cause. They told me they were all Irish, stript and wounded, turned out of the town, and that Collonel Jeffreys, with some others, had possessed themselves of the town for Cromwell.' Sir Richard was away in Kinsale, and his wife hurriedly scribbled him a warning, with a promise that she would secure his papers. The letter was entrusted to a faithful servant, 'who was lett down the garden wall of Red Abby, and sheltered by the darkness of the night he made his escape'.

Ann, who was pregnant again and in considerable pain from a broken wrist, now proceeded to pack up her husband's cabinet, 'with all his writings, and near £1,000 in gold and silver, and all other things both of clothes, linnin, and household stuff that were portable and of value'. At three o'clock in the morning she went out into the 'unruly tumult' in the town to find Colonel Jeffreys who, 'whilst he was loyall', had received several good turns from Richard Fanshawe, to ask him for a pass to allow her to leave for Kinsale. Fortunately this was forthcoming and, returning through 'thousands of naked swords' to Red Abbey, Ann hired a neighbour's cart, 'which carryed all that I could remove', and with her sister, her little daughter Nan, three maids and two menservants, 'sett forth at 5 a clock . . . having but 2 horses among us all, which we ridd on by turnes'. In this sad condition they left Cork, having had to abandon possessions worth £100, and travelled the ten miles to Kinsale 'in perpetuall fear of being fetched back'.

From Kinsale they went to Limerick to await further instructions from the king. By this time Ormonde's army had dispersed, he himself fled to Holland and the remaining Confederates left to fend for themselves; while Cromwell 'went through as bloodily as victoriously, many worthy persons being murdered in cold blood, and their familys quite ruined'. The Fanshawes stayed three nights with Lady Honor O'Brien, where Ann saw a ghost – a woman in white, with red hair and pale, ghastly complexion who leaned in through the bedroom window, spoke aloud in an unearthly tone, saying three times "a horse", and then vanished with a great sigh 'more like wind than breath'. Terrified, she woke her husband, who reassured her by telling her that such apparitions were quite common in Ireland, 'and we concluded the cause to be the great superstition of the Irish and the want of that knowing faith that should deffend them from the power of the Devill'.

After this unsettling experience they moved on to Galway, more from necessity than choice, for the plague had been so bad there the previous summer that the place was almost depopulated. But Sir Richard, who had now been ordered to Spain, had heard there was a Dutch ship in the harbour bound for Malaga and, in any case, with Cromwell 'pursuing his conquests at our backs', it seemed preferable to risk falling into the hands of God than the hands of man.

They were to stay in a merchant's house by the seaside, but as no horses were being allowed into the town, they had to pick their way on foot under the walls, 'over which the people during the plague, which was not yet quite stopped, had flung out all their dung, dirt, and rags'. When they finally reached their lodgings, the owner of the house, standing at the door, said: '"You are welcome to this desolate city, where you now see the streets grown over with grass, once the finest little city in the world." And indeed it was easy to think so,' wrote Ann, 'the buildings being uniformely built and a very fine markett place, and walkes arched and paved by the sea side for their merchants to walk on, and a most noble harbour.'

In spite of being almost eaten alive by fleas during the night, the family survived their sojourn in plague-stricken Galway, although, when they said goodbye to their kind host, they were somewhat startled to be told that he had buried nine persons out of his house within the last six months. They sailed for Spain at the beginning of February and, apart from the fact that the ship's captain was a drunken, foul-tempered man, 'a Dutchman, which is enough to say, but truly I think the greatest beast I ever saw of his kind', the voyage began smoothly, with prosperous winds. But Ann Fanshawe's adventures were by no means over. 'When we had just passed the Straights [of Gibraltar], we saw coming towards us with full saile a Turkish galley well man'd, and we believed we should all be carried away slaves', for although their ship had sixty guns she was so laden with merchandise that they were useless. However, the captain decided to fight rather than risk losing his valuable cargo and cleared the deck as well as he could. The women were sent below and ordered to keep out of sight, but when Ann discovered that 'this beast captain' had locked her in her cabin she was furious, and knocked and called until at last one of the crew came and opened the door. She, 'all in teares', bribed him with half a crown to give her his tarred coat and rough woollen cap, 'and putting them on . . . I crept up softly and stood upon the deck by my husband's side as free from sickness and fear as, I confess, from discretion . . . By this time the 2 vessels were ingaged in parley and so well satisfyd with speech and sight of each other's forces that the Turk's man-of-war tacked about and we continued our course.' When Richard Fanshawe looked round and saw his wife, 'he blessed himself and snatched me up in his armes, saying, "Good God, that love can make this change!" And though he seemingly chid me, he would laugh at it as often as he remembred this voyage.'

They landed safely at Malaga early in March, reaching Madrid on 13 April. They spent the summer there, while Richard tried unsuccessfully to extract a loan for his master from Philip IV, and Ann gave birth to a daughter who lived for only fifteen days. In September they set out on their travels once more, making for San Sebastian where they hired a ship to take them to Nantes. This was very nearly the end of them. 'We had not been a day at sea before we had a storme begun, that continued 2 days and 2 nights in a most violent manner, and being in the Bay of Biskey, we had a hurricane that drew the vessel up from the water, which neither had saile nor mast left.' It was not until the afternoon of the third day that they were finally driven aground by the tide about four leagues from Nantes and could hardly believe they had escaped with their lives. 'We often kissed each other as if yet we feared death, sighed, and complained of the cruelty of the rebells that forced us to wander. Then we again comforted ourselves in the submitting to God's will . . . and remembered the lott and present suffering of our king.'[16]

They reached Paris in November 1650 and in the New Year Ann returned to England after an odyssey which had lasted nearly two years. She settled in London with her two surviving children, four-year-old Nan and Richard, born in 1648. In June there was another baby, a girl christened Elizabeth. Ann now faced a period of acute anxiety about her husband, who had gone to join the king in Scotland. After the battle of Worcester she waited in agony for three days to hear if he was dead or alive before a messenger arrived with a letter telling her that he was a prisoner and 'very civilly used'.

He was taken to Whitehall, where he was kept in close confinement for the next ten weeks. 'During this time of his imprisonment', wrote Ann, 'I failed not constantly to goe when the clock struck 4 in the morning, with a dark lanterne in my hand, all alone and on foot from my lodging in Chancery Lane . . . to White Hall in at the entry that went out of King's Street into the bowling ground. There I would goe under his window and softly call him. He, that after the first time expected me, never failed to put out his head at first call. Thus we talked together, and sometimes I was so wet with rane that it went in at my neck and out at my heels.'

Ann was, of course, actively engaged in lobbying everyone from Cromwell downwards in the effort to secure her husband's release, and as he was by this time suffering from a bad case of scurvy, she was advised by the Lord General Cromwell himself to bring the Council of State 'a certificate from a physition that he was really ill'. This she did and, as a result Richard was released on bail of £4,000 at the end of November to the 'unexpressable' joy of his wife.

In March of the following year the Fanshawes were able to rent a house in Yorkshire, 'where we lived an innocent country life, minding only the country sports and the country affairs'. Sir Richard occupied his time by translating Luis de Camoens's long poem 'The Lusiads' from the Portuguese, while Ann found her neighbours 'very civil and kind upon all occasions, the place plentyfull and healthfull and very pleasant'. This happy, peaceful interlude ended abruptly in July 1654 when their eldest and 'most dearly beloved' daughter died of smallpox to the bitter grief of both parents. Two more babies had been born since Richard's release from prison and another was on the way, but Nan, the dear companion of all their travels and sorrows, had been special and 'we both wished to have gone into the grave with her'. Yorkshire being no longer either healthful or pleasant, the Fanshawes came south again and in November, when the High Court of Justice ordered Richard to stay within a five mile radius of London and appear before it once a month, they moved back into Ann's old lodgings in Chancery Lane.[17]

The shooting war may have finished at Worcester, but the war of ideas continued and one of the leading protagonists was that self-appointed resident thorn in the flesh to governments of all complexions, Free-born John Lilburne the Leveller. Lilburne had first been in trouble with the authorities as early as the 1630s and had enlisted in the parliamentary army at the outbreak of the war. He had been captured by Prince Rupert's men at Brentford in the autumn of 1642 and taken to Oxford Castle, where he and some other prisoners were accused of the treason of bearing arms against the king. Lilburne contrived to smuggle some letters out to his wife Elizabeth in London, and as soon as the House of Commons heard about his plight they issued a declaration of *lex talionis* – that is, a threat of retaliation in like manner on royalist prisoners of war. This was not published until Saturday 17 December and since the trial of the Oxford men had been set for the following Tuesday, there was not a moment to be lost. Elizabeth Lilburne, who had been presenting herself almost hourly at the bar of the Commons, undertook to deliver the Speaker's warning herself and, although with child, she immediately set out on the hazardous winter journey to Oxford, reaching the royalist headquarters in the nick of time after 'so many sad and difficult accidents, to a woman in her condition, as would force tears from the hardest heart', and having, by her 'wisdome, patience and diligence', saved her husband's life. Although reprieved, Lilburne's exchange was not arranged until the following May. He returned home to find that Elizabeth had secured him the offer of a lucrative government post worth £1,000 a year; but to her 'extraordinary grief' he refused to accept it, saying he must 'rather fight for eightpence a day till he saw the liberties and peace of England settled'.[18]

Lilburne ceased to fight for eightpence a day at the end of April 1645, when he left the army rather than take the Covenant, and embarked on a stormy career of opposition to all enemies of freedom and justice no matter where they were to be found. Inevitably he soon came into collision with the Presbyterian faction in Parliament and in August he was committed to Newgate. According to custom, his wife, who was pregnant again, was allowed to join him there, but during her absence the agents of the Stationers' Company, who ransacked the family home in Petty

France looking for dangerous and seditious writings, also made off with the precious childbed linen which had been carefully put away ready for her lying-in.[19] It is possible to feel extremely sorry for Elizabeth Lilburne.

In 1646 her husband was in trouble again, this time with the House of Lords, for uttering scandals against the Earl of Manchester and publishing pamphlets which did 'falsely and scandalously, and maliciously, charge the Peers in Parliament with Tyranny, Usurpation, Perjury, Injustice, and Breach of the Great Trust in them reposed'. This time Free-born John landed in the Tower, there to remain at their lordships' pleasure, and this time Elizabeth was not allowed to be with him, unless she agreed to become a prisoner too. John found their enforced separation a very great hardship. 'God hath so knit in affections, the hearts and soules of me and my wife, and made us so willing to help bear one another's burdens, that I professe, as in the sight of God, I had rather you should immediately beat out my braines, then deprive me of the society of my wife.'[20] His wife, though, was never one to stand idly by. Armed with a petition demanding justice for J. Lilburne, she and 'some scores of Gentlewomen her friends', picketed the House of Commons day by day until her visiting rights were restored and a Commons committee was appointed to look into her husband's case.

Although every precaution had been taken by the authorities, it was impossible to prevent John Lilburne from writing and publishing a steady stream of pamphlets. 'Liberty Vindicated Against Slavery', 'An Anatomy of the Lords Tyranny', 'London's Liberty in Chains' and 'The Charters of London' (which campaigned for reform of the City's government), and 'The Oppressed Man's Oppressions Declared' all appeared during the time when he was supposedly deprived of writing materials.

In February 1647 Elizabeth, too, was arrested for distributing her husband's books and ordered to appear with him before the Committee of Examinations (the direct descendant of the Star Chamber). John at once challenged the authority of the committee; if it were not a court of justice it had no right to try them, if it were, then he demanded a public hearing. At this point his exasperated wife interrupted, exclaiming in a loud voice: 'I told thee often enough long since, that thou would serve the Parliament, and venter thy life so long for them, till they would hang thee for thy paines, and give thee Tyburn for thy recompence, and I told thee besides, thou shouldst in conclusion find them a company of unjust, and unrighteous Judges, that more sought themselves, and their own ends, then the publique good of the kingdome.'[21]

This outburst might have had unfortunate consequences but, to his credit, John sprang to his wife's defence, asking the chairman 'to pass by what in the bitternesse of her heart being a woman she had said'. He also pleaded that as her husband he was responsible for her actions and the committee, possibly reluctant to take on two Lilburnes at the same time, decided to ignore Elizabeth as a scolding woman and discharged her.

Elizabeth Lilburne was luckier than Mary Overton, wife of Richard Overton, Lilburne's fellow dissident, pamphleteer and operator of one of the secret presses. Mary had been caught in the act of helping to stitch together the loose sheets of one of Overton's inflammatory works and, with her six-month-old baby in her arms, was 'most inhumanely and barbarously dragged headlong upon the stones through all the dirt and mire in the streets, and by the way was most unjustly reproached and vilified . . . with the scandalous, infamous names of wicked Whore, Strumpet, etc. and in that contemptible, barbarous manner was cast into the most reproachful Gaole of Bridewell'.[22]

Elizabeth continued to haunt army headquarters at St Albans and Kingston petitioning for her husband's release, but he remained in the Tower and took no part in the so-called Putney Debates of the autumn, when a number of Leveller proposals – religious toleration, freedom of speech, manhood suffrage and annual parliaments – as set out in 'The Case of the Army Truly Stated' and 'The Agreement of the People', were inconclusively discussed. Although the conditions of his confinement were progressively eased, he was not finally released until August 1648 and the Lilburnes enjoyed a brief period of domestic tranquillity.

In February 1649 Honest John was once more on the attack with 'England's New Chaines Discovered', followed in March by 'The Second Part of England's New Chaines', which in effect accused the new Council of State of having replaced one kind of despotism with another. The new regime, still feeling its way in the aftermath of the king's execution, and nervous of both economic unrest among the civilian population and disaffection in the lower ranks of the military, where Leveller sentiment was strong, reacted by arresting Lilburne and three other leading dissidents. This in turn resulted in a series of demonstrations and petitions for their release, in which 'divers well-affected Women inhabiting the City of London . . . and places adjacent' played a prominent part.

Five hundred of these women, variously described as 'the lusty lasses of the levelling party', 'the bonny Besses in the sea-green dresses' (sea-green being the colour associated with the Levellers), 'Ladyes errant of the Sea-green order', and 'the Civill-Sisterhood of Oranges and Lemmons and likewise the Mealy-mouth'd Muttenmongers Wives', laid siege to the House of Commons for three days at the end of April. On the second day the Serjeant-at-Arms was sent out to tell them that 'the Matter they petitioned about, was of an higher concernment than they understood . . . and therefore desired them to go home, and look after their own business, and meddle with their huswifery'. This provoked a mini-riot, and the women's tongues 'pelted hail-shot against the Members as they passed to and fro, whilst the Souldiers threw in squibs under their Coats'. One of the members was mobbed by angry women, who 'rounded him in a Ring' and refused to let him go until he swore he was for the liberties of the people; another, who rashly suggested they should stay at home and wash dishes, was told they scarcely had any dishes and were hardly sure of keeping those they had. Someone else remarked that it was strange for women to petition. 'It was strange that you cut off the king's head' came the reply, 'yet I suppose you will justify it.' At last, on 25 April, twenty ladies of the 'Sea-green order' were admitted to the lobby with their petition, which is said to have borne ten thousand signatures. It was not a very dignified occasion, the soldiers on guard throwing squibs and cocking their pistols in a threatening manner as they pushed and jostled the petitioners down the stairs, but one of the women, undismayed, grabbed hold of Oliver Cromwell by his cloak, demanding to be given 'those rights and freedoms of the Nation, that you promised us'.[23]

Although the agitation continued into the first week of May, John Lilburne stayed in prison. In October he was put on trial for treason and acquitted amid an explosion of popular rejoicing. But the Levellers, outmanoeuvred and overpowered by Cromwell and the other army commanders, were already in decline, and although he continued to enjoy considerable public support, Free-born John was destined to spend most of the rest of his life in exile or in captivity. He died in 1657, leaving only his debts and his reputation.

In one of his earlier pamphlets, John Lilburne had written that all men and women were 'by nature all equal and alike in power, dignity, authority, and majesty', but his exhausted widow, facing destitution with three small children and a newborn baby dependent on her, cannot have felt very equal, and for all her steadfast loyalty to her husband would surely have exchanged some of the fine words and high principles for the basic security of food and shelter for her little family. Indeed, as she later admitted, if Cromwell had not come to her rescue with a pension of two pounds a week, they would have starved. The Lord Protector was a powerful friend, and after his death Elizabeth transferred her supplications to his son, begging wistfully that after seventeen years' sorrows, she might have 'a little rest and comfort' with her fatherless children. Her pension was continued – it was still being paid in the spring of 1660 – and Parliament remitted the crippling fine imposed on John in 1651, but for how long Elizabeth survived to enjoy her rest and comfort does not appear to be recorded.[24]

The death of Oliver Cromwell in September 1658 produced an upsurge of somewhat premature euphoria among royalists at home and abroad, but it did bring an immediate improvement in the fortunes of the Fanshawe family. Both Richard and Ann had been seriously ill during the summer and in August had been given leave to go to Bath to recuperate. They were living in a rented house in Hertfordshire when they heard the news of Cromwell's death, upon which Richard 'began to hope that he should get loose of his fetters in which he had been seven years'. This was achieved through the good offices of the Earl of Pembroke, who wanted a reliable escort to take his eldest son to France and offered the job to Richard, promising to get his bail bonds cancelled in exchange. This offer was joyfully accepted and the following April Richard, now established in Paris, summoned his wife to join him.

Ann could not go without a pass, but when she applied to the High Court of Justice she was brusquely told that since her husband had got his liberty by a trick, she and her children should not stir on any condition. Ann was not so easily defeated, but she could not risk being turned back at the port, for then the authorities would 'ever after be more severe upon all occasions and it might be very ill for us both'. And yet she was all ready to go by the next tide, and if she only had a pass could be across the Channel before anyone knew she was gone. These thoughts suggested a plan.

'At Wallingford House the office was kept where they gave passes. Thither I went, in as plain a way and speech as I could devise. Leaving my maid at the gate, who was much a finer gentlewoman than myself, with as ill mien and tone as I could express, I told a fellow I found in the office that I desired a pass for Paris to goe to my husband. "Woman," says he, "what is your husband, and your name?" "Sir," sayd I, with many courtesys, "he is a young merchant, and my name is Anne Harrison." "Well," says he, "it will cost you a crown." Sayd I, "That is a great sum for me, but pray put in a man, my mayd, and 3 children." All which he immediatly did, telling me that a Malignant would give him £5 for such a pass.' So far so good, but the really tricky part was still to come. Clutching the precious pass, Ann hurried back to her lodgings, 'and with a penne I made the great H of Harrison 2 ff, and the 2 rr's an n, and the i an s, and the s an h, and the o an a, and the n a w, so compleatly that none could find out the change.' With all speed she hired a barge, and at six o'clock that night the little party was on its way downriver to Gravesend and from there by coach to Dover; 'where, upon my arrivall the searchers came and, knowing me, demanded my pass, which they were to keep for their discharge. When they had read it they sayd, "Madam, you may goe when you please." "But," says one, "I little thought they would give pass to so great a Malignant, especially in such a troublesome time as this."' From then on all was, literally, plain sailing. Ann, with her children and two servants, went on board the packetboat at about nine o'clock at night and by eight the following morning had 'landed safe, God be praised, at Callais'.[25]

In November the king came to visit his mother, who was then living at Colombes just outside Paris, and the Fanshawes went there to meet him. Charles was his usual charming self, telling Ann that if God pleased to restore him to his kingdoms, her husband 'should partake of his happiness in as great a share as any servant he had', and asking her a great many questions about England. By now things were at last beginning to move his way, and in the spring of 1660 Richard and Ann were at Breda to hear the good news of his forthcoming return home.

Early in May they went 'with all the court' to the Hague, where Charles and the rest of the royal family were being lavishly entertained and 'the business of state took up much time'. Then, on 23 May, the Fanshawes were commanded to wait on the king in his own ship, the *Naseby*, hastily rechristened the *Royal Charles*. 'The King imbarked about 4 of the clock, upon which we sett saile,' wrote Ann, reliving that never to be forgotten day. 'But who can sufficiently express the joy and gallantery of that voyage – to see so many great ships, the best in the world; to hear the trumpetts and all other musick; to see near an hundred brave ships saile before the wind with their wast clothes and streamers; the neatness and cleanness of the ships; the strength and jollity of the mariners; the gallantry of the commanders; the vast plenty of all sorts of provisions – but above all, the glorious Majesties of the King and his 2 brothers was so beyond man's expectation and expression. The sea was calme, the moon shined at full, and the sun suffered not a cloud to hinder his prospect of the best sight, by whose light and the merciful bounty of God hee was sett safely on shore at Dover in Kent upon the 25th of May, 1660.'[26]

When, four days later, Ann stood in the crowd in the Strand to see the king's entry into his capital, 'surely the most pompous show that ever was, for the hearts of all men in this kingdom moved at his will', it seemed like the best fairy-tale ending, and that surely all those who had suffered so long and so patiently for the royal cause would now live happily ever after.

Postscript

... his wife, who thought she had never deserv'd so
well of him [Colonel Hutchinson] as in the endeavours
and labours she exercis'd to bring him off, never
displeas'd him more in her life.

Lucy Hutchinson

All things considered, the Restoration of Charles II was remarkable for
the degree of magnanimity shown by the returning king. Indeed, some
people, who had seen their lives and fortunes wrecked by their loyalty to
his cause, felt he had gone rather too far with his policy of peace and
reconciliation. But there was one group which had put themselves
beyond the reach of pardon. Generous though he might appear towards
his enemies and anxious to let bygones be bygones, the second Charles
Stuart could not be seen to forgive the men who had killed his father.

Of the fifty-nine signatories of Charles I's death warrant, eighteen were
already dead, but that did not save the three principal culprits from the
vengeance of the more blood-thirsty Cavaliers. The corpses of Cromwell,
his son-in-law Henry Ireton, and John Bradshaw, the President of that
infamous court, were taken out of their tombs in Westminster Abbey to
be exposed all one day on the gallows at Tyburn. The heads were then
cut off and stuck on spikes on the facade of Westminster Hall – grisly
relics which were left to moulder there for another twenty years.

Of the forty-one surviving regicides, fifteen fled abroad, some to
Puritan New England, others to Germany, the Low Countries and
Switzerland. Some surrendered, hoping for mercy. With certain
exceptions, the king had offered an amnesty to those active republicans
who gave themselves up within forty days of his return. Some, a few,
neither fled nor surrendered, but waited quietly to be arrested, ready to
stand by their past actions and to die for them.

One of these would-be martyrs was Colonel John Hutchinson, but he
had reckoned without his wife who, seeing that 'he was ambitious of being
a publick sacrifice', resolved, for the first time in their married life, to

challenge his authority, 'for she sayd she would not live to see him a prisoner'. Since he had not been named among the first list of exceptions to the amnesty, many of the colonel's well-wishers were urging him to surrender in order to preserve his estates, but his wife 'would by no meanes heare of it', in spite of being accused of obstinacy in not giving him up. Having made him promise that he would not dispose of himself without her knowledge, she made it her business 'to sollicite all her friends for his safety', and decided to compose a letter in his name to the Speaker of the Commons expressing sorrowful repentance for the crime his 'ill-guided judgement' had led him into, and begging the House not to exclude him 'from the refuge of the King's most gracious pardon'.

Lucy had been on the point of taking this carefully crafted production to the colonel for his signature, when a friend came in to tell her that 'the House was that day in a most excellent temper towards her husband; whereupon she writt her husband's name to the letter, and ventur'd to send it in, being us'd sometimes to write the letters he dictated, and her character not much different from his'. Lucy's brother, Allen Apsley, was also busy pulling strings for the colonel and did not hesitate to use 'some artifice in engaging friends for him', while 'all the old sage Parliament men, out of very hearty kindnesse, spoke and labour'd very effectually to bring him cleare off'.[1] It could, of course, be argued in his favour that he had taken no part in public life during the Interregnum and had sat in the Convention Parliament which had recalled the king. It may also very likely have been the opinion in government circles that a man of such proven integrity would make an inconvenient martyr.

In the event, although expelled from parliament and disqualified from ever again holding any public office, John Hutchinson was included in the Act of Oblivion and Indemnity which presently passed both Houses and returned to Owthorpe a free man. He was not, however, a happy man, being 'not very well satisfied in himselfe for accepting the deliverance' – especially as the trials and executions of his fellow regicides proceeded. 'And his wife, who thought she had never deserv'd so well of him as in the endeavours and labours she exercis'd to bring him off, never displeas'd him more in her life, and had much adoe to perswade him to be contented with his deliverance; which, as it was eminently wrought by God, he acknowledg'd it with thankfullnesse, but while he saw others suffer, he suffer'd with them in his mind.'[2]

Although he was reluctantly brought to accept his escape as being part of the 'wonderfull over-ruling providence of God', the colonel could not be persuaded to give evidence against any of his former friends and his position remained precarious, as Lucy discovered the next time she had occasion to come to London. A kinsman of hers, 'fallen into the wicked Councells of the Court', came to visit her one evening, and having been 'so freely drinking as to unlock his bosome', told her that the king had recently been heard to say 'that they had sav'd a man, meaning Collonell Hutchinson, who would doe the same thing for him he did for his father, for he was still unchang'd in his principles, and readier to protect than accuse any of his associates'.

Lucy's visitor went on to suggest that if she would 'impart aniething that might shew her gratitude, she might redeeme her famely from ruine'. Her husband was known to have been intimate with the leading figures of the Commonwealth and she must have heard many of their secrets. But Lucy, like the colonel, scorned to become an informer and pleaded ignorance – 'she knew nothing of State managements, or if she did she would not establish her selfe upon any man's blood and ruine'. After all this, 'naturall affection working at that time with the gentleman', he advised her to persuade her husband to leave the country while he still could, for 'it was determin'd that if there were the least pretence in the world, the Collonell should be imprison'd and never be left loose againe'. Lucy passed on this warning, which was endorsed by several of his other friends, but John Hutchinson would not go out of England, saying 'this was the place where God had sett him and protected him hitherto, and it would be in him an ungratefull distrust of God to forsake it'.[3]

The inevitable knock on the door finally came in October 1663, when the colonel was arrested on the pretext of complicity in a minor uprising in Yorkshire, known as the Derwentdale Plot, where, according to Lucy, the discontented people had been stirred up to insurrection by *agents provocateur* 'to restore the old Parliament, gospell Ministry and English liberty . . . and abundance of simple people were caught in the nett; whereof some lost their lives, and others fled. But the Collonell had no hand in it, holding himself oblieg'd at that time to be quiet.'[4]

John Hutchinson was taken to the Tower, where he was held in close confinement for six months without charge or any prospect of a trial. But he 'was not at all dismay'd'. On the contrary, he told his wife that this captivity was the happiest release in the world to him, for he now considered himself freed from any obligations of honour or conscience laid upon him by the Act of Oblivion. He therefore forbade her to make any further applications to anybody on his behalf and she, 'rememb'ring how much she had displeas'd him in saving him before, submitted now to suffer with him according to his owne will'.[5] This did not mean that she was prepared to submit to the intimidation of officialdom and when Sir John Robinson, the corrupt Lieutenant of the Tower, tried to keep her from seeing her husband, Lucy, whose own father had once held that position, wrote Sir John 'a smart letter' threatening to expose some of his dishonest practices. As a result, she was positively entreated to come to visit and was able to spend a whole day alone with her husband.[6]

Not long after this, in May 1664, Colonel Hutchinson was transferred to Sandown Castle on the Kent coast, 'a lamentable old ruin'd place', and so damp that even in summer 'the Collonell's hat-case and trunkes, and every thing of leather, would be every day all cover'd over with mould'. Lucy did her best to get permission to stay in the castle with him, but when that was refused she took lodgings in Deal and walked to and fro every day from the town 'with horrible toyle and inconvenience'. The colonel, for his part, endured the discomforts of his situation so cheerfully 'that he was never more pleasant and contented in his whole life', and once, when his wife was lamenting his condition, told her he would not have been without this affliction, for if he had flourished while the other people of God suffered, 'he should have fear'd he had not bene accounted among His children'.[7]

Lucy had now taken a house in Deal, intending to bring the rest of her family to live there for the winter, and towards the end of August was obliged to go back to Owthorpe to collect the younger children and attend to matters at home. She left 'with a very sad and presaging heart', her greatest dread being that while her husband remained so near the coast he might be shipped off abroad to some 'barbarous place' during her absence. But when she went away he seemed 'exceeding well and chearfull', and so confident of seeing Owthorpe again that he gave her detailed instructions about the planting of trees and other things to do with the house and garden, so that she was quite unprepared for the news which reached her in September.

It seemed that the colonel had been walking by the seaside and came back feeling 'aguish, with a kind of shivering and payne in his bones, and went to bed and sweat exceedingly'. This 'feaverish distemper' with violent sweats, continued intermittently for a week. He remained conscious and sensible, but grew steadily weaker, until 'the Lord of Hosts sent his holy Angells to fetch him . . . up to his everlasting and blessed rest above; this being the Lord's-day, about 7 of the clock at night, the eleventh day of

September, 1664.' His two eldest sons took his body to London and from there he was brought home to Owthorpe 'with honor to his grave through the dominions of his murtherers, who were asham'd of his glories, which all their Tyrannies could not extinguish with his life'.[8]

John Hutchinson had sent 'a kind message' to his wife, bidding her 'as she is above other weomen, shew her selfe in this occasion a good Christian, and above the pitch of ordinary weomen'. Poor Lucy tried very hard to live up to his expectations and remember that she was 'under a command not to grieve at the common rate of desolate woemen'. It is not known exactly when she began to write her famous *Life* of her husband, but it seems reasonable to suppose that it was at least started soon after his death, at a time when she was 'studying which way to moderate my woe'.[9] The date and place of her death is not known either, although she was still living in 1675 in a world which she must surely have found an increasingly alien place.

Lucy Hutchinson and Ann Fanshawe never met (though Lucy's royalist brother, Sir Allen Apsley, was Governor of Barnstaple when the young Ann was eating cherries there in the summer of 1645), but in spite of the ideological gulf which divided them, those two brave and devoted women would have had a good deal in common. The Fanshawes' fortunes had not prospered quite as much as might have been expected after the Restoration. 'The King promised my husband he should be one of the Secrettaryes of State', wrote Ann indignantly, 'and both the now Duke of Ormond and Lord Chancellor Clarendon were witnesses of it. Yet that false man made the King break his word for his own accommodation, and placed Mr. Morice, a poor country gentleman of about £200 a year, a fierce Presbiterian and one that never saw the King's face.'[10] Lucy, too, blamed Edward Hyde, now Earl of Clarendon, for the persecution of her husband.

In 1661 Richard Fanshawe was sent on a special mission to Portugal to complete the arrangements for the king's marriage to Catherine of Braganza, and in 1662 his family packed up once again and set out for Lisbon, where he had been appointed ambassador. Two years later he was transferred to Madrid where, in August 1665, Ann's last child and only surviving son was born and where, the following June, her husband died at the age of fifty-eight.

Ann now had to undertake the last of her many pilgrimages, to bring home her husband's body, 'with my son of but 12 months old in my armes, 4 daughters, the eldest but 13 years of age' and a family of some threescore servants. She was forced to sell £1,000 worth of their own plate and spend the Spanish queen's parting present of 2,000 doubloons to pay for the journey, but left Madrid without owing so much as a shilling in debt, 'which every embassador cannot say'. She arrived in London in November to be welcomed 'by very many of the nobility and gentry, and also by all my relations in these parts', and on 23 November waited on the king and delivered her accounts to his majesty. 'He was pleased to receive me very gratiously and promissed me they should be paid, and likewise that His Majesty would take care for me and mine.' Unfortunately, like so many royal promises, this was not worth very much and Ann had to wait three years for the money owed to her – the arrears of her husband's salary and the nearly £6,000 he had laid out in the king's service. Even then she did not get it all, ending up over £2,000 out of pocket.

Ann Fanshawe found it hard not to be bitter. 'How far this was from a reward, judge ye, for near 30 years suffering by land and sea, and the hazard of our lives over and over . . . and the expence of all the monyes we could procure, and 7 years imprisonment, with the death and beggery of many eminent persons of our family, that when they first entered the King's service had great and clear estates.' But, as she told her son, 'God did hear, and see, and help me, and brought my soule out of trouble; and by his blessed providence I and you live, move, and have our being, and I humbly pray God that that blessed providence may ever supply our wants.'[11]

Providence notwithstanding, Lady Fanshawe had to live quite carefully to keep within her income. She took a lease of a house in Lincoln's Inn Fields but found it very difficult at first to adjust to her new circumstances. 'As it is hard for the rider to quit his horse in a full career, so I found myself at a loss that hindred me settling in a narrow compass suddenly, though my small fortune required it.' Sometimes she just wanted to renounce the world and 'shut myself up in a house for ever from all people' as a sacrifice to her husband's memory. But she had to think of her children, who were all young and unprovided for, and 'resolved to hold me fast by God, untill I could digest in some measure my afflictions'.[12]

Ann Fanshawe survived her husband by fourteen years, joining him at last in his vault in Ware parish church, near his old family home Ware Park in Hertfordshire, on 20 January 1680. For Ann, as for Lucy Hutchinson, life without her beloved partner had been an empty affair. 'We never had but one mind throughout our lives,' she wrote; 'our souls were wrapped up in each other . . . whatever was real happiness, God gave it me in him.'

Notes

CHAPTER ONE

1. Thomas Smith to Sir John Pennington, 11 February 1642, CSP Dom. 1641–3, pp. 282–3
2. Giovanni Giustinian to the Doge and Senate, 23 November 1640, CSP Venetian, vol. 25, p. 96
3. Same to same, 30 November 1640, CSP Venetian, vol 25, p. 97
4. Same to same, 14 December 1640, CSP Venetian, vol. 25, p. 103
5. Same to same, 8 February 1641, CSP Venetian, vol. 25, p. 119
6. Memoirs of Madame de Motteville, ed. M. Petitot (Paris, 1824), pp. 98–9
7. Clarendon, *History of the Rebellion*, vol. 1, ed. W. Macray, p. 329
8. Ibid., pp. 337–8
9. Giovanni Giustinian to the Doge and Senate, 24 May, 21 June, 28 June 1641, CSP Venetian, vol 25, pp. 151–2, 163, 166
10. *Lettres de Henriette-Marie de France à sa Soeur Christine*, ed. H. Ferrero, pp. 58–9
11. Clarendon, vol. 1 p. 338
12. Giovanni Giustinian at the Doge and Senate, 17 January 1642, CSP Venetian, vol. 25, pp. 275–6
13. de Motteville, p. 109
14. Rosalind Marshall, *Henrietta Maria the Intrepid Queen*, p. 94
15. *Memoirs of Sophia, Electress of Hanover*, p. 13
16. William Newton to Francis Newton, 18 March 1642, Henry Ellis, *Original Letters*, Series 2, vol. 3, p. 295
17. Henrietta Maria to King Charles, 17 March 1642, *Letters of Henrietta Maria*, ed. M. Everett Green, pp. 52–4
18. Same to same, March 1642, *Letters*, pp. 55–7
19. Same to same, 16 April 1642, *Letters*, pp. 60–1
20. Same to same, May 1642, *Letters*, pp. 63–5
21. Zuanne Zon to the Doge and Senate, 19 May, 26 May 1642, CSP Venetian, vol. 26, pp. 59 and 64; *Lives of the Princesses of England*, vol. 6, M. Everett Green, p. 131
22. Henrietta Maria to King Charles, 11 May 1642, *Letters*, pp. 68–9
23. Same to same, 11 May 1642, *Letters*, p. 70
24. Henrietta Maria to Madame St Georges, 28 May 1642, *Letters*, pp. 72–3
25. Henrietta Maria to King Charles, 4 June 1642, *Letters*, p. 77
26. Same to same, 9 June 1642, *Letters*, pp. 78–80
27. Same to same, 24 July 1642, *Letters*, p. 92
28. Giovanni Giustinian to the Doge and Senate, 18 July 1642, CSP Venetian, vol. 26, p. 103
29. Same to same, 25 July 1642, CSP Venetian, vol. 26, p. 109
30. Zuanne Zon to the Doge and Senate, 3 September 1642, CSP Venetian, vol. 26, p. 138
31. Giovanni Giustinian to the Doge and Senate, 5 September, 26 September, 17 October, 31 October 1642, CSP Venetian, vol. 26, pp. 142, 162, 178, 189
32. Henrietta Maria to King Charles, 23 July 1642, *Letters*, p. 91
33. Same to same, 13 September 1642, *Letters*, pp. 110–11
34. Same to same, 11 September 1642, *Letters*, p. 109
35. Same to same, 31 July 1642, *Letters*, pp. 93–4
36. Giovanni Giustinian to the Doge and Senate, 26 September 1642, CSP Venetian, p. 162; Henrietta Maria to King Charles, 8 September 1642, *Letters*, pp. 102–3

37. Henrietta Maria to King Charles, 19 September 1642, *Letters*, pp. 112–17
38. Same to same, 9 October 1642, *Letters*, p. 122
39. Same to same, October, 8 December 1642, *Letters*, pp. 123, 147
40. Same to same, 6 October 1642, *Letters*, pp. 126–7
41. Same to same, 11 October 1642, *Letters*, pp. 128–30
42. Zuanne Zon to the Doge and Senate, 3 December 1642, CSP Venetian, vol. 26, p. 204
43. Henrietta Maria to King Charles, 1 December 1642, *Letters*, p. 145
44. Same to same, 8 January 1643, *Letters*, pp. 152–3
45. Elizabeth of Bohemia to Sir Thomas Roe, May 1642, *Letters of Henrietta Maria*, p. 59
46. Strickland, *Lives of the Queens of England*, vol. 8, pp. 95–7; de Motteville, pp. 113–14; de Gamache, *Memoirs*, p. 350; *A True Relation of the Queenes Majesties Return out of Holland By one in the same Storme and Ship with her Majestie*; Zuanne Zon to the Doge and Senate, 11 February 1643, CSP Venetian, vol. 26, p. 239
47. Henrietta Maria to King Charles, 25 February 1643, *Letters*, pp. 166–8; de Motteville, p. 114
48. Gerolamo Agostini to the Doge and Senate, 13 February 1643, CSP Venetian, p. 240
49. Lord Fairfax to Henrietta Maria, Kingdom's Weekly Intelligencer, 14 March 1643, printed in *Letters of Henrietta Maria*, p. 170
50. *Letters of Henrietta Maria*, p. 171
51. *Mercurius Aulicus*, 17 January 1643, printed in *Letters of Henrietta Maria*, pp. 165–6
52. Henrietta Maria to King Charles, 30 March, 8 April 1643, *Letters*, pp. 177, 182
53. Same to same, 5 May 1643, *Letters*, p. 194
54. Gerolamo Agostini to the Doge and Senate, 5 June 1643, CSP Venetian, p. 280
55. Henrietta Maria to King Charles, 23 April 1643, *Letters*, pp. 189–90
56. Same to same, 23 April 1643, *Letters*, p. 188
57. Same to same, 14 May 1643, *Letters*, pp. 200–1

58. Same to same, 27 May 1643, *Letters*, pp. 209–10
59. Same to same, 18 May 1643, *Letters*, pp. 204–5
60. Same to same, 27 May 1643, *Letters*, pp. 208–9
61. Same to same, 27 June 1643, *Letters*, pp. 221–2
62. de Motteville, p. 115
63. C.V. Wedgwood, *The King's War*, pp. 207–8

CHAPTER TWO

1. *Memorials of Thomas, Lord Fairfax, An English Garner*, ed. E. Arber (London, 1903), vol. II, pp. 380–1
2. Ibid., p. 383
3. Ibid., pp. 385–6
4. *Mercurius Rusticus* No. 5, printed in Edmund Ludlow, *Memoirs*, ed. C.H. Firth (Oxford, 1894), vol. I, app. II, p. 447
5. The background to the Procession Picture is discussed in Chapter I of *The Cult of Elizabeth*, Roy Strong (Thames & Hudson, 1977)
6. Ludlow, *Memoirs*, vol. I, p. 51
7. *Mercurius Rusticus*, Ludlow, *Memoirs*, vol. I, app. II, p. 448
8. Ibid., pp. 448–51
9. Ludlow, *Memoirs*, vol. I, pp. 77–9
10. A.R. Bayley, *The Great Civil War in Dorset* (Taunton, 1910) p. 401
11. Mark Girouard, 'Wardour Old Castle', *Country Life*, 14 February 1991, pp. 44–9, 21 February 1991, pp. 76–9
12. Sir John Bankes to Mr Green, MP, 21 May 1642, printed in *A Dorset Heritage*, Viola Bankes (The Richards Press, 1953), p. 30
13. John Hutchins, *History and Antiquities of Dorset* (1861), vol. I, p. 495
14. Ibid., pp. 504–5
15. Ibid., pp. 505–7
16. Bayley, *Civil War in Dorset*, p. 270
17. Hutchins, *History and Antiquities of Dorset*, vol. I, p. 508
18. Ibid., p. 509
19. Bayley, *Civil War in Dorset*, p. 306
20. Hutchins, *History and Antiquities of Dorset*, vol. I, p. 495
21. George Bankes, *The Story of Corfe Castle* (London, 1853), p. 245

22. *Letters of Lady Brilliana Harley*, ed. T. Lewis (Camden Society, no. 58, 1854), Brilliana to Ned, 4 June 1642; J. Eales, *The Harleys of Brampton Bryan* (CUP, 1990), p. 144

23. Eales, *The Harleys*, pp. 146–7

24. Harley, *Letters*, p. 170, Brilliana to Ned, 20 June 1642

25. Ibid., pp. 182–3, Brilliana to Ned, July 1642; p. 180, same to same, 19 July, 1642

26. Ibid., p. 178, Brilliana to Ned, 15 July 1642; p. 180, same to same, 19 July 1642

27. Ibid., p. 181, Brilliana to Ned, 19 July 1642

28. Ibid., p. 175, Brilliana to Ned, July 1642; p. 169, same to same, 17 June 1642; Eales, *The Harleys*, p. 146; Harley, *Letters*, p. 178, Brilliana to Ned, 15 July 1642

29. Harley, *Letters*, p. 160, Brilliana to Ned, n.d.; p. 175, same to same, July 1642

30. Ibid., p. 187, Brilliana to Ned, 25 December 1642

31. Ibid., pp. 187–8, Brilliana to Ned, 28 January 1643

32. Ibid., pp. 188–9, Brilliana to Ned, 14 February 1643

33. Eales, *The Harleys*, p. 165

34. Harley, *Letters*, pp. 204–6, Brilliana to Ned, 30 June 1643; p. 202, same to same, 11 June 1643

36. Hist. Manuscripts Commission, *Marquis of Bath MSS* (London, 1904), vol. 1, p. 8, Henry Lingen and others to Brilliana, Lady Harley 26 July 1643

36. Ibid., p. 8, Lady Harley to Henry Lingen, 26 July 1643

37. Ibid., p. 9, Sir William Vavasour to Lady Harley, 28 July 1643

38. Ibid., p. 23, Priam Davies' narrative

39. Ibid., pp. 11–12, Lady Harley to Sir William Vavasour, 30 July 1643

40. Ibid., p. 12, Lady Harley to Sir William Vavasour, 31 July 1643; p. 12, same to same, 30 July 1643

41. Ibid., p. 23, Priam Davies' narrative

42. Ibid., pp. 24–5, Priam Davies' narrative

43. Ibid., pp. 14–18, King Charles I to Brilliana, Lady Harley, 21 August 1643; Lady Harley's petition to King Charles, August 1643; Lord Falkland to Lady Harley, 30 August 1643

44. Ibid., p. 7, narrative of the siege of Brampton Bryan

45. Ibid., pp. 26–7, Priam Davies' narrative

46. Eales, *The Harleys*, p. 177, Brilliana to Sir Robert Harley, 24 September 1643

47. Harley, *Letters*, p. 209, Brilliana to Ned, 9 October 1643

48. Hist. Man. Commission, *Bath*, vol. I, pp. 27–8, Priam Davies' narrative

49. Ibid., pp. 32–3

50. Eliot Warburton, *Memoirs of Prince Rupert and the Cavaliers* (1849), vol. I, pp. 391–2

51. D.R. Guttery, *The Great Civil War in the Midland Parishes* (Birmingham, 1951), pp. 35 and 40

52. Bayley, *Civil War in Dorset*, p. 129; A.L. Rowse, *The Early Churchills* (Macmillan, 1956), p. 33

CHAPTER THREE

1. S.R. Gardiner, *History of the Great Civil War* (Longmans Green, 1886), vol. 1, pp. 218–9 and note; Gerolamo Agostini to the Doge and Senate, 21 August 1643, CSP Venetian, vol. 27, p. 8

2. Revd G.N. Godwin, *The Civil War in Hampshire* (Southampton, 1904), pp. 121–2

3. J. Washbourn, *Bibliotheca Gloucestrensis* (Gloucester, 1825), p. lxviii

4. Washbourn, *Gloucestrensis*, p. 48; Antonia Fraser, *The Weaker Vessel* (Weidenfeld & Nicolson, 1984), p. 204; P.M. Higgins, *Women in the English Civil War*, Unpub. thesis, Manchester, 1965, pp. 31–2

5. Higgins, *Women in the Civil War*, pp. 37–8; Fraser, *The Weaker Vessel*, p. 204; Washbourn, *Gloucestrensis*, p. xlv; C.H. Firth, 'Siege and Capture of Bristol', *JSAHR*, 4 (1925), p. 204

6. Washbourn, *Gloucestrensis*, pp. 50 and 227

7. Higgins, *Women in the Civil War*, p. 39

8. Bulstrode Whitelocke, *Memorials of English Affairs* (Oxford, 1853), vol. 1, p. 258

9. A.R. Bayley, *The Great Civil War in Dorset* (Taunton, 1910), p. 191

10. Ibid., pp. 171–2

11. Ibid., p. 188
12. D.R. Guttery, *The Great Civil War in the Midland Parishes* (Birmingham, 1951), pp. 35–6; Higgins, *Women in the Civil War*, pp. 39–40
13. Antonia Fraser, *The Weaker Vessel*, p. 221
14. P.M. Higgins, *Women in the English Civil War*, pp. 42 and 47
15. *Sydney Papers, Letters and Memorials of State . . . from the Originals at Penshurst*, ed. Arthur Collins (London, 1746), vol. 2, pp. 667–8
16. Ibid., pp. 669–70
17. Ibid., pp. 670–1
18. Edward, Earl of Clarendon, *History of the Great Rebellion*, ed. W.D. Macray (Oxford, 1888), vol. 3, p. 177
19. Henry Sidney, *Diary of the Times of Charles II*, ed. R.W. Blencowe (London, 1843), vol. 2, pp. 319–22
20. *Sydney Papers*, vol. 2, pp. 671–2
21. *Memoirs of . . . Ann Lady Fanshawe*, ed. J. Loftis (OUP, 1979), pp. 110–12
22. Ibid., p. 115
23. Henrietta Maria to the Earl of Newcastle, *Letters of Henrietta Maria*, ed. M. Everett Green (London, 1857), p. 225
24. Henrietta Maria to the Marquis of Newcastle, 15 March 1644, *Letters*, pp. 237–8
25. Same to same, 5 April 1644, *Letters*, pp. 238–9
26. Clarendon *History of the Rebellion*, vol. 3, pp. 341–2
27. Gerolamo Agostini to the Doge and Senate, 6 May 1644, CSP Venetian, vol. 27, p. 97
28. Washbourn, *Gloucestrensis*, pp. lxxxvii and 329
29. *Letters of Henrietta Maria*, ed. Green, p. 243
30. Gerolamo Agostini to the Doge and Senate, 13 May 1644 and 20 May 1644, CSP Venetian, vol. 27, pp. 99 and 101
31. Henrietta Maria to Charles, 18 June 1644 (sic), *Letters*, p. 244
32. Same to same, 28 June 1644, *Letters*, pp. 247–8
33. *Letters of Henrietta Maria*, p. 246; CSP Venetian, vol. 27, 15 July 1644, p. 116; John Rushworth, *Historical Collections* (London, 1721), vol. 5, p. 684
34. Henrietta Maria to Charles, 28 June 1644, *Letters*, p. 248
35. Henry Jermyn to George Digby, 30 June 1644, CSP Domestic, Charles I, 1644, p. 318
36. A. Strickland, *The Queens of England*, vol. 8, Henrietta Maria, p. 113
37. Henrietta Maria to Charles, 9 July 1644, *Letters*, p. 249
38. *Letters of Henrietta Maria*, p. 250
39. Ibid., pp. 250–1
40. *Memoires de Madame de Motteville*, ed. M. Petitot (Paris, 1824), pp. 116–17
41. Henrietta Maria to Charles, 18 November 1644, *Letters*, pp. 263–4
42. Clarendon, *History of the Rebellion*, vol. 3, pp. 325–7
43. Lucy Hutchinson, *Memoirs of the Life of Colonel Hutchinson*, ed. James Sutherland (OUP, 1973), pp. 287–9
44. Ibid., pp. 28–34
45. Ibid., p. 37
46. Ibid., pp. 54–6
47. Ibid., pp. 62–3
48. Ibid., pp. 64–7
49. Ibid., pp. 75–6
50. Ibid., pp. 83–4
51. Ibid., p. 89
52. Ibid., pp. 95–6; Alfred C. Wood, *Nottinghamshire in the Civil War* (OUP, 1937), pp. 56–8
53. Hutchinson, *Memoirs*, p. 97
54. Ibid., p. 99
55. Ibid., pp. 103–4
56. Ibid., pp. 112–15; Wood, *Nottinghamshire in the Civil War*, pp. 64–5
57. Hutchinson, *Memoirs*, p. 158
58. Ibid., p. 173
59. Ibid., p. 166
60. Ibid., p. 189

CHAPTER FOUR

1. *Autobiography of Mrs. Alice Thornton*, ed. C. Jackson (Surtees Society, no. 62, 1875), p. 33
2. Ibid., pp. 36–8
3. R.H. Morris, *The Siege of Chester* (Chester Archaeological Society 1924), pp. 51–7; *Tracts Relating to Military Proceedings in Lancashire During the Great Civil War*, ed. George Ormerod (Chetham Society, no. 2, 1844, Lancs. Civil War Tracts), pp. 153–4; *Tracts Relating to the Civil War in*

Cheshire, ed. Revd J.A. Atkinson (Chetham Society, vol. 65, NS, 1909), pp. 110–11; S.R. Gardiner, *History of the Great Civil War* (Longmans Green, 1886), vol. 1, pp. 347–8; P.M. Higgins, *Women in the English Civil War*, (Unpub. thesis, Manchester, 1965), p. 45

4. Mary Rowsell, *The Life of Charlotte de la Trémoille, Countess of Derby* (Kegan Paul, 1905), p. 11

5. Ibid., pp. 19–20 and 32; Mme. Guizott de Witt, *The Lady of Latham* (London, 1869), pp. 24–5

6. de Witt, *Lady of Latham*, pp. 33–4

7. *Briefe Journall of the Siege Against Lathom, Lancs.*, Civil War Tracts, pp. 161–2

8. Ibid., p. 162; *A Discourse of the Warr in Lancashire*, Major Edward Robinson, ed. William Beamont (Chetham Society, no. 62, 1864), p. 46

9. *Briefe Journall*, pp. 162–7

10. *Discourse of the Warr in Lancashire*, p. 46; John Seacome, *History of the House of Stanley* (Manchester, 1767), quoted in E. Broxap, *The Great Civil War in Lancashire* (Manchester University Press, 1910), pp. 110–11

11. *Briefe Journall*, pp. 167–9

12. Ibid., pp. 170–1

13. Ibid., pp. 169–70

14. *Discourse of the Warr in Lancashire*, p. 47

15. *Briefe Journall*, pp. 172–5

16. *Discourse of the Warr in Lancashire*, p. 48

17. *Briefe Journall*, pp. 175–6

18. *Discourse of the Warr in Lancashire*, p. 48; E. Broxap, *The Great Civil War in Lancashire*, p. 108

19. *Briefe Journall*, pp. 176–8

20. Ibid., p. 180

21. Ibid., pp. 179–80

22. Ibid., pp. 180–1

23. Ibid., pp. 181–3

24. *An Exact Relation of the bloody and barbarous Massacre at Bolton in the Moors, Lancs.*, Civil War Tracts, pp. 191–4

25. *Discourse of the Warr in Lancashire*, p. 48

26. *Briefe Journall*, pp. 184–5; de Witt, *Lady of Latham*, p. 93

27. Joseph Hunter, *Hallamshire, The Topography of South Yorkshire*, 1819, pp. 111–12; *Savile Letters*, ed. W. Durant Cooper (Camden Society, no. 71, 1858), p. vii

28. Alice Thornton, *Autobiography*, pp. 44–7

29. *Memoirs of the Verney Family During the Civil War*, Frances Parthenope Verney (Longmans Green, 1892), vol. 2, p. 176

30. Ibid., pp. 74–7

31. Ibid., pp. 195–6

32. Ibid., pp. 199–200

33. Ibid., pp. 203–4

34. Ibid., p. 352

35. Henrietta Maria to Charles I, 27 January 1645, Agnes Strickland, *Lives of the Queens of England* (London, 1845), vol. 8, p. 129

36. *Memoirs of . . . Ann Lady Fanshawe*, ed. J. Loftis (OUP, 1979), pp. 114–17

37. *Memoirs of Sir Hugh Cholmley Kt. and Bart.*, 1787, p. 43

38. Ibid., p. 56

39. Ibid., p. 86

40. Ibid., p. 67

41. 'Sir Hugh Cholmley's Narrative of the Siege of Scarborough, 1644–45', ed. C.H. Firth (*English Historical Review*, vol. 32, 1917), p. 570; Cholmley *Memoirs*, pp. 67–8

42. Cholmley Narrative, p. 571

43. Cholmley *Memoirs*, pp. 68–9

44. Cholmley Narrative, p. 575

45. Cholmley *Memoirs*, p. 71

46. Ibid., p. 84

47. Cholmley Narrative, pp. 583–4; Cholmley *Memoirs*, p. 84

48. Cholmley *Memoirs*, pp. 83–4

49. Cholmley Narrative, pp. 584 and 586

50. Cholmley *Memoirs*, pp. 71–5 and 85

51. Ibid., pp. 86–7

52. Ibid., pp. 80–2

53. Ibid., pp. 91–2

CHAPTER FIVE

1. Charles to Henrietta Maria, 12 May 1645; *Letters of Henrietta Maria*, ed. M. Everett Green, pp. 303–4

2. Clarendon, *History of the Rebellion*, ed. W. Macray, vol. IV, p. 46

3. Ibid., p. 45

4. C.V. Wedgwood, *The King's War* (Collins, 1958), pp. 427–8 and p. 637, n. 59

5. R.H. Morris, *The Siege of Chester*, pp. 85–6

6. G.N. Godwin, *The Civil War in Hampshire* (Southampton, 1904) p. 112
7. Ibid., pp. 117–18
8. Clarendon, *History of the Rebellion*, vol. III, pp. 408–11
9. *Civil War in Hampshire*, pp. 250–1, 255–6, 258–9; W. Emberton, *Love Loyalty*, 1972, pp. 70–5
10. *Civil War in Hampshire*, p. 324
11. Ibid., p. 347
12. Ibid., pp. 352–3
13. Ibid., pp. 354–8
14. Ibid., pp. 359–61
15. *Memoirs of . . . Ann Lady Fanshawe*, ed. J. Loftis, pp. 118–19
16. M. Everett Green, *Lives of the Princesses of England*, vol. 6, pp. 403–4
17. Ibid., pp. 407–8
18. T. Birch, *The Court and Times of Charles I*, vol. 2, pp. 409–10
19. Frances Parthenope Verney, *Memoirs of the Verney Family During the Civil War* (Longmans Green, 1892), vol. II, p. 240
20. *Memoirs of . . . Ann Lady Fanshawe*, p. 119
21. *Memoirs of the Verney Family*, pp. 237–40
22. Ibid., p. 239
23. Ibid., pp. 245–6
24. Ibid., pp. 248–9
25. Ibid., pp. 250–3
26. *Memoirs of the Verney Family*, p. 255
27. Ibid., p. 263
28. Ibid., pp. 258–60
29. Ibid., pp. 268–9 and 274
30. Ibid., pp. 285–7 and 292–3
31. Ibid., pp. 78, 369–70, 383–4 and 388
32. Ibid., pp. 294–7
33. Ibid., pp. 303–7
34. Ibid., pp. 308–10 and 317
35. Ibid., pp. 414–16
36. *The Family of Twysden – Sir John Ramskill Twysden*, completed by C.H. Dudley Ward (John Murray, 1939), pp. 151–62; 'The Diary of Isabella Twysden', *Transactions of the Kent Archaeological Society*, vol. LI, 1939, pp. 117 and 131
37. Mary Rowsell, *Life of the Countess of Derby*, p. 158
38. *Life of William Cavendish, Duke of Newcastle by Margaret, Duchess of Newcastle*, ed. C.H. Firth (London, 1886), pp. 296–8
39. *Memoirs of . . . Ann Lady Fanshawe*, p. 120
40. Anthony Wood, *Athenae Oxonienses*, ed. P. Bliss, 1913, p. xxviii; William Lilly, *History of his Life and Times* (London, 1822), p. 140
41. Godwin, *Civil War in Hampshire*, pp. 27–8
42. *Athenae Oxonienses*, p. xxix, Lilly, *History of his Life and Times*, pp. 141–2; G. Hillier, *Narrative of the Attempted Escapes of Charles I from Carisbrooke Castle* (London, 1852), pp. 130–1, 136–7 and 140
43. A. Fraser, *The Weaker Vessel*, p. 210; Charles Carlton, *Charles I* (Routledge & Kegan Paul, 1983), pp. 333–4
44. *Memoirs of Anne Lady Halkett*, ed. J. Loftis, pp. 23–8
45. Clarendon, *History of the Rebellion*, vol. IV, p. 486; C.V. Wedgwood, *The Trial of Charles I* (Collins, 1964), pp. 154–5
46. *Letters of Henrietta Maria*, pp. 348–9
47. Green, *Lives of the Princesses of England*, vol. 6, p. 369; *The Trial of Charles I*, p. 178
48. Green, *Lives of the Princesses of England*, vol. 6, pp. 370–1
49. Ibid., p. 370, note.
50. Pauline Gregg, *Charles I* (Dent, 1981), p. 443
51. Birch, *Court and Times of Charles I*, vol. 2, p. 381–2
52. Agnes Strickland, *Lives of the Queens of England*, vol. 8, pp. 182–3

CHAPTER SIX

1. M. Everett Green, *Lives of the Princesses of England*, vol. 6 pp. 372–3
2. Ibid., p. 382
3. *Memoirs of Anne Lady Halkett and Ann Lady Fanshawe*, ed. J. Loftis (OUP, 1979), pp. 53–6
4. Charles Carlton, *Going to the Wars* (Routledge, 1992), pp. 204–7
5. Allan Fea, *After Worcester Fight* (John Lane, 1904), *Tract I, The King's Own Narrative*, pp. 5–18; *Tract II, Thomas Blount's Boscobel*, part 1, pp. 70–98
6. Fea, *After Worcester Fight, The King's Narrative*, pp. 22–3
7. Ibid., *Blount's Boscobel*, part 2, p. 127
8. Ibid., *The King's Narrative*, pp. 26–9
9. Ibid., *Tract IV, The King's Concealment at Trent*, pp. 184–6

10. Ibid., *The King's Concealment at Trent*, pp. 190–3, 195–200, 202, 206–7, 209; *Tract V, Mr. Ellesdon's Letter to Lord Clarendon*, pp. 223–5, 228; *The King's Narrative*, p. 32; A.M. Broadley, *The Royal Miracle* (Stanley Paul, 1912); Abraham Jenings, *Miraculum Basilicon*, pp. 132, 134, 135, 137

11. Broadley, *The Royal Miracle, Robert Phelipps' Narrative*, pp. 199–202; Fea, *After Worcester Fight, The King's Narrative*, pp. 35–6; *Blount's Boscobel*, part 2, pp. 140–1

12. Allan Fea, *The Flight of the King* (John Lane, 1897), *Tract V, Colonel Gounter's Narrative*, pp. 283–7, 294–5, 303; Fea, *After Worcester Fight, The King's Narrative*, pp. 37–8

13. *The Stanley Papers*, part 3, ii, p. ccxxvi (Chetham Society 67, 1867), ed. F.R. Raines

14. Guizott de Witt, *The Lady of Latham*, pp. 207, 209

15. Ibid., p. 275

16. *Memoirs of . . . Ann Lady Fanshawe*, ed. J. Loftis, pp. 122–31

17. Ibid., pp. 134–6

18. Pauline Gregg, *Free-born John* (Harrap, 1961), pp. 102–4; M.A. Gibb, *John Lilburne the Leveller* (Lindsay Drummond, 1947), p. 93

19. Gregg, *Free-born John*, p. 122

20. Ibid., pp. 141 and 143

21. Ibid., p. 153

22. Ibid., p. 151

23. Ibid., pp. 271–2; A. Fraser, *The Weaker Vessel*, pp. 267–9; P.M. Higgins, *Women in the English Civil War*, pp. 174–5; Gibb, *John Lilburne the Leveller*, p. 259

24. Gregg, *Free-born John*, pp. 347–8; Gibb, *John Lilburne*, pp. 345–6

25. *Memoirs of . . . Ann Lady Fanshawe*, pp. 137–9

26. Ibid., pp. 140–1

POSTSCRIPT

1. Lucy Hutchinson, *Memoirs of the Life of Colonel Hutchinson*, ed. James Sutherland (OUP, 1973), pp. 229–31

2. Ibid., p. 234

3. Ibid., pp. 237–8

4. Ibid., pp. 246–7

5. Ibid., pp. 255–6

6. Ibid., p. 261

7. Ibid., p. 265

8. Ibid., pp. 268–70, 272, 274–5

9. Ibid., pp. 271 and 1

10. *Memoirs of . . . Ann Lady Fanshawe*, ed. J. Loftis (OUP, 1979), p. 140

11. Ibid., pp. 188–9

12. Ibid., p. 190

Select Bibliography

Adair, John, *By the Sword Divided: Eyewitnesses of the English Civil War* (Century Publishing Co. Ltd, 1983)

Arber, Edward (ed.), *Memorials of Thomas, Lord Fairfax, An English Garner*, (London, 1903)

Ashley, Maurice, *The English Civil War*, rev. ed. (Alan Sutton, 1990)

——., *The Battle of Naseby* (Alan Sutton, 1992)

Bagley, J.J., *The Earls of Derby 1485–1985* (Sidgwick & Jackson, 1985)

Baillie, Robert, *Letters and Journals*, 3 vols, ed. David Laing (Bannatyne Club, Edinburgh, 1841–2)

Bankes, George, *The Story of Corfe Castle* (John Murray, 1853)

Bankes, Viola, *A Dorset Heritage – The Story of Kingston Lacey* (The Richards Press, London, 1953)

Bayley, A.R., *The Great Civil War in Dorset* (Taunton, 1910)

Bence-Jones, Mark, *The Cavaliers* (Constable, 1976)

Birch, Thomas, *The Court and Times of Charles I*, 2 vols (London, 1849). (Vol. 2 contains the *Memoirs of the Mission in England of the Capuchin Friars* by Fr. Cyprien de Gamache)

Bond, Thomas, *History and Description of Corfe Castle* (Bournemouth, 1883)

Bone, Quentin, *Henrietta Maria: Queen of the Cavaliers* (Peter Owen, 1973)

Broadley, A.M., *The Royal Miracle* (Stanley Paul, 1912)

Broxap, E., *The Great Civil War in Lancashire* (Manchester University Press, 1910)

Bryant, Arthur, *King Charles II* (Collins, 1955)

Calendar of State Papers Domestic, Reign of Charles I, ed. William Douglas Hamilton, 1641–3 and 1644 (HMSO, 1887 and 1888)

Calendar of State Papers, Venetian, ed. Allen B. Hinds et al. vols 25, 26 and 27 (1925–6), 35 vols (HMSO, 1864–1940)

Carlton, Charles, *Charles I: The Personal Monarch* (Routledge, 1983)

——., *Going to the Wars – The Experience of the English Civil Wars* (Routledge, 1992)

Cartwright, Julia, *Sacharissa – Some Account of Dorothy Sidney, Countess of Sunderland* (London, 1893)

Cavendish, Margaret, *Life of William Cavendish, Duke of Newcastle to which is added The True Relation of my Birth Breeding and Life by Margaret, Duchess of Newcastle*, ed. C.H. Firth (London, 1886)

Chapman, Hester, *The Tragedy of Charles II* (Jonathan Cape, 1964)

Charles I in 1646: Letters of King Charles I to Queen Henrietta Maria, ed. John Bruce (Camden Society, no. 63, 1856)

Charles II's Escape from Worcester – A Collection of Narratives Assembled by Samuel Pepys, ed. William Matthews (G. Bell & Sons, 1967)

Cholmley, Hugh, *Memoirs of Sir Hugh Cholmley Kt, and Bart.* (1787)

'Sir Hugh Cholmley's Narrative of the Siege of Scarborough, 1644–45', ed. C.H. Firth (*English Historical Review,* no. 32, 1917)

Tracts Relating to the Civil War in Cheshire, ed. J.A. Atkinson (Chetham Society, no. 65, New Series, Manchester, 1909)

Clarendon, Edward, Earl of, *The History of the Rebellion and Civil Wars in England,* 6 vols, ed. W.D. Macray (Clarendon Press, Oxford, 1888)

A Discourse of the Warr in Lancashire (Major Edward Robinson?) ed. William Beamont (Chetham Society, no. 62, 1864)

Eales, Jacqueline, *Puritans and Roundheads: The Harleys of Brampton Bryan and the Outbreak of the English Civil War* (CUP, 1990)

Emberton, Wilf, *Love Loyalty – The Close and Perilous Siege of Basing House, 1643–1645,* (W.J. Emberton, 1972)

Fea, Allan, *The Flight of the King* (John Lane, 1897)

——., *After Worcester Fight* (John Lane, 1904)

Fraser, Antonia, *Cromwell Our Chief of Men* (Weidenfeld & Nicolson, 1973)

——., *King Charles II* (Weidenfeld & Nicolson, 1979)

——., *The Weaker Vessel – Woman's Lot in Seventeenth-century England* (Weidenfeld & Nicholson, 1984)

Gardiner, S.R., *History of the Great Civil War,* 4 vols (Longmans Green, 1886)

Gibb, M.A., *John Lilburne the Leveller* (Lindsay Drummond, 1947)

Girouard, Mark, 'Wardour Old Castle', *Country Life,* 14 Feb. and 21 Feb. 1991

Godwin, G.N., *The Civil War in Hampshire and the Story of Basing House* (Southampton, 1904)

Graham, E., Hinds, H., Hobby, E. and Wilcox, H. (eds), *Her Own Life, Autobiographical Writings by 17th Century Englishwomen* (Routledge, 1989)

Green, M.A. Everett, *Lives of the Princesses of England,* 6 vols (London, 1855)

Gregg, Pauline, *Free-born John* (Harrap, 1961)

——. *King Charles I* (J.M. Dent, 1981)

Guttery, D.R., *The Great Civil War in the Midland Parishes* (Birmingham, 1951)

Hamilton, Elizabeth, *Henrietta Maria* (Hamish Hamilton, 1976)

Haythornthwaite, Philip, *The English Civil War, An Illustrated Military History* (Blandford Press, Poole, 1983)

A True Relation of the Queenes Majesties Return out of Holland By one in the same Storme and Ship with her Majestie (Oxford, 1643)

Hibbert, Christopher, *Cavaliers and Roundheads* (HarperCollins, 1993)

Higgins, P.M., *Women in the English Civil War* (Unpublished thesis, Manchester University, 1965)

Hill, Christopher, *God's Englishman, Oliver Cromwell and the English Revolution* (Weidenfeld & Nicolson, 1970)

Hillier, George, *Narrative of the Attempted Escapes of Charles I from Carisbrooke Castle* (London, 1852)

Historic Manuscripts Commission, *Marquis of Bath MSS*, vol. 1 (HMSO, 1904)

Hunter, Joseph, *Hallamshire – Topography of South Yorkshire* (1819)

Hutchins, John, *History and Antiquities of the County of Dorset*, 4 vols (1861)

Hutchinson, Lucy, *Memoirs of the Life of Colonel Hutchinson*, ed. James Sutherland (OUP, 1973)

Kenyon, John, *The Civil Wars of England* (Weidenfeld & Nicolson, 1988)

Tracts Relating to Military Proceedings in Lancashire During the Great Civil War (Civil War Tracts) ed. George Ormerod (Chetham Society, no. 2, 1844)

Laurence, Anne, *Women in England 1500–1700* (Weidenfeld & Nicholson, 1994)

The Letters, Speeches and Proclamations of Charles I, ed. Sir Charles Petrie (Cassell, 1935)

Letters of Brilliana, Lady Harley, ed. Thomas Taylor Lewis (Camden Society, no. 58, 1854)

Letters of Queen Henrietta Maria, ed. M.A. Everett Green (1857)

Lettres de Henriette Marie de France à sa Soeur Christine, ed. H. Ferrero (Rome, 1881)

Lilly, William, *History of his Life and Times* (London, 1822)

Lodge, Edmund, *Portraits of Illustrious Personages of Great Britain* (London, 1850)

Ludlow, Edmund, *Memoirs*, 2 vols, ed. C.H. Firth (Clarendon Press, Oxford, 1894)

Ludlow, Patrick, *Bloody Ludlow* (Kensal Press, Oxford, 1988)

Marshall, R.K., *Henrietta Maria the Intrepid Queen* (HMSO, 1990)

Memoirs of Anne Lady Halkett and Ann Lady Fanshawe, ed. John Loftis (OUP, 1979)

Memoirs of Sophia, Electress of Hanover, trans. H. Forester (1888)

Memoires de Madame de Motteville, ed. M. Petitot (Paris, 1824)

Morris, R.H., *The Siege of Chester*, ed. and completed by P.H. Lawson (Chester Archaeological Society, 1924)

de Motteville, Madame, *Memoir of the Life of Henrietta Maria*, ed. M.G. Hanotaux (Camden Miscellany 8, Camden Society NS 31, 1883)

Nicholls, H.G., *The Forest of Dean* (John Murray, 1858)

Ollard, Richard, *The Escape of Charles II After the Battle of Worcester* (Hodder & Stoughton, 1966)

——., *This War Without an Enemy: A History of the English Civil War* (Hodder & Stoughton, 1988)

Oman, Carola, *Henrietta Maria* (Hodder & Stoughton, 1936)

Pugh, R.B. and Saunders, A.D., *Old Wardour Castle* (HMSO, 1968)

Richardson, M.A., *Reprints of Rare Tracts and Imprints of Ancient Manuscripts*, 3 vols (1847)

Roots, Ivan, *The Great Rebellion, 1642–1660*, rev. ed. (Alan Sutton Publishing Ltd, 1995)

Rowsell, Mary, *The Life Story of Charlotte de la Trémoille, Countess of Derby* (Kegan Paul, 1905)

Rushworth, John, *Historical Collections*, 8 vols (1680–1701)

Savile Letters, ed. William Durant Cooper (Camden Society 71, 1858)

Seacome, John, *History of the House of Stanley* (Manchester, 1783)

Sidney, Henry, *Diary of the Times of Charles II*, ed. R.W. Blencowe, 2 vols (London, 1843)

Spalding, John, *History of the Troubles and Memorable Transactions in Scotland in the Reign of Charles I* (Aberdeen, 1829)

Stanley Papers III, ed. Revd F.R. Raines (Chetham Society, no. 67, 1867)

Stenton, D.M., *The Englishwoman in History* (New York, 1977)

Strickland, Agnes, *Lives of the Queens of England: Henrietta Maria*, vol. 8 (1845)

Sydney Papers, Letters and Memorials of State . . . from the Originals at Penshurst, 2 vols, ed. A. Collins (London, 1746)

Thornton, Alice, *Autobiography*, ed. C. Jackson (Surtees Society, no. 62, 1875)

Trease, Geoffrey, *Portrait of a Cavalier: William Cavendish, First Duke of Newcastle* (Macmillan, 1979)

'Diary of Isabella Twysden', ed. Revd F.W. Bennit, *Transactions of the Kent Archaeological Society*, vol. 51 (1939)

Twisden, J.R. (completed by C.H. Dudley Ward), *The Family of Twysden and Twisden* (John Murray, 1939)

Warburton, Eliot, *Memoirs and Correspondence of Prince Rupert and the Cavaliers* (1849)

Washbourn, John, *Bibliotheca Gloucestrensis* (Gloucester, 1825)

Wedgwood, C.V., *The King's Peace* (Collins, 1955)

——., *The King's War* (Collins, 1958)

——., *The Trial of Charles I* (Collins, 1964)

Whitelocke, Bulstrode, *Memorials of the English Affairs*, 4 vols (Oxford, 1853)

de Witt, Madame Guizot, *The Lady of Latham – The Life of Charlotte de la Trémoille, Countess of Derby* (London, 1869)

Wood, Alfred C., *Nottinghamshire in the Civil War* (OUP, 1937)

Wood, Anthony, *Athenae Oxoniensis*, ed. P. Bliss (London, 1813)

Index